The Japanese Century

Challenge and Response

by

Thomas R. Zengage

C. Tait Ratcliffe

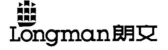

Longman 朗文

Published by
Longman Group (Far East) Ltd
18/F, Cornwall House
Tong Chong Street
Quarry Bay
Hong Kong
and associated companies throughout the world

ISBN 0 582 99969 3

Printed in Hong Kong

CONTENTS

Thomas R. Zengage is Managing Director of IBI, Inc. (International Business Information) in Tokyo, where he directs the firm's Research and Consulting Group and Financial and Corporate Communications Group. Fluent in Japanese and a long-term American resident of Tokyo, Zengage has written numerous articles and consulting reports on Japan's financial markets as well as on industrial and high technology-related topics. Educated at Columbia University and with an MBA from the University of Washington, he serves as a consultant to many international corporations, financial firms, and government agencies.

Dr C. Tait Ratcliffe is founder and President of IBI, Inc. and Director of its Financial Services Group. He has lived and worked in Japan for 25 years and is fluent in Japanese. A former Fulbright scholar, Dr Ratcliffe has taught in the Department of Economics at Stanford University and engaged in extensive consulting with the Boston Consulting Group. Dr Ratcliffe's books on finance in Japan include *Japanese Corporate Finance* (1977) in English and his latest book, *Zaitech (Financial Technology)*, in Japanese.

ACKNOWLEDGEMENTS

In the preparation of this book, we have drawn on the resources of our firm, IBI, Inc., the largest management and corporate communications consultancy based in Japan. Founded in Tokyo in 1972, IBI, Inc. today employs over 100 people full time in Japan. IBI's services span market research, strategy consultation, and the development of corporate communications programs principally in the fields of investor relations and public relations.

Portions of this book have been adapted from industry studies which appeared in IBI's *Japan Industry Research* series, the longest-running and most comprehensive program of independently-originated research of its type. Some other sections appeared as part of a regular feature on the editorial pages of Japan's *Mainichi Daily News*. The chapter on yen internationalization is based on work originally done for the Institute of Foreign Bankers in Japan, and the chapter on Tokyo as a financial center first appeared in a Euromoney publication.

We would like to thank our colleagues on the professional staff at IBI, former staff members, and our other associates for their help in the preparation of *The Japanese Century*: Kimio Yoshizaki, John Gregory Brockelbank, Mark S. Brown, Shuzo Yamamoto, Tran Van Tho, Chizuko Kume, Miho Nishio, and others.

Finally, we are grateful for the support of our colleague, Edwin F. Hauxhurst, for his valuable counsel.

TABLES

We are on the threshold of the Japanese Century. Notwithstanding the emergence of the Asian newly industrializing economies (NIEs) and the future importance of China, the internationalization of Japan's economy will have a profound impact worldwide. Specifically, Japan's rising influence will become especially pronounced in key strategic industries such as semiconductors, in the global financial markets, and, ultimately, in the geopolitical balance of power.

The most important change that Japan's rising dominance will bring about is acceleration of the declining influence of the US and, perhaps, a fundamental reordering of the US economy. Ironically, throughout the postwar period, the US has focused its attention on competing with the Communist Bloc, only to discover a far more serious threat to US influence emerging in the form of Japan. While the US lost its sons and, some would say, its national will in the quagmire that was Vietnam, Japan was quietly but purposefully building its industries into world-class competitors.

One central fact needs to be stressed: economics has replaced ideology as a key theme of the Japanese Century.

Challenge of and Response to the Japanese Century

The objective of this book is to provide a basis for a fuller understanding of the challenges of the Japanese Century and to offer suggestions as to how other countries might respond. The views expressed are based on more than 25 years' combined experience in providing consulting assistance to Japanese companies internationally and to non-Japanese companies in Japan.

Challenge

The list of challenges offered to the rest of the world by the Japanese Century is impressive.

Japan as the Leading Creditor Nation
What price in the future might Japan extract from the US for continuing Japanese willingness to finance the massive twin fiscal and trade deficits of the US?

Financial
What are the implications for the global capital markets now that the Tokyo Stock Exchange is the world's largest?

Currency

Is the yen likely to continue to appreciate, or will the US dollar rebound as the US reduces its trade surplus? And can the yen become *the* international currency if Japan continues to shirk its responsibility to take on an international political role?

The Manufacturing Base of the US

What is the effect of the continuing willingness of the US to sell off to Japan its technological and manufacturing base in exchange for adding a relatively few blue-collar jobs in the US?

The Japanizing of the US Economy

Perhaps no question is more important than the eventual impact of the massive flows of Japanese direct investment into manufacturing capability in the US.

As Japan's economy and political influence internationalize, so does the US economy. Already the threat of a potential Japanese lack of participation in US government bond auctions has directly influenced interest rates in the US. In the not-too-distant future, will Japan be able to dictate the terms of fiscal and monetary policy in the US? One wonders if, in effect, Japan's Ministry of International Trade and Industry (MITI) is not already by default partially writing US industrial policy, as Japanese company after Japanese company establishes ever-increasing market shares in the US market.

The most basic question is: what will be the long-term impact of rising Japanese economic power on the quality of life in the US?

Questions of Military Power

All of the above, together with the waning world influence of the US, begs the question: Can economic power be naked of military power? The answer seems to be, quite simply, no.

A further aspect of the Japanese Century may be additional pressure on Japan to assume a larger role in its own defense. In fact, the component pieces of military power are already at hand in Japan, albeit in unassembled form. Such factors include Japan's aircraft and defense industries, advanced defense electronics capabilities, participation in the US Strategic Defense Initiative (SDI), its healthy space program (represented by the Japanese Space Shuttle scheduled to fly in the 1990s), and rising military expenditures. These issues deserve in-depth treatment in a separate book.

Response

What should be the response of the West? Or should the West even have a response? The European response in some cases has been one of protectionism, which seems to have kept Japan at bay. A well-known Japanese industrialist has remarked succinctly that Japan's economic fundamentals compel it to grab at more and more of the world economic pie until its hand is slapped.

National Economic Security: The Case for Economic Self-defense

An unavoidable conclusion may be that, for the US, a well-formulated industrial policy and some form of economic self-defense of critical sectors may be critical to long-term national security. It is too simplistic a response to argue that the taking of strong, selective steps to protect vital US industries will somehow plunge the world into a new economic depression. There are markets in the world today that for all intents and purposes are closed, and there are governments which practice some form of protectionism. Moreover, vigorous policies of protectionism for many different industries have characterized much of Japan's postwar economic history.

In practical terms, we are calling for a careful review of what we might call 'sector-selective' economic self-defense, or the preservation of industries thought critical to national defense as well as to long-term prosperity. Such vital industries might include semiconductors, computers/communications, steel, machine tools, and others. Sector-selective economic self-defense of this type in the US might lead to the following scenario: the reduction of imports, which would in turn cause inflation, raise interest rates, reduce consumption, and strengthen the dollar. In this context, the sharp devaluation of the dollar may have been a huge mistake, since the US appears to be running out of capacity for manufactured exports. Japan, for its part, has been able to accelerate direct investment in plant and equipment in the US, thereby shielding these new, well-managed Japanese factories from import controls.

US Management Mistakes

Why is it that Honda can successfully hire thousands of persons in the US, build cars, and then ship them back to Japan? Half the answer lies in an open US market. But Japanese factories in the US and Europe boast productivity rates about as high as those in Japan. The story in Asia is similar. In other words, Japan did not beat Detroit, Silicon Valley and the US rust belt all on its own. While Main Street has run its companies into the ground, Wall Street has put too much premium on non-productive endeavors.

What many fail to see is that Japanese managers have all but lost respect for American and, to a lesser extent, European management because of what they view as slipshod practices. When the Japanese say that the US must first heal itself, they are really indicting US management for mismanaging US companies.

Japanese opinion makers are also fond of saying that the US economy is like someone whose house is on fire but does not know it. Put bluntly, US fiscal, monetary and, if it has one, industrial policy must stop being used to cover up the mistakes of US management. Mindless protectionism is probably not the answer, and neither is failing to implement measures to preserve vital strategic industries in the US. Instead, the US needs an industrial policy which identifies and sets out programs for the long-term preservation and development of vital high-technology and manufacturing sectors.

If the Japanese Century is a crisis for the US, what are some of the concrete steps the US might take? If it is not too late, the response must center on measures to limit consumption and to increase savings and capital spending. Some of the specific measures might include taxes on consumption and the reinstatement of investment tax credits. The goal should be to rebuild the US industrial base to make a dollar-for-dollar balance between Japanese sales in the US and US sales in Japan – on a sector-by-sector basis – a reality.

Clearly, then, Japan will be among the key challenges facing the successors to the Reagan administration, not only in the US but also elsewhere around the world.

1

When the history of the 1980s is eventually written, two points may become clear. The first is that the external pressure on Japan to open its markets has had an ambiguous and not clearly positive effect. It has led to a very rapid relaxation of the restrictions on financial markets, some progress in certain industrial product sectors, and a prolonged stalemate in beef and oranges. The theory current at the time of the Japan-US Yen-Dollar Committee discussions – that the yen may have been undervalued because of the lack of availability of yen assets for investment – may have been proved by subsequent events. The moves to internationalize the yen, as well as other measures, have resulted in a much sharper rise in the yen's value than was initially thought.

The second point that historians will certainly note is that the events of 1985–87, a period when the yen doubled in value, did not really make Japan a more accessible and open market. Tariff and non-tariff barriers can be removed, but if the cost of investment and operations is too high in yen terms, non-Japanese corporations will hesitate to participate actively in the Japanese market, particularly if major investments are required to carve out a market position.

Rather than become an active participant in the world community of nations, Japan in the latter half of the 1980s may therefore have become more isolated in some respects. Even if current events in Japan are quite different from its historical periods of strict isolationism, Japan still appears to lack an urgent and aggressive desire to play its appropriate role in the international economy. Although in behind-the-scenes discussions many groups in Japan have welcomed external pressures, historians may write that greater efforts on the part of Japan appropriate to its current international economic status, as well as more focused pressures from abroad, might have benefited both Japan and the rest of the world.

The Changing Structure of Japan's Economy

Until early 1988, economists were seriously concerned about the prospects for the Japanese economy because of the adverse effects of the appreciation of the yen. However, virtually all the economic indicators have picked up, and some economists have even proclaimed that Japan has moved into a new 'high-growth' phase of its development. The driving force for GNP growth since 1987 has shifted away from exports and towards the domestic market, as consumer spending, private housing investment, and private capital investment have become the principal forces contributing to economic expansion.

Capital investment especially has been very strong, as corporations have invested in increased capacity in order to meet higher domestic demand and introduce new products; in machinery and equipment with the aim of raising productivity and remaining competitive in export markets; and in research and development facilities so as to take the lead in introducing new products. Most surveys of new plant construction show a boom in progress characterized by signs of a movement outside the Tokyo and other central urban areas, rising expenditures in order to set up facilities to respond to increased domestic demand, and a surprisingly large percentage of new facilities dedicated to research and development.

Domestic Investment

One of the first reactions to the strengthening of the yen and the rise in overseas direct investments was that Japanese industry might be subjected to a 'hollowing out'. There is ample evidence that many lower value-added manufacturing operations have been, or are in the process of being, moved overseas. However, domestic investment is also up by a substantial margin.

Growth in Japan's real domestic capital investment dropped to only 0.1% for the first quarter of 1986. Since then, however, it has risen at an accelerating pace, to 1.8% for the last quarter of 1986, then to 4.1% (about 17% at an annual rate) in the last quarter of 1987. Over this period, private capital investment in real terms has risen from about ¥55 trillion (19% of real GNP) to ¥63 trillion (almost 20% of GNP).

Separate data, covering only incorporated enterprises, indicate that the shift away from investments in manufacturing to the non-manufacturing sector is being reversed, a fact which casts some doubt on the expectations of many economists in the US and elsewhere that a post-industrial, service-oriented economy would inevitably develop in Japan. According to data of the Economic Planning Agency, the rate of growth in manufacturing investments has been about double that of non-manufacturing investments, and this trend is likely to continue at least until late 1988.

Investment in R & D Centers

According to a survey of more than 2,500 listed and unlisted corporations conducted in early 1988, more than 250 companies have acquired or are actively looking for new plant sites. In addition, 100 companies have purchased or are looking for sites for new R & D facilities, and 84 have investigated or purchased new distribution centers. Some of the significant trends evident from the survey are:

- Although a large percentage of the new plants will be located in the proximity of Tokyo and other major urban centers, there is a slight shift towards other areas, including Kyushu and Shikoku. The bullet train linking Tokyo with Sendai and Niigata also appears to be encouraging more investment in areas within two hours of Tokyo by train.
- The percentage of planned investment in R & D centers is very high by previous standards and reflects the growing drive among Japanese companies to develop their own technologies in pharmaceuticals, chemicals, and other industries.
- A large percentage of new plants are aimed at meeting the increased demand in domestic-oriented industries, such as food products, apparel, and plastics.
- Planned investment in distribution centers reflects the strong attention which Japanese companies are directing at substantially increasing the efficiency of their distribution systems.

From a somewhat different perspective, the number of industrial park developments, sponsored by both private interests and regional governments, is also significant. According to the same survey, 472 such large-scale developments are underway in various parts of Japan. About 40% of the sites in these industrial parks have been taken, and the remainder are still to be developed. The largest number of these industrial parks in a single area is 61, in Hokkaido; Niigata has 50 and Fukushima 25. Both of the latter sites are within two hours of Tokyo by bullet train.

Foreign Investment

The number of non-Japanese companies adding plant capacity is still small. However, according to the same survey, the number is rising, despite the increased cost of setting up manufacturing operations in Japan following the appreciation of the yen. According to Ministry of Finance data, after dropping back to about US$500 million in fiscal 1983 from $800 million a year earlier, foreign direct investment in Japan climbed to almost $1.5 billion in fiscal 1987. Foreign investment in plant and facilities in Japan, for example, amounted to $345 million in the January–March quarter of 1988, an increase of more than 53% over the figure for the previous year.

Such trends suggest that the 'hollowing out' of the Japanese economy may be much less of an issue than was originally thought. Even with the yen worth twice what it was in mid-1985, Japanese companies are still adding capacity in order to meet rising domestic demand, and non-Japanese companies are still being attracted, in apparently increasing numbers, by the country's high technological level, the availability of skilled labor, and the strong industrial base.

Withstanding the 'Yen Shock': Lessons in Resilience

The amazing strength of the Japanese economy has made life increasingly difficult for those doomsayers who have been forecasting the demise of Japan as a result of the sudden and steep appreciation of the yen since September 1985. For a while, pessimists could attract an audience by pointing to what seemed to be a high level of dependence on government spending in order to sustain economic growth in Japan, as well as to the specter of rising prices and a host of other dire consequences of any further appreciation of the yen. Our own analyses suggest that these more pessimistic points of view need to be rethought, as the Japanese economy is clearly showing an exceptional ability to adapt and grow over the long term.

Recovery of the Export Sector

For example, Japan's export sector was presumably severely affected by the appreciation of the yen from around ¥240 to the dollar in mid-1985 to around ¥123 in early 1988. While it is true that Japan's export-dependent corporations have been under intense pressure to adapt to the stronger yen through cost-cutting, the introduction of new products, and the setting up of manufacturing operations overseas, overall economic data suggest that Japan's export sector is making the necessary adjustments. From a wider perspective, the Japanese economy as a whole also adapted quickly and flexibly to the upward revaluation of the yen, and was able to move into a period of moderately rapid real GNP growth (in excess of 4% in 1988). Unfortunately, in the process of adaptation, the full benefits of the yen appreciation were not passed on to Japanese consumers.

The best evidence of adaptation in the export sector is the data available on Japan's exports. There are three kinds of aggregate data: the value of Japanese exports stated in dollar terms, the value of exports in yen terms, and an index of the volume of exports. The value of Japan's exports in dollar terms has never in fact declined. Because of the 'J-curve' phenomenon, growth in exports in dollar terms was actually in the double-digit range for a good part of 1986, and double-digit growth resumed in 1988. Thus, even though there has been much discussion of a 'hollowing out' of the Japanese economy, the export sector appears to be holding its own.

Costs of Recovery

Needless to say, the competitiveness of Japan's export sector has not been sustained without some costs. One clue to this has been the trends in export prices in foreign currencies and in yen terms. The price index for exports in contractual currency terms remained relatively stable between September 1985 and into 1988.

Price figures suggest that exporting corporations have adopted a number of measures, including accepting lower profits, or even losses, on some exports, stepping up cost-cutting activities, and automation of production. Since there are no figures that reveal profitability on exports versus domestic sales, the extent of losses on exports is very difficult to determine. Aggregate corporate profits, however, were able to stage a strong recovery. While some of this profit may stem from increased domestic sales, improved profits (or reduced losses) from exports was also a contributing factor for many corporations.

Other Evidence of Long-term Strength

Many other indications of strong recovery attest to Japan's amazing ability to adapt. These indicators include growth in consumer spending, expansion of retail sales, an increase in the level of housing starts to an annual rate of well over 1.7 million in 1987, growth in industrial production, a continued marked uptrend in orders for machinery from the private sector and in orders for construction from the private and public sectors, and aggressive investment plans.

Much of this growth is in strong contrast to the performance of the US economy, where the impact of the stock-market drop on consumption may have been more lingering than in Japan and where interest rates are higher, thus ruling out some growth possibilities.

Japan's Productivity Success Story

According to comparative statistics prepared by the Bank of Japan, Japan led the other industrialized nations in manufacturing productivity growth from 1976 to 1986. However, a more recent comparison, based on 1980, shows Japan beginning to lag somewhat in productivity growth because of a slowdown in 1985 and 1986 as the country slipped into a recession induced by the appreciation of the yen. Data for 1987 and 1988, however, show a sharp acceleration in labor productivity, reflecting the taking up of slack as production levels recovered from the recession and the continued high level of capital investment in Japanese industries.

Some Erosion in Productivity Growth

From 1976 to 1986, growth in Japan's labor productivity index consistently exceeded that of the US, France, the UK, and West Germany. But one of the costs of the recession induced by the appreciation of the yen was a decline in Japan's productivity growth to 4.2% in 1985 and 2.3% in 1986, compared with nearly 10% growth in 1984.

As a result of this slowdown in 1985 and 1986, comparative productivity indexes based on 1980 indicate that Japan's manufacturing sector produced only 15.7% more per manhour in 1986 than in 1980. The performance in the

US was well above this level. US workers increased productivity by 23.6% and UK workers posted an increase of 30.7% over the same period. West Germany and France also showed bigger gains in productivity from 1980 to 1986.

One of the costs of increased output per employee in the US and other industrialized nations, however, has been high unemployment. The percentage of jobless in the UK rose from 6.8% in 1980 to 11.9% in 1986. Over this same period, unemployment figures rose from 3.8% to 9% in West Germany, from 6.4% to 10.4% in France, and from 7.6% to 11.1% in Italy. Only the US showed little change (from about 7% in 1980 to 6.9% in 1986), even though the jobless rate rose temporarily to 9.5% in both 1982 and 1983. In contrast, the unemployment rate in Japan rose only from 2% to 2.8%. Even though this figure is biased downward because of the reluctance of Japanese companies to lay off employees, one can still argue that the social costs of increased labor productivity in other industrialized nations were higher. Corporations bore the cost of the slack in Japan. Elsewhere, the cost had to be paid by the public sector and individuals.

Despite the slippage in positioning from 1980 to 1986, Japan's labor productivity increased much faster in 1987 and 1988. In January 1987, the index of labor productivity was up 1.7% over the previous year. However, by October 1987, the index was up more than 10%. One of the main factors accounting for this rise was an increase in the demand for manufactured goods, which led to greater utilization of the capacity of plants and the labor force.

High Japanese Investment Levels

Another factor leading to increased productivity has been the continued high level of private capital investment. From 1980 to 1986, investment by the private sector rose from about ¥38 trillion, or nearly US$300 billion, to ¥53.4 trillion, or more than $400 billion. As a percentage of real GNP, private capital investment climbed from 15.6% in 1980 to 18.6% in 1986. By way of comparison, private non-residential fixed investment in the US in 1986 was $444 billion and rose only to $447 billion in 1987. The total investment of both the private and government sectors in the US was 18.4% in 1986, compared to 18.6% for the private sector alone in Japan.

Many economists have pointed to the long-term connection between the increase in manufacturing productivity and currency valuations. This disparity in the percentage of GNP put back into investment in Japan has persisted throughout most of the postwar period. The latest data suggest that it may continue unless the US adopts a different set of priorities in the allocation of its resources.

One factor that will give the US a respite, however, will be the strength of the yen. For example, in yen terms, Japan's wage cost index – which shows the real increase in wages after adjustment for productivity increases – was up by only 8% in 1986 from 1980. This is roughly comparable with the increase in the same index for the US in dollar terms. The same index rose by 15.6% in the UK and 35% in France (1980–83 only). However, Japan's wage cost index increased between 1980 and 1986 by an enormous 45%, because wages in dollar terms had risen by nearly 70% over that period. This figure compares to an increase of 34% in the US, and declines in wage levels, when converted to dollars, in the UK and West Germany.

Strategy Needed

Although the temporary slowdown in Japan's productivity growth and the appreciation of the yen are providing a strategic opportunity for US companies to regain world market share in some industries, these companies must be aware that this window of opportunity will not be open forever. Growth in productivity has essentially recovered in Japan. If the wage cost index expressed in dollars in Japan was up by 45% in 1986 over 1980 and the US wage cost index was up by 8%, then in very general terms the US had a 37% advantage in early 1987. But with productivity in Japan up by 10% or more in 1987, this advantage was reduced to 27%.

If past patterns hold, this lead could be whittled away even further. Furthermore, if the current export-led uptrend in the US leads to substantially higher wage costs and the high cost of imports is used by US companies as a reason to raise prices in the home market to show quick profits, the US lead will diminish even faster. In other words, the advantage gained from having the yen appreciate from ¥250 to the dollar to about ¥130 (which translates into an increase for an item costing ¥100,000 from $400 to $769, or about 90%) may be lost. Unfortunately, much of the rhetoric in the US tends to focus on criticizing Japan rather than pointing to the need for US management to take advantage of the opportunity they have to regain some measure of industrial leadership.

Japan's Impressive Consumer Market

The growth in Japan's imports of consumer goods has accelerated substantially in recent years, boosted by the stronger yen. Thus, even though oil and other raw materials still account for a substantial share of Japan's imports, finished consumer products are beginning to make a stronger contribution to the gradual reduction in its trade surplus. Although many problems remain before Japan can be described as an open market, present and potential foreign suppliers of imported consumer goods to the Japanese market should perhaps renew their awareness and appreciation of the size of the market and its major features. A better awareness of the potential might lead to a somewhat earlier arrival of the day when Japan relies on overseas sources for an important part of its needs in significant finished consumer product areas.

Doubled Spending Power

Japan's population is now more than 122 million, making it one of the five most populous nations in the free world. In early 1988, its current price GNP was

¥360 trillion, or about US$2.8 trillion, thus placing it second after the US, where GNP was about $4.7 trillion. Total consumer spending in early 1988 was running at an annual rate of ¥205 trillion, or about $1.6 trillion, compared to $2.6 trillion in the US. Since the population of Japan is about half that of the US, the value of consumer spending per capita, as well as per capita GNP, expressed in dollars, was somewhat higher for Japan.

This comparison does not imply, however, that the standard of living is identical in the two nations, especially in the field of housing. The floor area of Japanese houses in 1985 averaged about 81 square meters versus about 135 square meters in the US. In addition, the size of urban rental dwellings was substantially below the average for Japan as a whole, at only 43 square meters. By early 1988, updated figures showed only slight increases for Japanese homes.

Despite this handicap in housing, by virtually all other measures the Japanese consumer is quite affluent, and the international purchasing power of yen incomes has risen very sharply since the beginning of the 1980s because of the combination of a gradual increase in yen terms and the sharp appreciation of the yen. For example, over 98% of all households have refrigerators, washing machines, and color television sets. Almost 34% of households have video-cassette recorders. In terms of material possessions, the average household is as well or better off than households in the US or Europe. Medical care and health facilities are at a high level, with per capita data on the number of hospital beds and nurses comparing favorably with those of other industrialized nations. And, as is pointed out later, an important factor contributing to the quality of life is that the likelihood of injury or serious loss of property because of crime is relatively low.

Perhaps the most important development over the course of the 1980s, however, has been the rise in the international purchasing power of the Japanese consumer. In calendar 1980, Japanese consumers spent about ¥141 trillion, or US$642 billion (at 1980 exchange rates). Since then, consumer spending has risen to about ¥205 trillion, or $1.6 trillion. Thus, over this period, consumer spending per capita, in dollar terms, rose to approximately $13,000, compared to $5,400 in 1980, a jump of almost 140%. About 45% of this increase was accounted for by higher total consumer spending in yen terms; the remainder was a result of the stronger yen.

Growing Concern with the Quality of Life

One of the trends working in favor of new market entrants in Japan is the desire for greater individuality in consumption and a higher perceived quality of life. As a result of a number of developments, personal consumption patterns are continuing to evolve and new market opportunities are emerging.

One of these developments is the aging of the population. Japan's first baby-boom generation, born between 1947 and 1949, is now turning 40. Compared with previous generations, this group has proved more willing to try new lifestyles and to travel overseas. Many of the women in this generation are returning to work, now that their children are in middle or high school. Wives are therefore contributing more to the family income and are spending more time on continuing education, sports, and other leisure activities.

The first members of the second baby-boom generation, born between 1971 and 1974, are now approaching 20. In a few years, they will be entering the work force and becoming 'aristocrat singles' in their twenties, with a high level of purchasing power.

At the other end of the age spectrum, by the year 2000, more than 16% of the Japanese population will be over 65 years of age, as opposed to less than 11% in 1986. This 'grey generation' has already been targeted by many companies in travel, leisure, and health-care services.

Along with these changes in demographics, there is clearly a growing concern with increasing the quality of life. As the yen has appreciated, the topic of how much of the benefits of a stronger yen have actually been passed on has been discussed frequently on national television and in the other media. Although data show that per capita GNP in Japan is now higher than in the US, the vast majority of Japanese refuse to take these numbers at face value.

Remaining Problems for Market Entry

The real question confronting Japan and its trading partners is whether the current strength of the yen will enable more and more imported consumer products to establish a market position in Japan. After all, the strong yen only allows exporters, especially those in dollar-based economies, to export more cheaply to Japan. Lower prices are an important competitive weapon, but not the only requirement, since Japanese consumers are renowned for being extremely particular about quality and features.

Foreign companies interested in breaking into the Japanese market will still face considerable resistance. Domestic competitors are firmly entrenched in most product areas. The mentality of *jimae shugi* – that is, that Japan should be virtually self-sufficient in all important product areas – is as strong as ever. And industries which US and European companies would have moved offshore have maintained strong positions in Japan through increased automation and product innovativeness. The problem of entrenched suppliers is also compounded by the related one of imitators, who are generally the entrenched suppliers. An embarrassment for foreign suppliers is that the imitations are sometimes better than the original imported products.

While it is true that imports of finished consumer products are increasing and that the Japanese consumer is gaining the benefits of some lower cost imports, even with the yen in the ¥120–130 range, it will be far from easy for potential exporters to Japan to expand and hold on to a significant market share.

Japan's Egalitarian Economic System

Is Japan a 'Wealthy' Country?

Japan has been called the ultimate classless society, where roughly 90% of the population identifies itself as middle class. While this perception no doubt contains a fair amount of illusion, it is by no means false. Income distribution has been highly equitable throughout the postwar period, reaching a peak in evenness of distribution some time in the 1970s at the end of the era of accelerated economic growth and acute labor shortage. Although income differentials have tended to expand during the 1980s, Japan's income distribution still compares very favorably with that of the US and some of the European market economies. In this context, the importance and benefits of Japan's egalitarian economic system is often misunderstood, both in Japan and in the West.

Traditional Japanese Value of Social Equality

Macroeconomic questions aside, Japan consistently exhibits a strong preference for maintaining close internal social parity and equality. A compelling internal calculus exists for compensating weaker participants, while at times restraining those who are strong and aggressive. This quest for parity is everywhere evident in Japanese social and economic life, and is firmly entrenched in its institutional framework. It is perhaps nowhere more evident than in Japan's educational system, where it has elevated the average standards of education to the world's highest levels, while at the same time extracting, according to some critics, a numbing human toll as the great leveller of people.

Furthermore, some foreign observers have cynically referred to the phenomenon of social equality as Japan's 'egalitarian obsession'. In the area of international economic relations, these critics argue that a major shift in this traditional Japanese value is inevitable if Japan is to proceed with internationalization and market liberalization.

Egalitarianism as Market Barrier?

The problem with Japan's egalitarian formulation with respect to economic matters is that the system simply jams when it is called upon to cede any of its component parts to foreign competition. In the parlance of economists, there exists an 'interdependence of utility functions'. That is, specifically, the dislocation suffered by any one participant automatically subtracts from the welfare of all other participants. The ensuing process of equitably re-allocating the cost and emotional pain of shutting down, or otherwise disadvantaging, any sector of the economy, whether coal-mining or whaling, is just too time-consuming. (The West has been led to believe that it is in this field of unjamming the system that current Prime Minister Takeshita excels as a politician.) Meanwhile, the symbolic importance of conceding to foreign pressures tends to be blown far out of proportion compared to the real economic ramifications. So, in a sense, the egalitarian obsession constitutes yet another form of non-tariff barrier, and as with all trade barriers today, the question is can Japan afford to maintain them? Nevertheless, interdependent utility functions are not without their merits.

Japan's Rationale for Egalitarian Economics

Japan's egalitarian obsession prioritizes parity, equality, and uniformity at the expense of rational allocation, reward of merit, and creativity. Obviously, this phenomenon has deep cultural roots. With respect to economic matters, however, two relatively recent events have fueled the postwar belief in the value of equitable distribution and growth, or egalitarian economics. One is the postwar US-induced exercise in 'economic democratization', which the Japanese have often carried forward with the zeal of a convert. The other is the protracted war effort which stigmatized consumption while lionizing mutuality and sacrifice.

Factors Supporting Japanese Egalitarian Economics

Japan's egalitarian economics draws its momentum from several important sources. Probably the most important of these is the framework of the labor market, which traditionally has tended to discount disparities in individual abilities. Even in the current phase of slow and uneven growth, the labor market remains committed to maintaining a broadly based balance of wages throughout the economy. Steeply graduated income and estate taxes are other factors which make it difficult to escape the confines of the omnipresent middle class. Consumer behavior is swayed by the virtues of saving, and is marked with the vestiges of 'non-conspicuous consumption', or, much to the chagrin of Japan's trading partners, just plain non-consumption. Finally, industrial policy has played no small role in perpetuating egalitarian economics. While promoting new hi-tech growth industries, the Japanese government has been no less sensitive to the needs of laggard sunset industries. The long-suffering tolerance for certain inefficient economic sectors, and the curious absence of countervailing consumer movements, outline the general acceptance of the obligation to carry or support certain sectors in the name of internal parity and equity.

Why Japan is a 'Wealthy' Country

Egalitarian economics has of course done much more than just to provide Japan with a handsome Lorenz curve. The Japanese economy's special achievement is that its *average* standard of living is so uniformly high. However, the payoff has been substantial. This point is all too often lost on the casual observer who, cringing at the inferior stock of social and residential capital, bemoans the poor quality of life in Japan. From the Japanese observer, this calls forth the all-too-familiar 'Japan is a poor country' reaction; from the foreigner, we hear Japanese homes described as 'rabbit hutches'. But if so many urban dwellers are confined to 'rabbit hutches', we are assured that the streets at night are not populated by the homeless and by professional muggers. These factors are, then, the two most significant by-products of the Japanese obsession with internal parity: a relatively crime-free society, and the absence of serious social polarization. If these intangibles could be fitted into our calculations of a nation's quality of life, certainly Japan would fare much better in international comparisons, notwithstanding the shortage of parks and sewers. We may therefore conclude that Japan is indeed a wealthy country, although not in strictly Western terms.

Japan as Leading Creditor Nation

Japan's export of capital, in the form of portfolio investments in bonds and stocks and in the form of direct investment in plant and equipment, has continued to rise at a rapid pace, according to the most recent data. This rise reflects a number of developments, including the large volume of monetary assets in Japan, the activities of financial institutions engaged in 'monetariza-tion' of the gains in the value of real estate over the past one or two years, and the very rapid relaxation of restrictions on investment in overseas securities and real estate by large institutional investors since the publication of the Japan-US Yen-Dollar Committee report in 1984.

These capital exports are having a diverse range of effects on the economy of Japan and on the countries receiving the investment. In the US and elsewhere, many of these investments are assisting in revitalization and economic development. In some areas, however, there have been criticisms of overpresence, as Japanese companies are buying their way into certain over-seas markets. From the Japanese point of view, increased investment in foreign securities represents an important step by trust banks and insurance companies in diversifying their investment portfolios. Increased direct investment in the US and other markets is one means by which Japanese companies – under pressure because of the stronger yen – can maintain their positions in overseas markets.

Despite these generally beneficial effects of Japan's capital exports and the rising prestige that accompanies ownership of overseas assets, some of Japan's opinion leaders are raising the question of whether priorities should not be readjusted so as to assure that a larger portion of Japan's monetary surplus goes into improving the quality of life in Japan.

Increase in Capital Outflows

The growth in Japan's capital outflows has probably been higher thus far than for any other country in the history of the world. Long-term capital outflows in fiscal 1986, ending in March 1987, amounted to nearly US$145 billion, up approximately twofold from $73 billion in fiscal 1985. In fiscal 1987, capital outflow continued at a high $119 billion. This increase in long-term capital outflows has gone into massive purchases of foreign bonds and stocks and substantially higher investment in overseas plant and equipment.

When converted to US dollar terms, purchases of foreign bonds by Japanese investors in fiscal 1986 amounted to $1,473 billion, up from $513 billion in fiscal 1985 and $77 billion in 1984. In 1988, purchases continued to be very high, at $1,228 billion. Since investors are very active in both buying and selling, net purchases have been much smaller, amounting to $99 billion in fiscal 1986 and $64 billion in 1987. Despite the smaller net figure, there is no denying that Japanese capital has assumed an important role in determining the success of some US treasury bond issues. Although Japan would perhaps prefer to preserve some degree of neutrality, at least in economic matters, Japanese investors have in fact become very important in financing the fiscal expenditures of the US, including its defense costs.

Investment in stocks has generally lagged behind bonds because of the greater perceived risk and the lack of experience of Japanese investors in foreign equity markets. However, growth since fiscal 1985 has been very rapid. Purchases of foreign stocks in fiscal 1987 rose to US$76 billion versus $32 billion in fiscal 1986 and $7 billion in fiscal 1985. Compared with investments in Japanese stocks, which have yields of well under 1%, Japanese investors have discovered what they perceive as bargains (for example, US electric power utility stocks, some of which have yields of 7–8%). Despite the dampening effects of Black Monday, in the long term, Japanese institutional investors are likely to continue to diversify their equity portfolios into foreign stocks.

Similarly, data released on overseas direct investments show very impressive increases. These investments were fluctuating around US$7–8 billion annually during the end of the 1970s and into the early 1980s. But in 1984, overseas direct investments moved above $10 billion, then to $12 billion in 1985. With the sharp appreciation of the yen in late 1985 and 1986, Japanese manufacturing companies in particular came under pressure to move a portion of their manufacturing facilities to overseas markets. As a result, overseas direct investment jumped to $22 billion in fiscal 1986 and to $33 billion in fiscal 1987.

Need for Different Priorities

Ironically, a proportion of the capital that Japan is exporting is going into real estate development in the US and Europe, and into the financing of mortgage loans in the developed nations, most of which have a higher standard of housing than Japan. Thus, Japan, a nation where sharply higher real estate prices have put housing ownership out of reach for many, is actively financing investments to improve the quality of life in the US and Europe.

This fact has not escaped the attention of many opinion leaders in Japan. In the years ahead, we can probably expect more and more calls for increased use of Japan's financial resources at home. But careful thought should be given to creating the proper incentives and to taking steps to prevent the redirecting of liquidity to the home market from adding to inflationary pressures on land prices. One partial solution to the perceptions of inequality that may arise might be to provide more incentives for Japan's hard-working salaried class to enjoy the benefits of the country's wealth. The European experience of government-directed mandatory vacation time might be wisely considered in Japan.

The Problem of Double Deficits in the US

If the Japanese economy has rebounded strongly to the challenge of a sharply appreciated yen, how has the US fared? Some commentators in the US in particular have seen a connection between the trade and budgetary deficits, suggesting that a reduction in the budgetary deficit might somehow lead to a decline in the trade deficit. It may come as a surprise to these commentators, but Japan also has a large government budgetary deficit, though with a trade surplus and an appreciating currency. Our analyses in fact suggest that basic differences exist between Japan and the US in this regard. These include a very different composition of government expenditures, a decline in the size of deficits in Japan versus an increase in the US, and a much higher domestic savings rate in Japan which is generating more than enough financial resources to cover the government's requirements.

Japan's Budget Deficit

The expansion in Japan's budgetary deficit dates back to the mid-1970s, when the government sought to hasten recovery after the first oil crisis by expanding public works spending. The government budget deficit swelled from ¥880 billion, or only 4.6% of the total budget, in 1974, to a peak of ¥13.5 trillion in 1980, when it accounted for more than 30% of the budget, the highest level among the industrialized nations.

However, since then, the Japanese government has been successful in reducing the deficit to just over ¥11 trillion, or about 21% of the total government budget. As a percentage of the total government budget, the deficits in Japan and the US were virtually the same in 1985 and 1986, or just over 20%. In value, however, the US deficit in both years was over $200 billion, versus just under $90 billion for Japan. Relative to the size of the two economies, however, these deficits are close to being comparable as a percentage of GNP. But in contrast to the downtrend in the budget deficit in Japan, the US deficit has risen steadily from about $70 billion in 1980 to more than $170 billion in 1987.

The principal difference between the two nations is in the ratio of the deficit to net savings. Japan has a much higher rate of savings in the private sector to cover the excess of government spending over revenues. Although the ratio of net private sector savings has dropped to just under 14% in Japan, versus about 17% in the late 1970s, it still remains much higher than the 6–8% recorded in the US since the early 1980s.

The ratio of the government deficit to net private sector savings in Japan was about 26% in 1986, versus almost 94% in the US. As a result of this very basic difference in the ability to finance a budgetary deficit, not to mention the ability to control it, Japan is in a much better fiscal position. Savings in Japan cover the deficit of the public sector, finance the substantial investments of the private sector – which are a key to maintaining competitiveness – and resources are left over to export huge volumes of liquidity to finance deficits and investments in other countries.

Guns or Butter?

Another major difference between the budget deficits of Japan and the US is a stronger orientation towards investment of total expenditures. The US spends nearly 28% of its total budget on national defense. US defense expenditures alone amount to nearly 60% of the total Japanese national government budget. Another important difference is a much lower percentage of expenditures on social security. These expenditures still represent only about 20% of government expenditures in Japan, versus about 44% of the total budget in the US. Thus, government expenditures are more directed towards defense and welfare in the US, accounting for over 70% of the budget. These two items account for only about 26% of the national budget in Japan. This leaves a larger share of the budget available for government public works expenditures.

The smaller percentage of domestic savings absorbed by the budget deficit in Japan also has other implications. Other things being equal, we would expect interest rates to be much lower in Japan than in the US, which of course they are. Lower interest rates and the greater availability of funds have made it possible for Japan to keep the ratio of private capital investment to GNP at a high level. About 16% of the GNP in Japan is accounted for by private capital investment, versus only 10% in the US. In absolute terms, the US invests more – the dollar equivalent of ¥59 trillion, versus ¥53 trillion in Japan – but relative to the size of the economy, Japan invests substantially more. Government and private sector investment accounts for nearly 28% of the GNP in Japan, versus 18% in the US.

One useful observation from the Japanese experience is that a higher level of capital formation in the public, and particularly in the private, sector would contribute to sustained recovery in competitiveness in the US. The challenge for the US is to devise workable methods to increase total investment without incurring added costs to the government.

The US as Almighty Debtor

If Japan has moved to a position of prominence as the leading creditor nation, whither the United States? Unless some unforeseen developments appear on the horizon between now and the early 1990s, the net external debt position of the US will move from the current level of close to $300 billion to more than $1 trillion. Economists are still pondering what the full implications of this massive shift in the net external asset position of the US will be. Until relatively recently, the US was the world's largest creditor nation, a position now held by Japan.

Some economists in the US tend to play down the significance of this development, noting that US investments overseas are undervalued, that the inflow of capital from overseas does not materially affect the ownership structure or the operation of the US economy, and that the external debt of the US is only a small proportion of GNP. Our analysis suggests that their point of view may not take full account of some fundamental problems.

For example, it appears that one result of the growing external indebtedness of the US has been a sharp decline in the value of the dollar. Prospects for increasing external indebtedness have also created the perception that unless the US adopts the right monetary and fiscal policies and is successful in reducing its current account surplus by regaining its competitiveness, the dollar may continue to decline in value in the long term. In short, the dollar will be far from 'almighty' in the years ahead, and it is far from clear how the US will continue to maintain its position in the future as it goes further into debt to foreigners and must pay a growing proportion of its export earnings to service its external debt.

Causes of the Deficits

In today's international monetary system, countries such as Brazil and Mexico, which have large external borrowings in dollars, are obliged to meet those obligations in dollars. This means in effect that they must run balance of payment surpluses to pay interest and make payments on the principal. These countries are under a strong obligation to pay their way by remaining competitive in exports.

For the US, the implications are slightly different, since its obligations can be met in its own currency. However, like Brazil and Mexico, the US is gradually beginning to lose some of its autonomy in monetary and fiscal policy. One of the best examples of this was the newspaper coverage given in Japan to statements by certain large Japanese institutional investors that they would not participate in US Treasury Bond issues unless interest rates were above a specified level.

The causes of the growing external borrowings of the US include its large current account deficit and strong funds demand, stemming in large part from the substantial government deficit.

Neither of these problems appears likely to be solved in the foreseeable future. The record shows that the yen/dollar relationship is very much affected by trends in the US current account. For example, improvement in figures for May 1987 led to a stronger dollar in June and July, but the announcement of an increase in the current account deficit in June led to a weaker dollar in late August of that year. In the future, therefore, this sensitivity to developments in the US current account may have a strong effect on the relationship of the two currencies.

The process of reducing the US current account deficit may be quite lengthy unless stronger policy measures are adopted. There are signs that US exports have strengthened somewhat, as the weakening of the dollar since mid-1985 has restored some of the competitiveness of US industry. But a new development is that the growth in export industries is bringing higher growth in incomes, and this in turn is resulting in an increase in imports into the US. The US consumer is apparently willing to pay a large premium for what is perceived as a substantial quality differential between US and Japanese products. A contributing factor is that US manufacturers appear to be using the weakening of the dollar and the increase in the prices of imports as a reason for increasing prices and boosting short-term profitability, rather than trying to regain market share from Japanese manufacturers.

Similarly, the fiscal deficit is very likely to be difficult to reduce, since, for political and other reasons, it will continue to prove difficult to lower spending.

Prospects for Twin US Deficits

In what is probably a best-case scenario, the US government may achieve some gradual reduction in its fiscal deficit and succeed in increasing exports sufficiently to bring about a gradual fall in the balance of payments deficit. Under this scenario, the dollar may remain weak against the yen and show further gradual, but moderate, decline as the current account deteriorates because of rising interest payments to foreigners holding US debt.

However, in order to bring about this scenario, decisive action is needed in the next few years before the value of the dollar declines further. In a less-than-best-case scenario, the US would continue to experience an increase in its indebtedness and would increasingly be forced into the uncomfortable position of having foreign creditors dictate, or at least exert a growing influence on, interest rates.

As the dollar continues to decline in value, creditors such as the Japanese may begin to demand that a portion of their exposure be denominated in yen terms. This would mean an even faster increase in debt service payments in dollars, because in addition to an increase in the volume of outstanding debt, Americans would be forced to convert to an appreciating currency to pay interest and repay principal.

As debt service payments rise, the US will be under increasing pressure to expand its exports to cover its financial payments and reduce the current account deficit. In addition, since the US will be obliged to pay higher interest rates, US industry may continue to have to bear a higher cost of capital.

There is a tendency amongst some economists to play down the importance of the growing external debt of the US by comparing it with the GNP. Even with net external debts of US$1 trillion, the ratio of these debts to the US GNP will be smaller than for Brazil and Mexico. These arguments should be examined more critically. Many of the implications for the US and for its relationship with Japan and other allies appear to be quite serious, unless the current course of events can be reversed.

Introduction

Japan's game plan for domination of key strategic industries worldwide spans steel, automobiles, semiconductors, computers, robotics, biotech, and other fields. Japan's story is one of targeting key manufacturing industries and high technology.

The term 'high technology' covers two areas: applied versus basic technologies. By basic technology, we refer to high-cost, high-risk endeavors, such as ocean or space development, where the returns from a particular investment are much less than certain. We can contrast basic with applied technologies, where companies commercialize technologies that have already been established. Permitted a broad generalization, we would submit that high technology in Japan has often been developed outside Japan and then assimilated by Japanese companies, which have succeeded in commercialization and mass production. In a word, the current success of Japanese high technology is in applied technology, which, of course, spells competition with non-Japanese companies in the marketplace.

What are the driving factors behind Japan's success in commercializing high technology? Several issues are important. One is the educational system. The educational system in Japan is very strong through the secondary level and provides a thorough grounding in math and the sciences. Subsequently, company-sponsored training plays a key role.

We might also note governmental actions that have had an impact on high technology in Japan. Close government/business ties and articulated industrial policies have had a major impact. The basic policy is to make Japan less dependent on trade, while developing a more knowledge-intensive economy that will promote the diffusion of high-value-added products and services in Japan. However, certain failures and shortfalls over the years suggest that Japanese government policy is indeed fallible. If we examine the different projects funded, most to date have been for projects with rather immediate commercial payoffs. Another feature of Japanese industrial policy is to promote co-operation initially and then to encourage competition among Japanese companies. The key insight is that Japanese high-tech policy is almost always market driven.

We can see some of the results of the high-tech push in computers. Japan has the second largest computer industry and market in the world. In the world market for computer systems, the US leads with the largest share of the market;

all other countries account for the remainder. We have to keep Japanese achievements within perspective, however. One point to keep in mind is the slow progress the Japanese have made in computer exports. But the key factor is IBM, which has a world market share of about 60%. Historically, IBM has been perceived by Japanese companies as the major competitor, both in Japan and overseas. To date, at least, Japan's success in the international computer market has been mixed.

The Japanese share of the semiconductor market has grown even larger than its share of the world computer market. The general strategy of the Japanese integrated circuit industry is to be the first to level up into the next generation of high-density MOS memory devices. This was done very successfully in the 64K-DRAM, 256K-DRAM and 1M-DRAM fields. Generally speaking, Japanese producers have achieved very high volumes of production, enabling Japanese producers to reduce costs very quickly, to underprice US companies and, in the process, to capture market share.

We shall also look at Japanese robotics in our overview of Japanese high technology. According to most sources, Japan is the world leader in the production and installation of industrial robots. However, on the R & D side, Japan and the US are considered by many to be at roughly the same level.

Traditional biotechnology is an area in which the Japanese are very strong. Biotechnology refers to the use of fermentation technologies to produce substances such as antibiotics, enzymes, and amino acids. Japan's position derives from its long experience with fermentation technologies used to produce foods such as soy sauce, fermented soy beans, and other foods. New biotechnology usually refers to cell fusion, bioreactors, recombinant DNA, and certain other areas.

Let us tally the scorecard. The Japanese have been highly successful in integrated circuits and industrial robotics. In those sectors, Japan has achieved internationally competitive positions – a trend which is likely to continue in the foreseeable future. While biotechnology is lagging in the US, Japan is making rapid gains. In computers, the Japanese clearly will continue to be major players in the local home market. Exporting computers, however, is more difficult due to problems associated with software, service/support, and marketing and distribution channels.

We have now established a basis for comparing Japan's position in applied versus basic technologies. The Japanese have been successful in applied technologies, in part perhaps because of an educational system that is excellent through the secondary level, but weak at the graduate level. To be more successful in the basic technologies, a significantly improved postgraduate educational system would have to emerge in Japan.

Management style would have to be changed so as not to reward seniority, but rather to reward creativity. These practices, too, are culturally bound and unlikely to change very quickly. The Japanese have invested considerable time and effort in mass-production technologies. Therefore, shifting to the small-lot production, which the most advanced technologies may require, is something that is unlikely to occur very quickly or easily. The outlook is that while Japan will continue to be successful in applied technologies, there are apparently significant gaps regarding progress made in basic technologies.

We might also note the role of the Japanese government in summarizing future direction in planning documents which present its vision of the future for particular industries. Such documents are produced almost every year, reflecting subtle changes in attitude. What Japanese government planners seem to be saying currently is that it is imperative to shift from the present orientation as a trade-centered economy and to move to one that is more knowledge intensive.

To be sure, this concept has been around for years. In comparison to the past, however, one major difference is apparently a growing recognition that foreign companies and governments may be less willing to sell technology to Japan. This shift makes it essential for Japan to allocate more resources for work in basic technologies.

In short, the Japanese will likely continue to be successful in the applied technologies. This will affect US, European, and other companies most immediately in the integrated circuit and industrial robot marketplace. Success in the basic technologies, however, is an issue to consider for the mid-to-long term, as was the case with semiconductors and industrial robots ten years ago.

MITI and the Future of Japan's Industrial Structure

Japan's Ministry of International Trade and Industry (MITI) is the primary agency for formulating Japanese government policies to promote Japanese business and industrial development. The specific organ which formulates and publicizes MITI's industrial policy is the Industrial Structure Council. The Council is composed of representatives of academic and industrial circles, consumers, and labor unions, and works with MITI bureaucrats in the formation of industrial policy statements.

The first such statement, entitled *The Vision of MITI's Policies in the 1970s*, was published in 1971. The report forecast that, in the 1970s, Japan's industrial structure would become more sophisticated, with the growth of many technology- and knowledge-intensive industries, compared to the 1960s, which were characterized by the development of chemical and heavy industries. In 1979, the Industrial Structure Council began to consider Japanese industries in the 1980s. The results were published in March 1980 as *The Vision of MITI's Policies in the 1980s*. Revised in late 1987, the basic plan is still in force, and consists of the following basic directives:

- The degree of Japan's interdependence with both advanced and developing countries must be increased. Japan will have to avoid trade conflicts with advanced nations, and enlarge the domestic market for imports of low value-added products from developing countries. The upgrading of Japan's industrial structure towards a more sophisticated product mix is one way the

Japanese government is seeking to attain this goal.

- Japan must diversify its sources of oil supply, develop both alternative and new energy sources, and increase energy fuel stockpiles and conservation efforts.
- Japan must promote the development of innovative and original technology in order to stabilize its economic base. For the 1980s, the Japanese government has given itself the task of overseeing the country's transformation from a net importer of foreign technology to a technology-innovative nation, dependent on high-technology areas for economic growth.

According to the Industrial Structure Council, the knowledge-intensive industrial structure aimed for in the 1970s must be promoted further in the 1980s, with an emphasis on developing indigenous technological strengths. Technology intensification is being emphasized in most sectors of the Japanese economy, not only in such industries as computers, aircraft, and other machinery, but also in the energy-intensive sectors and in other basic industries.

Consequently, Japanese industrial policy has two overall thrusts. One is the promotion of high-technology or knowledge-intensive industries; the other is the gradual phasing out of basic, energy-intensive, low-growth industries.

The Promotion of Knowledge-intensive Industries

It is often heard in both industry and MITI circles that Japan was able freely to import foreign technology until the mid-1970s. However, since then, foreign companies have become acutely aware that Japanese companies have used imported technology to competitive advantage. And since foreign companies have come to demand stricter conditions for technology licensing, such as joint venture arrangements, MITI has started to encourage Japanese industry to develop greater expertise in basic research.

Most of MITI's attention and subsidies are directed towards the information sector, which includes the computer, software, telecommunications and semiconductor industries. Japanese government support of the domestic computer industry consists of government subsidies for joint R & D projects and the promotion of computer use through support of a specialized computer rental company, the JECC (Japan Electronic Computer Co).

While most government-sponsored initiatives have met with success, at least one major blunder can be noted. In 1984, MITI proposed a new and highly controversial software protection law which seeks to place software under a system of protection closer to patent, as opposed to copyright, provisions. The US and Canadian governments criticized numerous features of the MITI proposal: a short protection period of only 15 years as opposed to the 50 years plus life of the author formula available under copyright law; an unspecified right to modify software developed by third parties; and a compulsory licensing provision for software packages. Informed observers agreed that enactment of the proposal would have placed Japan outside internationally agreed-upon standards for software protection, and would enable Japanese companies, perhaps unfairly, to acquire software developed outside Japan. This was clearly a protectionist policy, and MITI's proposal was for the most part abandoned in the face of foreign pressure and criticism from other Japanese government ministries.

MITI's efforts to contribute to the future competitiveness of Japan's semiconductor industry are perhaps best symbolized by the New Function Semiconductor Element Program, which is part of the Next Generation Industries Basic Technologies R & D Program. A long-term undertaking lasting from 1981 to 1990, about ¥25 billion in government funding has reportedly been allocated for this program.

The Japanese government also supports R & D programs in other advanced fields, including biotechnology, robotics, and new materials.

Policies for Basic Industries

Just as MITI targets high-technology and key strategic industries, policies for basic and so-called 'sunset' industries are also carefully planned. MITI's overall policies and targets for Japan's basic industries during the 1980s include stabilizing supply sources, conserving energy, and diversifying business activities and technological development.

Japan is dependent on foreign sources for about 90% of its primary energy requirements (75% comes from imported oil). One of Japan's greatest national priorities is therefore to establish long-term energy security. As energy-intensive sectors, basic industries have more potential than other industries for conserving energy and diversifying energy sources. Thus, one goal is to reduce the importance of basic industries in Japan's industrial structure, while promoting energy conservation and alternative energy use by basic industries.

Another goal is to aid structurally depressed basic industries, such as the petrochemical, oil refining, and textile industries. MITI's overall objective is to ease the impact of chronic market stagnation and excess competition, which characterize these industries, as the importance of their position in the Japanese economy as a whole declines.

In order to achieve the objectives of conserving consumption and diversifying energy sources, MITI is urging Japan's basic industries to implement the following three fundamental policies:

- *Large-scale systematization.* This includes improvement of existing production processes and the development of new processes, such as biotechnical processes.
- *Specialty orientation.* During the 1980s, basic materials produced in Japan should require less energy and resource inputs, and be higher in value added. R & D efforts should be directed towards developing new materials with better performance and more sophisticated functions. Examples include specialty steels and chemicals, as well as special quality cement.

- *Diversification of raw materials.* The basic thrust of this policy is to lower the dependence of basic industries on oil as a raw material, and to diversify Japan's supply sources for other raw materials. This policy includes import-sourcing strategies, and the promotion of investment by Japanese firms in resource development projects overseas.

MITI has implemented the following measures in order to realize the policy goals outlined above:

- Tax measures to stimulate energy conservation.
- Subsidies to private firms undertaking R & D for new production processes or new products, such as programs in biotechnology, and C1 chemistry and heavy oil cracking projects.
- Government financing for both national and private projects to develop natural resources overseas. In all overseas projects carried out under the 'develop-and import scheme' (including projects for the development of raw materials and processed basic materials), companies have access to loans from the Ex-Im Bank at lower interest rates than those given by commercial banks.

Japan's Steel Industry: Why Japan is Number 1 in the Free World

Measured by its value of output, the steel industry ranks fifth in Japan behind the electronics, transportation equipment, general machinery, and chemical industries. In 1985, the steel industry accounted for 6.7% of manufacturing output and 7.7% of exports. Owing to the influence of the strong yen and foreign competition, steel exports fell to 6.1% of all Japanese exports in 1986.

Internationally, Japan has ranked second to the Soviet Union in steel production every year since 1982. The production of crude steel in Japan in 1986 amounted to 98.3 million tons, compared with 160.5 million tons in the Soviet Union and 74 million tons in the US (Figure 1).

Supported by MITI, and fueled by a rapidly increasing demand, Japan's steel industry grew at a phenomenal pace in the decade to 1973. There has been a slight decline in annual production of crude steel since the first oil crisis, but Japan still leads the free world in both output and exports of steel.

Recovery Led by Construction Demand

Japanese production of crude steel fell below 100 million tons in both 1985 and 1986, but effectively exceeded that mark in 1987. More than any other factor, the construction of office buildings and infrastructure projects is responsible for the upturn. About one-half of the steel consumed in Japan is used by the construction industry, and this proportion is expected to rise in the next few years. Growth in the construction industry was about 6% in 1987–88.

Figure 1   Crude Steel Production in 10 Leading Nations, 1986

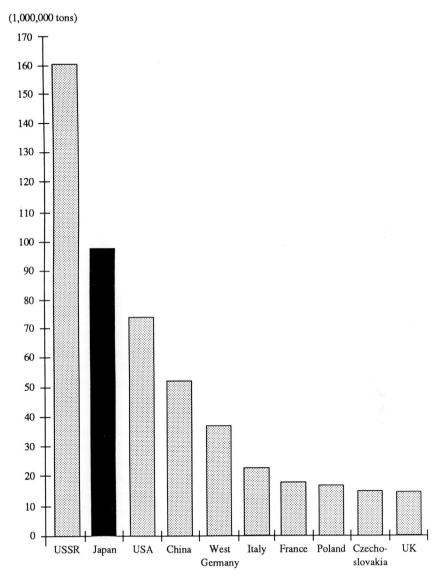

(1,000,000 tons)

Source: Tekko Tokei Yoran.

A Slowdown in Output Expected

Even with a strong demand from the construction sector, however, it is unrealistic to expect continued long-term growth in Japanese steel production. The appreciation of the yen is perhaps the most important factor militating

25

against a long-term recovery in the steel industry. The major steel companies have yet to restructure their operations to the point that they can export profitably at an exchange rate of ¥150 to the US dollar. Since about 30% of Japan's steel output has been shipped overseas in recent years, the inability to earn a profit on exports is clearly damaging to the industry.

Auto Industry Moves Offshore

The strong yen is driving domestic users of steel to set up factories overseas in order to take advantage of lower labor and material costs. From the viewpoint of steel makers, the most important example of an industry migrating to a more favorable business environment is Japan's auto industry. By 1990, the Japanese auto industry, now the second biggest consumer of steel in the country, will have established factories with production capacity of 1.9 million vehicles per year in North America alone. Working at full capacity, these auto factories in North America could cut Japanese auto exports by almost 30% from their level of 1986.

Strong Yen Driving Import Growth

The strong yen is also making it easier for foreign producers to export steel to Japan. The yen-based price of imported steel dropped sharply and almost continuously throughout 1985 and 1986, while the amount of steel imported shot up by 17% in 1986 and by about 30% in 1987. Almost 10% of the steel consumed in Japan is now cast in foreign mills.

Numerous Participants

There are about 60 companies traded publicly in Japan which are engaged wholly or primarily in the manufacture of steel. Fifteen of these companies have sales of ¥100 billion or more. The exclusive group of five companies with sales of more than ¥900 billion in fiscal 1986, ending March 1987, is often referred to in the press as 'the big five'.

Corporate Performance Depends on Rationalization

Japanese steel companies are making strenuous efforts to meet the challenge posed by the yen's appreciation and rising imports. Rationalization plans at the five biggest companies call for personnel cuts amounting to 20% or more of all employees. Old and relatively inefficient plants will be closed and production concentrated in fewer centers. In order to diversify, some steel companies set up as many as 10 or 12 new businesses in 1987 alone, many in areas unrelated to steel. None of the new businesses are expected to contribute significantly to profits before 1990, but they will absorb excess personnel at little cost to their parent companies.

The looming question for the Japanese steel industry is whether the respite from falling demand provided by the construction boom will last long enough to allow rationalization and diversification plans to bear fruit. The industry's goal, of course, is to restore its competitive edge. In other words, steel makers must aim to be profitable at a less favorable exchange rate than ¥150 to the dollar and at an annual production volume of less than 100 million tons of crude steel per year.

Guidance from the Government

MITI has long played a role in organizing cartels in the steel industry whenever excessive price cutting seemed likely to break out. Since many in the government view steel as one of Japan's key industries (a title it can still rightfully claim), support for current retrenchment efforts is likely to be strong. However, financial support is not likely to be forthcoming.

Steel Makers in a Strong Financial Position

For their part, the five major steel companies are well-armed for the struggle that lies ahead. The fact that they carry relatively heavy debt loads means that support for diversification will likely be forthcoming from the city banks. The top five steel companies also hold land and securities that may be worth several trillion yen at current market values. As a result, the so-called 'big five' have immense borrowing power and can well afford to run up large losses during this difficult period of restructuring.

Long-term Production Downtrend

Worldwide steel production reached a peak in 1974 and again in 1979, only to be brought down in both instances when oil prices were pushed to heights that

Figure 2 Worldwide Crude Steel Production, 1966–86

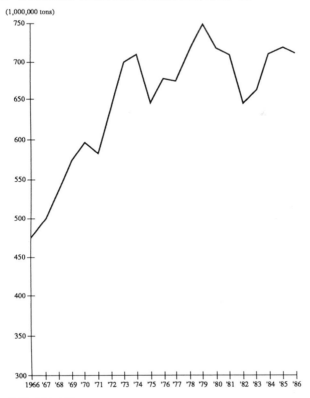

(1,000,000 tons)

Source: Tekko Tokei Yoran.

caused a global recession (Figure 2). Japan's steel output, like that of most industrialized countries, has declined since 1973–74, while the combined output of China, Brazil, South Korea, and Taiwan has more than doubled in the same period. Overall, a rough balance has been preserved in the 14 years since the first oil crisis, as worldwide steel production has neither risen nor fallen by more than 10% in any given year from the level of 1973.

Special Characteristics of the Steel Industry in Japan

Problem of Excess Capacity

The Japanese steel industry has long been plagued with excess capacity. The operating ratio of the industry as a whole has fallen below 70% in all but two years since 1975. The Industry Structure Council, an advisory organ of MITI, suggested that major producers should expand their capacity in the 1970s in order to meet expected domestic demand for 152 million tons of crude steel in fiscal 1978, ending March 1979. Although the resurgence in demand never materialized, nine extra-large furnaces were constructed between 1975 and 1979. The smallest of these new furnaces had a volume of 3,890 cubic meters, while six had volumes of between 4,000 and 5,000 cubic meters, and two exceeded 5,000 cubic meters in volume.

Complex Role of the Government

The fact that Japanese steel makers expanded their production capacity at an inopportune time solely on the advice of MITI may suggest to some that MITI controls the industry in all but name. Actually, the relationship is somewhat more complex. Japan's steel industry, though considered by many in government to be vital to the nation's welfare, has received very little in the form of direct subsidies during the postwar period. Comfortable and usually non-adversarial ties have been promoted by the following two practices:

- The government, and MITI in particular, helps steel companies to ride out cyclical downturns in the industry by arranging cartels and by setting price and output guidelines. Open defiance of a consensus reached with MITI guidance is extremely rare, not because the companies are subservient, but rather because they are willing to co-operate in times of crisis.
- It is common for elite bureaucrats in Japan to take executive positions in key industries after retiring at an early age from government jobs. A few of these retirees find their way into steel companies each year and, consequently, ties between these companies and MITI, for example, are very close.

Exports

Japan is the Top Exporter

Japan has been the world's leading exporter of steel since it overtook West Germany in 1969. Its exports of steel peaked in 1976 at 37.2 million tons, or about 39% of domestic crude steel production. In every year since 1971, Japan's exports of steel have been at least one-third higher than those of West Germany, which is still Japan's closest rival. The 30.4 million tons of steel exported in 1986 accounted for 32% of the country's crude steel production in that year. The destinations of Japanese steel exports are shown by country in Figure 3.

Figure 3   Destination of Japanese Steel Exports, 1981–86

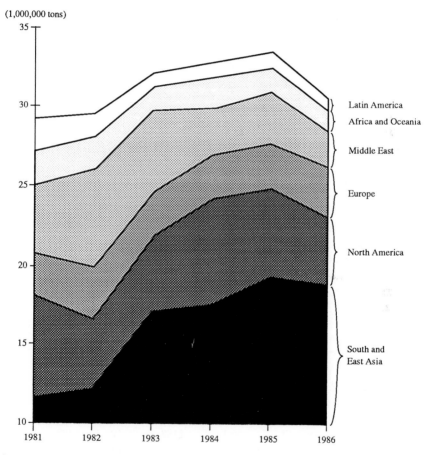

(1,000,000 tons)

Source: Tekko Tokei Yoran.

But Exports are Declining

Regardless of whether Japanese steel exports are measured by weight, percentage of domestic production, or yen-based value, they are clearly in decline. There are four main reasons for this decline in exports of steel from Japan:
•   effects of the strong yen;

- decline in Middle East buying power;
- expanding capacity in developing nations; and
- export restraints.

Imports

Rising Import Competition
The appreciation of the yen has not only made Japanese steel less attractive to potential overseas buyers, but has also made domestic steel makers more vulnerable to imports. In 1976, the year that Japan's steel exports peaked at more than 37 million tons, steel imports hit a low of 937,000 tons, or only 2.5% of exports. The amount of steel imported into Japan has increased rapidly since then, totaling more than 5 million tons in 1984 and 1986, or about 17% of steel exports.

Domestic Demand by Industry

The oil crisis of 1973 had a profound effect on industries requiring steel as a raw material. For example, the shipbuilding industry moved into a prolonged recession after high oil prices and subsequent conservation measures cut the demand for oil tanker services. Growth in the machinery industries declined, along with slower growth in private capital investment. The construction industry also shifted to a slower pace of expansion. The auto industry, however, continued to grow through the early 1980s as overseas demand for fuel-efficient Japanese vehicles increased (Tables 1 and 2).

Table 1   Domestic Consumption of Steel Products by Industry, fiscal 1984–86

(1,000 metric tons, %)

	1984	%	1985	%	1986	%
Shipbuilding	3,646	6.2	3,521	5.9	2,058	3.5
Automobiles	10,832	18.5	11,454	19.3	11,281	19.3
Industrial machinery	5,127	8.8	5,364	9.0	4,823	8.2
Electrical machinery	4,172	7.1	4,182	7.0	4,182	7.1
Construction	25,857	44.2	26.216	44.1	27,862	47.6
Secondary processing	4,255	7.3	4,200	7.1	3,958	6.8
Other	4,575	7.8	4,536	7.6	4,358	7.4
Total	58,464	100.0	59,473	100.0	58,522	100.0

Source: Tekko Tokei Yoran.
Notes: 1. Other includes household appliances, office equipment, containers, and rolling stock.
2. Figures for 1986 are provisional.

Table 2   Forecast for Domestic Consumption and Production

		1986	1990(a)	1990(b)
	1985	(Actual)	(Pessimistic)	(Optimistic)
Shipbuilding	3.5	2.1	0.5	1.0
Automobiles	11.5	11.3	7.2	9.0
Industrial machinery	5.4	4.8	4.7	4.7
Electrical machinery	4.2	4.2	4.5	4.5
Construction	26.2	27.9	32.6	32.6
Secondary processing	4.2	4.0	3.6	3.6
Other	4.5	4.4	4.0	4.0
Total domestic consumption (Product basis)	59.5	58.7	57.1	59.4
Exports	32.1	29.8	24.0	28.0
Imports	4.9	5.3	9.8	7.8
Domestic production (Crude steel basis)	103.8	96.4	82.3	91.2

(1,000,000 tons)

Source: Japan Iron and Steel Federation and IBI forecast.

Factors Affecting Performance of Japanese Steel Industry

Cost of Raw Materials

High Import Dependence

Japanese steel makers are dependent on foreign suppliers for more than 99% of the iron ore they use and more than 95% of the coal. As shown in Figure 4, the prices of these commodities fell sharply in yen terms in 1986 after drifting downwards for several years. In December 1986, the price of imported iron ore was only 53% of what it had been in 1982. In the same month, the price of imported coking coal fell to 55% of its 1982 price. Figure 4 also shows that the price of imported iron ore was fairly stable in the first 10 months of 1987, rising for five months and falling for five months.

Although iron ore and coal are the two most important raw materials in the production of steel, energy sources such as electricity, oil, and natural gas are also indispensable to the process. The yen-based price of energy, like that of other imports, has been slashed by the yen's appreciation. The price of imported oil, for example, plunged 78% between March 1985 and August 1986, and subsequently recovered only a fraction of that loss.

Figure 4 Price of Iron Ore and Coal Imported into Japan, 1982–87

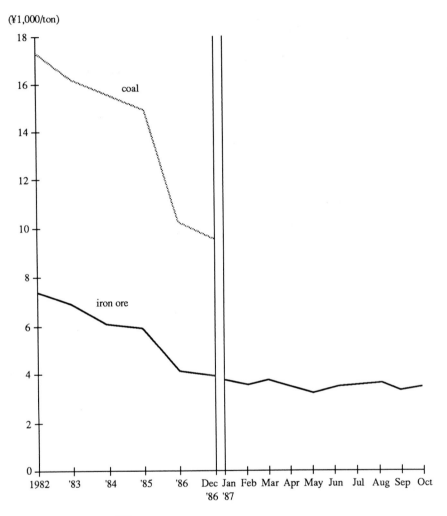

Source: Ministry of Finance.

Mixed Effects of the Strong Yen

The appreciation of the yen has clearly reduced raw material costs for Japanese steel makers. Nevertheless, benefits derived from the strong yen have not been enough to offset wage, salary, and equipment payments made domestically, all of which have risen sharply in US dollar terms since 1985. The important point here is that the overall effect of the yen's appreciation on the Japanese steel industry has been negative, although not as one-sidedly as is commonly thought.

Technological Advances

Japan has been in the forefront of efforts to curb energy consumption ever since the oil crisis of 1973 made the precarious nature of the country's energy supply abundantly clear. In 1973, Japanese steel makers used 5.4 million kilocalories of energy to produce one ton of steel, but by 1986 this figure was trimmed to 4.2 million kilocalories (Figure 5). This represents a 22% reduction in energy consumption per unit of finished steel in only 13 years.

Figure 5 Energy Consumption per Ton of Finished Steel, 1973–86

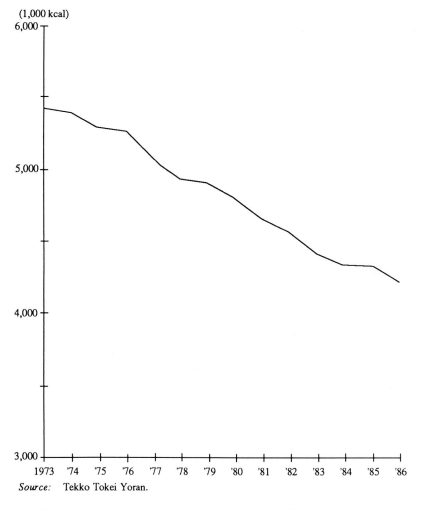

Source: Tekko Tokei Yoran.

    The continuous casting process was instrumental in helping Japanese steel companies to cut their energy consumption. Under this process, steel slabs are made directly from molten metal and then rolled and shaped into other products. Under older processes, molten steel is first cast as an ingot and cooled. It must then be reheated for further processing. The continuous casting process is far more energy-efficient and economical. As of 1986, only three minor players in steel production—Greece, Denmark, and Ireland—made all of their steel by the continuous casting process. The proportion of Japanese steel made by continuous casting in 1986 was 93%, higher than in any other major industrialized country (Figure 6).

Figure 6 Percentage of Steel Produced by Continuous Casting Method in
(%)   10 Leading Nations, 1986

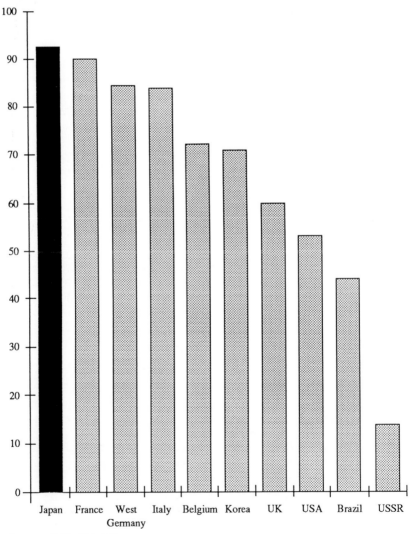

Source: Tekko Tokei Yoran.

34

Japanese steel companies are internationally regarded as being in the forefront in developing such new high valued-added steel products as rust-resistant electrogalvanized sheets for use in automobiles. One fairly good measure of the sophistication of a country's steel industry is the percentage of crude steel production that is accounted for by the output of specialty steel. At 18%, Japan leads both the US (13%) and the EC (17%).

Rationalization

The top five steel companies are attempting to move their operations into the black again by implementing medium-term rationalization plans. Central to

Figure 7 Employment in the Japanese Steel Industry, 1977–87
(1,000 employees)

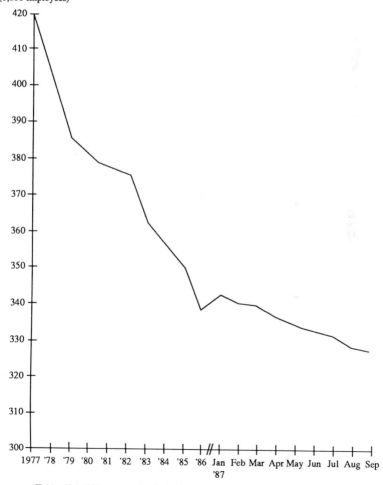

Sources: Tekko Tokei Yoran and Tekko Tokei Geppo.

each company's plan is a large-scale reduction in personnel. Old, inefficient plants will be closed, and companies will concentrate on raising their output of high value-added steel products.

Reduction in Personnel

As shown in Figure 7, total employment in the Japanese steel industry fell by 81,000 between 1977 and 1986. Personnel cuts continued at an even more rapid pace in 1987, with month-to-month drops in employment of more than 1,000 being recorded several times.

Corporate Strategies

Steel Production Overseas

The acquisition of companies overseas and the establishment of joint ventures in the US and elsewhere have been very limited compared to some other Japanese industries. This is believed to be a result of the lack of international orientation of the steel companies, many of which depend on trading companies for overseas marketing. Another concern is labor problems with the generally more fractious unions of the US and Europe.

In spite of their lack of experience in this field, all the big five except Kobe Steel are now actively engaged in overseas steel production. No specific plans have been made public regarding the expansion of overseas production facilities, but conditions appear ripe for further growth, particularly in North America. Interviews in the auto industry suggest that Japanese companies prefer to use Japanese suppliers; therefore, the invasion of North America by Honda et al could make the purchase or construction of more steel plants there almost irresistible for the major Japanese steel companies.

Gradual Diversification

Many of the new businesses set up by steel companies are not expected to add significantly to the parent company's profitability, but rather are meant to create new jobs for current employees. In-house services such as translation, security, and maintenance are often the first new businesses to be spun off. The new subsidiaries are smaller and therefore tend to have lower pay scales than parent companies, which makes their establishment very attractive to cost-conscious steel makers. If new businesses are successful, they can absorb more workers at no cost to the parent company.

Some new businesses are intended to become major revenue sources supporting the parent company. These tend to be larger and better financed than the former in-house services described above. The operations of major new business ventures may be closely related to steel, or in unrelated areas that have been chosen because they make good use of company assets or promise to be profitable.

Carbon fiber is a good example of a major new business area that is closely related to steel. Oil burned in steel production leaves a carbon residue that can be processed into carbon fiber. At present, the carbon fiber industry is suffering from overcapacity, so the success of steel makers in this competitive field depends on their ability to develop new composite materials.

Several steel and/or closely affiliated companies are already producing silicon wafers, thus showing that they are willing to take the plunge in business areas unrelated to steel. Growth is running at about 7% per annum in the semiconductor industry as recovery proceeds from the slump that began in 1984.

Automobiles: New Inroads into the US Market

The year 1980 marked a turning point in the Japanese automobile industry. The number of vehicles (including passenger cars, trucks, and buses) produced in

Figure 8 Annual Auto Production in Four Major Countries, 1977–86

(Unit: million vehicles)

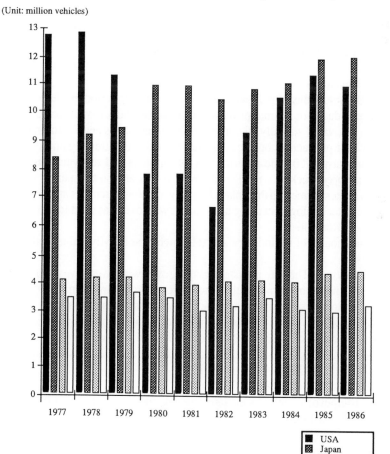

Source: Automotive News, 1987 Market Data Book Issue.

Legend: USA, Japan, W. Germany, France

the US that year plunged by more than 3 million units from 11.4 million in 1979. Smaller production cuts were recorded in West Germany, France, Italy, Canada, and the UK. Among major auto producers in the non-communist world, only Japan raised its production. The number of vehicles produced in Japan surged from 9.6 million units in 1979 to 11 million units in l980 (Figure 8). After more than a decade of finishing second to the US in annual vehicle production, Japan was suddenly thrust into the position of world auto industry leader. Since then, it has never looked back.

Continued Dominance

Japan turned out 12.3 million vehicles in 1986, thus maintaining its number 1 ranking in the world auto industry for a seventh consecutive year. Although Japanese auto makers now account for more than one-quarter of all vehicle production in the world, Japan's share has actually declined by 1–2% since 1980, owing largely to the resurgence of the American auto industry. Sharp production increases by auto makers in South Korea and Italy also squeezed the Japanese share in 1986.

Historical Perspective

Early Development

Although the auto industry in Japan dates from the prewar period, its development into an industry of international standing began in about 1956. Prior to the war, Japan cultivated virtually all of the peripheral industries needed for truck and war vehicle production, but the consumer market was extremely limited in size. By the early 1950s, the industry and its suppliers had recovered sufficiently to produce trucks for the Korean War. It was also in this period that major auto makers firmed up their plans for entry into the passenger car market, some through technology licensing agreements with overseas producers such as Austin and Renault.

The early course of the industry's development was heavily influenced by two factors

- *Protectionism* The auto industry in Japan, even with protective tariffs of 40%, was not competitive with imports from the US in the mid-1950s, which led to an early drive to achieve greater economies of scale.
- *Targeting of Small Cars* Also as a result of competition from overseas, Japanese auto makers decided to concentrate on the small car market. Small cars were more suited to road conditions in Japan, and their low operating costs appealed to Japanese consumers.

Large Role in the Japanese Economy

The annual output of vehicles by the Japanese auto industry increased 178-fold between 1955 and 1985. As a consequence of this expansion, employment in auto manufacturing reached 844,000 in 1986, with hundreds of thousands more people employed in related fields such as sales, leasing, and repairs. Production

Figure 9 Manufacturing Industries: Output by Sector, 1985

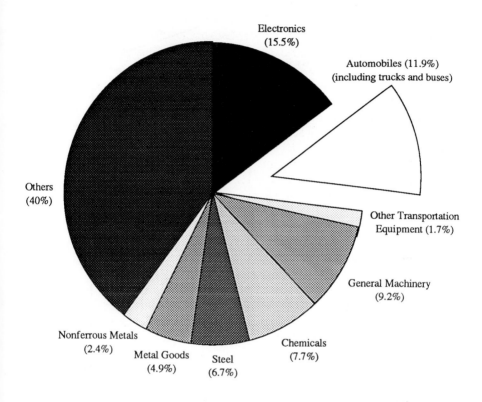

Source: Japan Automobile Manufacturers Association.
Note: Total value = ¥ 265,632 billion.

of vehicles is now the second largest manufacturing industry in Japan (Figure 9). More than half of Japan's vehicle production is exported, and these exports account for more than 25% of the country's total exports (Figure 10). In fact, nearly half of all exported vehicles in the world are Japanese. Although the US is often portrayed as the nation most infatuated with cars, Japan has come to be far more dependent than the US on its auto industry for continued economic health.

Figure 10   Export Value of Seven Main Industrial Sectors, 1986

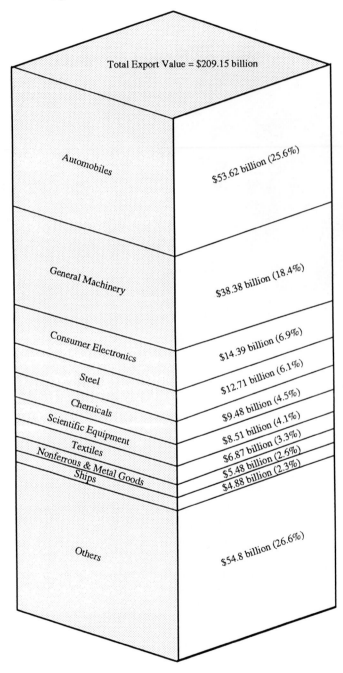

Total Export Value = $209.15 billion

Automobiles — $53.62 billion (25.6%)

General Machinery — $38.38 billion (18.4%)

Consumer Electronics — $14.39 billion (6.9%)

Steel — $12.71 billion (6.1%)

Chemicals — $9.48 billion (4.5%)

Scientific Equipment — $8.51 billion (4.1%)

Textiles — $6.87 billion (3.3%)

Nonferrous & Metal Goods — $5.48 billion (2.6%)

Ships — $4.88 billion (2.3%)

Others — $54.8 billion (26.6%)

Source: Japan Automobile Manufacturers Association.

The Japanese Auto Market

Second Largest National Market

Four-wheel vehicle sales in Japan totaled 5.7 million units in 1986, or about 46% of domestic vehicle production. With 48 million vehicles licensed for use on its roads, Japan ranks second in the world in vehicle ownership (Figure 11).

Figure 11   Ownership of Four-wheel Vehicles in 16 Major Countries (end of 1985)

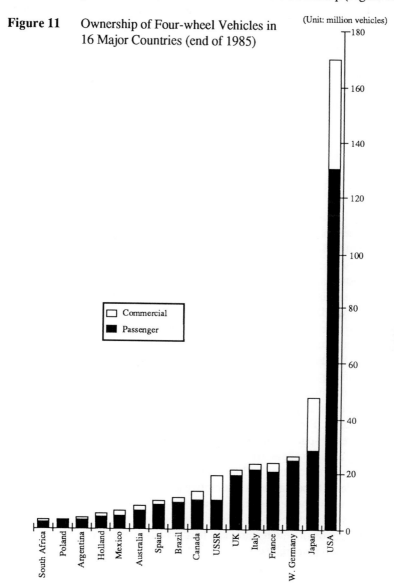

Source: Japan Automobile Manufacturers Association.

41

This vast market remains almost inaccessible to imports in spite of the efforts of foreign auto makers to sell more of their vehicles in Japan. In 1986, non-Japanese auto makers sold fewer than 70,000 units in Japan.

Reason for High Vehicle Turnover

Overall, there are fewer than 30% as many vehicles licensed for use on the road in Japan as in the US, yet unit vehicle sales in Japan are typically 35% or more of the US level each year. Government regulations play an important role in curtailing the average useful life of a new vehicle in Japan to about 80% of the US vehicle average. These regulations, which take the form of a periodic inspection called *shaken*, also go a long way towards maintaining domestic vehicle sales at a high level. No vehicle may be driven on public roads if it does not meet rigorous *shaken* standards three years after purchase and every two years thereafter. Rather than pay for the expensive tuning and repair work indicated by *shaken* after five or seven years, many motorists prefer to buy new vehicles. Though this system has its merits, it has been criticized as a form of collusion between government and industry.

Passenger Cars

Mature Market

The Japanese passenger car market is said to be mature. In concrete terms, this means that 80% of new cars are bought as replacements for cars that are being traded in or discarded. About 70% of Japanese households already own a car, and a substantial 15.6% of households own two cars. Although auto makers are pinning rather large hopes on a surge in the number of two-car families, it must be remembered that the number of people per household is decreasing, and that second cars are almost invariably less expensive than first cars. As one might expect in a mature market, passenger car sales, which account for 55% of all new vehicle sales in Japan, have not shown exceptional growth in recent years.

Technology as a Sales Weapon

The trend towards new features and increasing technological sophistication is indicative of an important tactic that auto makers use to stimulate sales in a mature market. Four-wheel steering, for example, was introduced by Honda and has greatly spurred sales of the Prelude model. Four-wheel drive has been offered by all Japanese auto makers since 1984, and sales of vehicles equipped with this feature increased by 36.4% from 1985 to 1986. Now that the Japanese are considered to be leaders in automotive technology, they are in a position to introduce innovative features almost at will. This may not be the decisive factor that makes or breaks major players in the auto industry, yet the development and introduction of new features can hardly be ignored in a market where the overall growth potential is small.

Japan's Domestic Market Outlook

Clear Upward Trend

All indicators point to a growing domestic market in Japan. Paradoxically, the strength of the domestic market derives largely from the weakness of the export market. Faced with a strong yen and 'voluntary' export restraints, auto industry executives are placing great emphasis on increasing their market share in Japan. Competition heated up in late 1986, when Toyota launched a corporate 50th anniversary program aimed at seizing a 50% share of the domestic market. Toyota achieved its goal for a brief period, but profit margins were cut to a level that rendered the victory meaningless.

Vehicle sales in Japan will likely remain solid but unspectacular for the next two to three years. Measures to stimulate the domestic economy will have a positive effect on overall sales growth, but will benefit companies that specialize in trucks more than those that produce mainly passenger cars. Under present circumstances, it would not be unreasonable to expect annual growth of more than 5% in truck sales.

Minicar sales will rise or fall along with the number of two-car families, which means that they will probably rise faster than the industry average in the short term, and flatten out in the 1990s as replacement purchases become the driving force in the market. About 3% growth per year in minicar sales is expected until the end of the decade.

Japanese Vehicle Exports

Historical Perspective

Until the oil crisis of 1973–74, Japan was one of three countries exporting between 1 and 2 million vehicles per year. West Germany, which exported over 2 million vehicles in 1973, was the world leader in this field. With the onset of the first oil crisis, the demand for inexpensive, fuel-efficient automobiles increased dramatically in oil-importing countries all over the world. The Japanese fully exploited this 'windfall', exporting more vehicles than the West Germans not only in 1974, but also in every year since then (Figure 12). In 1986, vehicle exports from Japan exceeded those of West Germany, still the runner-up, by a factor of 2.4 in unit terms. The average export ratio of Japanese auto makers, about 54%, is compared with those of other countries in Figure 13.

Resistance to Japanese Exports is High

Japanese auto makers are now facing a level of resistance to export sales that is unprecedented since their vehicles first gained widespread overseas recognition 15–20 years ago. The most important barriers to export sales are the strong yen, competition from South Korea and other newly industrializing countries, and export restraints on both the American and European markets. Japanese auto makers are responding with a strategy that stresses (1) overseas production, and (2) strengthening of their position in the domestic market.

Figure 12   Annual Auto Exports of Major Countries, 1970–86

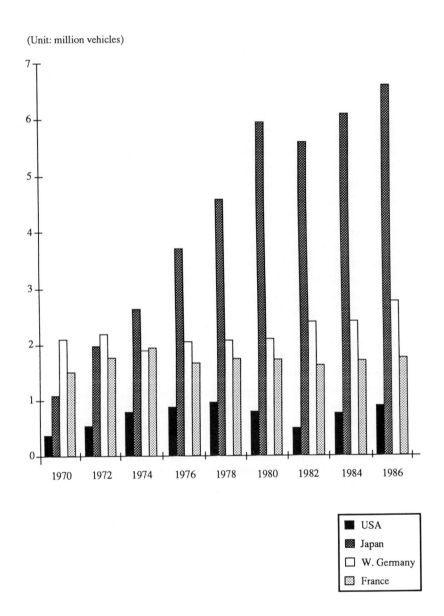

(Unit: million vehicles)

Source: Japan Automobile Manufacturers Association.

Figure 13   Four-wheel Vehicle Export Ratio of Major Industrial
Nations, 1986

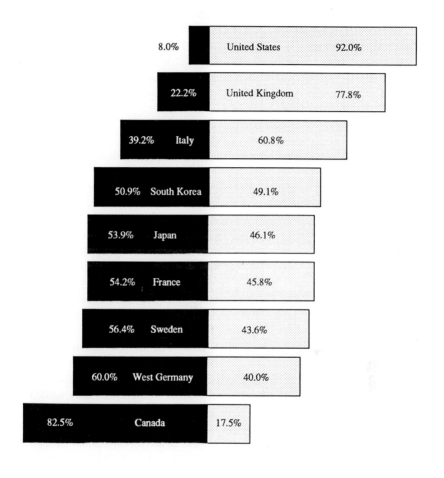

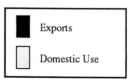

Source: Japan Automobile Manufacturers Association.

Export Destinations

Slightly more than half of all vehicles exported from Japan in 1986 were sent to the US. This seems reasonable when one notes that the US is the largest auto market and the largest import market in the world. Although they expended great effort in getting established in the US, Japanese auto makers have by no means ignored other markets. In 1986, almost 24% of vehicles exported from Japan were destined for Europe, and another 11% were sent to Southeast Asia and Oceania. With a strong presence in the relatively small auto markets of the Middle East, Africa, and South America, Japanese vehicles have, if not conquered, at least gained a foothold in every non-communist market in the world.

Adjustment to Yen Shock

No discussion of recent trends in Japanese vehicle exports would be complete without mention of the severe blow dealt to the entire industry by the yen's sharp rise in value. In mid-1985, the exchange rate was ¥249/US$1, but two years later it had moved to ¥147/$1. The yen's upward revaluation rendered old production and export strategies obsolete within a period of months. It is to the credit of auto makers in Japan that vehicle exports were higher in dollar terms, albeit slightly lower in unit terms, in 1986 than in 1985. In the process of adapting to the strong yen, Japan's auto industry has gone through some revolutionary changes, the most significant of which are explained below.

Declining Exports

As mentioned above, exports of Japanese vehicles declined from 1985 to 1986. The decline amounted to only 1.9% of 1985 vehicle exports, or 126,000 units, but coming after three consecutive years of positive export growth, the reversal appeared devastating at first, especially in light of the yen's continuing rise. Year-to-year sales figures deteriorated most in the final quarter of 1986, a development that can be attributed to price increases made late in the year by auto makers attempting to recoup at least some of the losses they sustained because of higher production costs in terms of dollars.

The downturn in vehicle exports from Japan continued and even picked up speed in 1987. Just over 3.2 million four-wheel-drive vehicles were exported in the first half of 1987, down 6.2% from the same period in 1986. Combined Japanese vehicle exports to the US declined 11.2% from the first half of 1986, while passenger car exports to the US were down by 13.7%.

Squeezed Profit Margins

The only reason the export decline has not been worse is that Japanese auto makers have apparently been willing to reduce profit margins significantly in order to maintain their overseas market share. Price increases of Japanese vehicles in the US were held at 18–25% in the period from September 1985 to July 1987, in spite of the fact that the value of the yen rose 70% in the same period.

As recently as 1985, it was highly profitable for Japanese auto makers to export passenger cars to the US. The exchange rate was favorable and the number of Japanese vehicles shipped to the US under export restraints fell short of demand. Each auto maker's quota within the overall restraint figure was set by negotiations, which severely limited competition between companies. This is no longer true. The appreciation of the yen has put some added pressure on the ability of the Japanese to export. Cost-cutting alone will not solve this problem, as Japanese auto makers cannot compete in their traditional market with low-cost South Korean producers.

Japanese Move Upmarket

The number of passenger cars with engine displacement greater than 2,000cc exported from Japan in the first half of 1987 was 36.4% higher than in the same period of 1986. Meanwhile, the number of small cars exported from Japan in the export sales of all Japanese passenger cars has come under pressure. Buffeted by market trends that discriminate against small vehicles, Fuji Heavy Industries announced that it will stop selling small trucks in the US because it cannot meet the price of other imports or domestically produced models.

In fact, it is becoming economically unjustifiable for Japanese auto makers to keep exporting the small, inexpensive cars and trucks that made them famous. American auto makers have trimmed production costs to a competitive level, and South Korean auto makers — relatively unaffected by damaging currency fluctuations — are assuming a larger role in the North American market for economy cars. Pushed from two sides, the Japanese are planning their move into full-size luxury cars, a market where high-level technological skills are required and profit margins are wider.

Company Strategies for Upmarket Passenger Cars

European performance luxury imports command an annual 500,000 unit market in the US, and it is towards this market that Honda, Toyota, and Nissan in particular are aiming. Honda's Acura division is already producing a line of US$20,000-plus luxury cars that the company expects will match Daimler or Volvo in US sales volume. Toyota and Nissan will follow suit with full-size cars of their own, possibly in 1989. Toyota reveals that its new V-8 sedan is likely to be 200 inches or more in length, as opposed to 197 inches for the Buick Electra or 196 inches for the 98 Regency Brougham.

Because image is of great importance in marketing luxury cars, Honda decided to sell its Acura line only through exclusive outlets that do not handle economy cars. Market research suggested that Honda luxury cars suffer by association with less glamorous models. By 1989, Honda intends to increase the number of its Acura outlets in the US to 600 from a current 200. Two or more sales networks per auto maker may become the rule when Toyota and Nissan introduce their upmarket models.

Knockdown Sets and Overseas Production

At an exchange rate of ¥150 to the dollar, most Japanese auto makers find that they can produce vehicles as cheaply in the US as in Japan. However, the first few Japanese auto factories in the US were planned long before the yen began its ascent. Their original purpose was to ease the sting of export restraints.

One side effect of the establishment of overseas production facilities has been a rapid increase in the number of knockdown sets exported from Japan. The five Japanese auto factories operating in North America procure, on average, more than 50% of their parts locally, but the remaining 40–50% are still shipped from Japan. In other parts of the world, production of Japanese autos involves markedly less local content. At the end of 1986, there were Japanese auto production facilities in 41 countries around the world, most of which were 'screwdriver factories', where local employees assembled auto kits from Japan. As long as the yen stays at a high level, Japanese industry participants report that it makes more sense, for example, to assemble Japanese autos destined for Thailand in Thailand.

Exports of knockdown sets reached 1,315,755 units in 1986, or 31.2% higher than in the previous year. The US was still the number one destination for Japanese knockdown sets, but it took only about one-third (456,255 units) of the exported total. Australia (158,138 units) and Taiwan (139,656 units) were the next biggest importers. In the first five months of 1987, exports of knockdown sets were running 35.9% ahead of 1986's record-setting pace.

Outlook in Overseas Markets

Over the next several years, the Japanese yen will probably continue to grow stronger relative to the dollar, although at a much slower rate than in the recent past. This will make it less economical for Japanese auto makers to produce vehicles in Japan for export. The practice of assembling vehicles in overseas plants near their point of sale may become more desirable not only because it allows auto makers to get around import/export controls, but also because it will make increasingly good sense as a means of controlling production costs.

Rise in Offshore Capacity

Along with an increase in the number of overseas production facilities, double-digit growth in knockdown set exports has been recorded through 1988. Between mid-1987 and late 1989, six new Japanese production facilities are scheduled to open in North America. These plants will absorb a huge number of auto components from Japan, but the stimulus provided to producers in Japan by these plants will likely be short-lived. The six plants mentioned here will have a combined production capacity of about 1 million vehicles per year, which will undoubtedly play a large part in exacerbating the predicted oversupply of up to 4 million units per year in the North American market by 1990. Furthermore, it is the stated intention of Japanese auto makers operating in North America to procure an increasing percentage of parts locally, which means, of course, that fewer parts will be shipped from Japan. Nevertheless, a rapid increase in knockdown set exports, even though a short-term phenomenon, will prevent Japanese auto makers from coming down with a bump as their exports of finished vehicles erode from under them.

As for exports of finished vehicles, the outlook is not bright. In unit terms, vehicle exports in 1987 were below the previous year's level, and all indicators point to a continuation of the same trend in 1988. As Japanese auto makers retreat upmarket, and production costs increase along with the value of the yen, the market for vehicles exported from Japan will grow more restricted with each passing year. Furthermore, prospective auto buyers in many countries will have little reason to purchase Japanese imports if locally produced Japanese autos are also readily available.

A Sign of the Times
Honda started selling American-made Accords in Japan in 1988. Other auto makers made similar announcements shortly after Honda.

Overseas Vehicle Production

Industry-wide Trend
The number of vehicles sold under Japanese brand names each year is considerably greater then the number of vehicles made in Japan. All Japanese auto makers are now involved to some extent in overseas vehicle production, one of the most rapidly evolving fields in the industry. In 1982, Honda became the first Japanese auto maker to open a large factory in its major foreign market, the US. Even prior to that, however, a number of Honda's rivals were operating vehicle assembly plants with limited output in Southeast Asia.

US Production
Honda, Nissan, and Toyota all established production facilities in the US at a time when the yen-dollar exchange rate made exports from Japan very profitable. The purpose of these first factories was not to make operations more cost-efficient, but rather to allow the auto makers to sell more passenger cars in the US than was permitted by export restraints.

Export Restraints
Export restraints were 'voluntarily' adopted by Japanese auto makers in 1981 as a means of deflecting the resentment of protectionist-minded legislators in the US. From 1981 to 1983, Japanese passenger car exports to the US were limited to 1.68 million units per year. The export ceiling was lifted in each of the next two years, first to 1.85 million units and then to 2.3 million units, where it has remained thus far. Restraints applied not only to the Japanese auto industry as a whole, but also were divided into yearly quotas for each company. Honda, realizing that US demand for its passenger cars was much higher than its export quota, accelerated plans to establish a factory in the US. Honda of America started production in November 1982.

The upward revaluation of the yen, which continued almost unbroken throughout 1986, was extremely propitious for Japanese auto makers who had just invested heavily in US production facilities. At an exchange rate of ¥150 to the dollar, most Japanese auto makers now state that they can manufacture vehicles as cheaply in the US as in Japan. In 1987, the yen surged briefly beyond ¥140 to the dollar, which means that auto makers have managed to add the benefit of low production costs to the originally planned benefit of higher US sales.

Japanese auto factories in North America differ from other overseas production facilities in both their scale of operations and their reliance on local parts suppliers. Nevertheless, Japanese production facilities in other countries cannot be disregarded, as they contribute significantly to total output. Southeast Asian factories in particular have a major role to play in the global strategy of their parent companies. Taiwan, for example, serves as an actual or planned production site for Daihatsu, Nissan, Mitsubishi, and Fuji Heavy Industries. Some of the vehicles manufactured in Taiwan by these companies are destined for export to the US and Europe, where, it is hoped, they will not arouse the same protectionist backlash as if they were manufactured in Japan. A comparison of North American and Southeast Asian operations might be in order at this point.

New Japanese Auto Factories in North America

Since Honda commenced auto production at its Ohio factory in 1982, there has been a flood of Japanese investment into North American auto factories (Table 3). North American output capacity of Japanese vehicles, which stood below 360,000 units per year when Honda was the only player, swelled to approximately 900,000 units per year at the end of 1987, and to more than 1,900,000 units per year in 1991. The actual output of Japanese vehicles in North America was roughly 350,000 units in 1986, not including the Chevrolet Novas built from Toyota knockdown sets at the NUMMI factory. By 1990, seven of the nine Japanese companies that manufacture passenger cars will have operations in the US.

Honda's Strategy

Honda has good reason to be more ambitious than its competitors in establishing and expanding North American production facilities. In 1986, Honda sold 690,000 vehicles in the US, as opposed to 508,000 in Japan. Furthermore, the company expects its sales to grow faster in the US than in Japan for the next several years. As the strong yen cuts into Honda's exports of finished vehicles from Japan, the company intends to increase US production significantly from the 1986 level, which was about 245,000 units per year, in order to make the US a base for Honda exports to other countries. Honda of America already ships motorcycles to 15 countries, and passenger cars to Taiwan.

Japanese auto makers are taking action to defuse the politically explosive issue of local content in the vehicles they produce in the US. Until now, virtually all safety-related and high value-added components, such as engines and drive trains, have been imported from Japan for assembly in North America. Honda, a perennial trendsetter, announced at the beginning of 1987 that it would start producing engines in the US for use in its North American vehicles. This, along with other measures, will raise the local content of Honda's vehicles to two-thirds in 1989 from about one-half in early 1987. In 1987, Toyota announced that it would include 60% local content in the passenger cars it will begin manufacturing at its facility in Kentucky by early 1988. Periodically, other Japanese auto makers announce that they will begin procuring door handles, dashboard clocks, etc, locally. The trend towards higher local content can be expected to continue apace, as it is both politically expedient and causes little or no increase in production costs at the current exchange rate.

Mixed Outlook

A problem arises in predicting the output of Japanese auto factories in North America. While capacity can be predicted with relative confidence, actual output has been two-thirds of capacity. Since the US market for new passenger cars was under pressure in 1987 and 1988, albeit with a slight growth in the market for foreign cars, it seems improbable that the scheduled capacity increases of Japanese auto makers in those years will be used efficiently. However, it is also unlikely that all Japanese auto makers will suffer equally from the looming oversupply. On the one hand, Honda may actually improve its capacity utilization rate in spite of dismal market conditions. Honda's vehicles are still growing in popularity in North America, and Honda procures a higher percentage of its parts locally than any of its Japanese competitors, which puts the company in a good position to cope with the expected long-term strengthening of the yen. On the other hand, both Toyota and Nissan reportedly fell behind sales goals in 1987; Nissan even cut back 20% on light truck production at its Tennessee factory. The inventory of completed vehicles carried by each of these companies in the US gives some idea of how well they are performing relative to their expectations. In early 1987, Honda was carrying its usual 10- to 12-day inventory, while Toyota carried a 30-day inventory and Nissan struggled with a 61-day inventory.

Auto Imports into Japan

Negligible Amounts

Sales of imported vehicles in Japan are very low relative to overall vehicle sales. In 1986, fewer than 70,000 foreign vehicles were sold in Japan, as opposed to more than 5.6 million domestically produced vehicles. At first

Table 3   Japanese Auto Makers in North America

Japanese Manufacturer	Honda Motor	Nissan Motor	Mazda Motor	USA Mitsubishi Motor
Production form	Independent	Independent	Independent	Joint venture with Chrysler
Japanese manufacturer in the US	Honda of America Mfg Inc	Nissan Motor Mfg Corp USA	Mazda Motor Manufacturing (USA) Corp	Diamond Star Motors Corp
Date established	February 1987	July 1980	January 1985	October 1986
Capitalization	US$478 million	US$375 million	US$200 million	US$15 million at first and US$150 million at final stage
Capital ratio	Honda of America 97%, Honda 3%	Nissan, USA 80% Nissan 20%	Mazda 100%	50/50
Location	Marysville, Ohio	Smyrna, Tennessee	Flat Rock, Michigan	Bloomington-Normal, Illinois
Site area	1.05 million square meters	3.17 million square meters	2 million square meters	2.57 million square meters
Model	Accord Civic	Nissan truck (1t) Sunny	Capella-class project	1,800–2,000cc 2-door hatchback sports specialty car (initially)
Startup date	First line in November 1982. Second line in April 1986	Nissan truck, June 1983 Sunny, March 1985	Autumn 1987	Autumn 1988
Capacity	360,000 units per year (in full production)	240,000 units a year	240,000 units a year	240,000 units a year
Work force	About 2,600	2,540	3,500	About 2,900
Investment	US$256 million (First line) US$280 million (Second line)	US$745 million	US$110 billion	About US$600 million
Local content	Above 60%	Above 60%	Above 60%	50–60% (planned)

Source: Japan Automobile Manufacturers Association.

Toyota Motor	Toyota Motor	Fuji Heavy Ind. Isuzu Motors	Honda Motor	Canada Toyota Motor	Suzuki Motor
Joint venture with GM	Independent	Undecided	Independent	Independent	Joint venture with GM Canada
New United Motor Mfg Inc NUMMI	Toyota Motor Manufacturing USA	Undecided	Honda of Canada Mgf Inc	Toyota Motor Manufacturing Canada Inc	CAMI Automotive Inc
February 1984	January 1986	Spring 1987	June 1984	January 1986	December 1986
US$200 million	Undecided	Undecided	C$203 million	–	C$202.5 million
50/50	Undecided	Fuji 51% Isuzu 49%	Canada Honda 100%	–	50/50
Freemont, California	Georgetown, Kentucky	Lafayette, Indiana			
810,000 square meters	6.07 million square meters	3.52 million square meters	1.82 million square meters	1.50 million square meters	1.60 million square meters
Nova	Passenger cars	Light trucks	Accord	Passenger cars	Custom Gimny
December 1984	1988	End of 1989	November 1986	1988	April 1989
240,000 units a year	240,000 units a year	50,000 Carolla cars a year	80,000 units a year (in full production)	50,000 units a year	200,000 units a year
About 2,500	About 3,000	About 1,700	About 700 (in full production)	About 1,000	2,500–2,800
About US$400–500 million	About US$600 million	About US$80 billion	C$200 million	C$400 million	C$615 million
About 60%	Undecided	Initially 50–60%	About 50%	Undecided	About 50%

glance, the share of foreign vehicles in the Japanese market may seem to be of extremely minor importance, yet all indicators point to considerable sales growth in the future.

The Japanese Challenge in Industrial Robotics

Introduction

Japan's production of industrial robots, estimated at around ¥300 billion in 1987–88, is still small in scale but is growing (Table 4). Increasingly faster production growth, both in volume and value, occurred during the 1970s. Between 1975 and 1980, production value for industrial robots increased faster than production volume, indicating a growing share of higher-grade, more expensive industrial robots in total robot production. Higher-grade robots account for over 50% of industrial robot production in value terms. However, the overwhelming majority of the installed industrial robot population base is of lower-grade varieties, performing relatively simple tasks.

Industrial robots are a combination of various technologies. This results in a substantial level of inter-company sourcing and other transactions, since no one company is able to produce all the necessary parts and technology for robot production. Industrial robots are classified by input method or by area of application. The latter is important since Japan's industrial robot industry is segmented by application area. Application technology is vital for the introduction and operation of robots within a particular production process. This necessitates specialization on the part of the robot producer. The introduction of industrial robots is part of a broader trend towards full factory automation, the other components of which are numerically controlled machine tools, computer-aided design/computer-aided manufacturing systems, and automated warehouses.

Factors Promoting Growth

Factors promoting the growth of Japan's industrial robot market include:
- Technological advances that have led to greatly improved industrial robot reliability, increased economy relative to labor costs, and a growing variety of applications.
- The increase in demand for flexible factory automation, of which industrial robots are a vital part, due to the increasing need for production rationalization, improvements in the work environment, and the growing trend towards small lot production and frequent model changes.
- Stagnation in the supply of blue collar labor in general, and shortages of skilled labor in particular, resulting in additional demand growth for industrial robots.

Table 4 Production and Shipment of Industrial Robots in Japan

(Value in ¥ millions)

		1977	1978	1979	1980	1981	1982	1983	1984	1985	1986
Production	Value	21,549	27,349	42,420	78,426	107,781	148,428	181,753	247,394	300,147	278,703
	Units	8,613	10,100	14,535	19,873	22,069	24,782	30,544	40,923	48,490	42,066
Shipment	Value	21,128	26,613	38,080	76,928	104,848	143,870	183,787	255,593	302,325	286,776
	Units	8,613	9,166	13,801	19,409	21,572	23,990	30,244	40,080	47,820	42,285
Export	Value	960	751	705	1,971	5,954	20,563	33,391	50,057	59,913	57,392
	Units	388	301	273	1,170	1,072	2,488	4,276	7,235	8,528	7,788
Export ratio (%)	Value	4.45	2.75	1.67	2.51	5.52	13.85	18.37	20.23	19.96	20.59
	Units	4.50	2.98	1.88	5.89	4.86	10.04	14.00	17.68	17.58	18.51

Source: Japan Industrial Robot Association.

- Government policies that promote the introduction of industrial robots by small and medium-sized manufacturers, and include the establishment of the Japan Industrial Robot Leasing Co (JAROL).

Industry Structure

There are over 150 robot producers in Japan, of which at least 70% are unlisted companies. The vast majority of these companies initially started industrial robot production for internal use, and entered the industry from diverse fields. For Japanese producers of industrial robots, corporate size is not always a crucial factor for survival and growth; what is necessary is that an industrial robot maker accumulate both hardware expertise and application know-how in a specialized area of application because competition within the industry is largely segmented by application area. Furthermore, there is a rough division of labor between large and small producers of industrial robots, not only by application area but also, in some cases, within the same application area.

In general, production of industrial robots is not profitable for most companies due to small lot production and the high sales and general administrative expenses, coupled with increasing price competition in some cases. However, such companies expect profitability to improve along with an increase in demand and improved technology, and a resulting decrease in per unit production costs. Those companies which already find robot production profitable generally: (a) have achieved volume production; (b) cater to markets in application areas with little competition; or (c) emphasize higher value-added product packages, such as systems engineering.

The industry is currently evenly divided between those producers which rely on outside agents and those which sell their robots themselves. As a rule, the smaller companies are more dependent on outside sales agents, mainly trading companies specializing in machinery.

Historically, the principal users of industrial robots have been large companies in the automobile and electrical machinery industries. These two industries together account for a substantial share of industrial robot shipments. Other major users include producers of plastic and metal products.

Definitions

Industrial robots, which at present are used almost exclusively in the manufacturing sector, are a combination of various technologies, the two most important being mechanics and electronics (the combination of which is often referred to in Japan as *mechatronics*). The implication of this is that no one company is able to marshal all of the necessary technology and produce all of the necessary parts itself. Instead, there is a substantial amount of inter-company sourcing and other transactions, in the form of outright purchases and tie-ups, both domestically and internationally. Given the growth potential expected for the industry, the substantial growth of peripheral industries and parts suppliers is also expected.

In Japan, industrial robots are classified by the Japan Industrial Robot Association (JIRA) according to their method of input. This classification is important for statistical purposes and for observing trends in the degree of sophistication of Japanese industrial robots. Simple robots, such as manual manipulators and fixed-sequence robots, which are essentially mobile auto-mated machines, are not considered to be robots in the US and Europe. Such robots are basically suited to mass production in which there are few model changes.

Variable-sequence robots, playback robots (which are instructed through physical guidance), numerically controlled robots, and intelligent robots are distinguished from conventional automated machines by the fact that they can be easily reprogrammed for product model changes. The more restrictive classifications of the Robot Institute of America correspond to these four types of industrial robots. International comparisons of industrial robot populations and production must take into account these definitional differences. When the terms high-grade or sophisticated robots are used, they refer to playback, numerical control, and intelligent robots.

Full Factory Automation in Japan

Industrial robots are part of a broader trend of continuing factory automation, as indicated by the growing awareness of the concept of full factory automa-tion. The major components of full factory automation are industrial robots, numerically controlled machine tools, CAD/CAM (computer-aided design/ computer-aided manufacture) systems, and automated warehouses and trans-fer equipment (unmanned carriers, etc). Parallel growth patterns can be seen in the demand for numerically controlled machine tools, industrial robots, and CAD/CAM systems. Numerically controlled machine tools, which have led the way in the march towards full factory automation, have begun to show some signs of slower demand growth due to their greater rate of diffusion. The demand for industrial robots, as well as for CAD/CAM systems, however, is still growing.

International Comparison

Japan is by far the world leader in the production and use of industrial robots, whether one uses the much broader Japanese definition or the more restrictive definition of robots in use in the US.

Japan's large accumulated base in robot instalment has given it the lead in application know-how. In Japan, application technology has been developed to a greater extent through industrial robot producer and user co-operation in product development than in other countries. In the US, users generally must develop application know-how by themselves or through a third party, such as an engineering firm, while the producer supplies only the hardware.

In R & D and basic research, Japanese, US, and European industrial robot producers have different strengths. This fact has been a major force in encouraging international tie-ups in robotics. For example, Kawasaki Heavy Industries introduced basic industrial robot technology from Unimation in 1968. Yaskawa Electric Manufacturing and Machine Intelligence Corporation (MIC) reached an agreement to set up joint ventures in both Japan and the US for R & D, manufacture, and sales of intelligent industrial robots, with Yaskawa providing the hardware production technology, while MIC provides the visual sensor technology.

For sophisticated industrial robots, market concentration is high in both Japan and the US. Most reports on Japan's robotics industry have stated that compared to the US, Japan's industrial robot market concentration is low. However, this is true only if the large number of producers of low-grade robots (manual manipulators, and fixed and variable sequence robots) are included. Only a handful of companies dominate the market for high-grade robots in both the US and Japan.

Factors Promoting Growth

Three main factors have led to the growth in demand for industrial robots in Japan: advances in technology, socio-economic factors, and demographic factors. An additional factor for small and medium-sized firms is direct government low-interest loans for industrial robot introduction and special depreciation allowances for robots.

Advances in Technology

Substantial advances have been achieved in the reliability of industrial robots since they were first introduced into Japan in the late 1960s. This advance in technology is indicated by the greatly increased mean time between failures (MTBF). In 1968–69, MTBF was only about 150 hours. By the early 1980s, however, MTBF was between 1,000 and 1,500 hours. This dramatic improvement in reliability has promoted demand by significantly improving the reputation of industrial robots among users.

Concomitant with the improvements in reliability, technology advances have consistently reduced the price of industrial robots relative to labor costs. The 1970s saw a consistent decline in the ratio of the average cost of a playback robot to average labor cost in manufacturing, when calculated on the basis of single shift operation. The decline in this ratio was actually much greater, given the fact that industrial robots can be used around the clock.

Finally, technological advances have considerably broadened the range of industrial robot applications in recent years through increased speed and precision, lighter weight, and smaller size. Substantial improvements in memory capacity and control mechanisms have also been realized, allowing for a greater variety of improved functional capabilities. Recent examples include the development of robots capable of rapid and accurate circuit board assembly, and robots with a sense of touch for handling soft food items.

Socio-economic Factors

Due to the slower economic growth of the 1970s, especially after the first oil crisis, Japanese manufacturers came under increasing pressure to cut costs through rationalization of production. This need for greater production rationalization increased the demand for industrial robots. Nine out of 10 Japan's robotics producers initially developed industrial robots in order to automate their own production lines.

The increasing demand for improvements in the safety and quality of the workplace has also stimulated the demand for industrial robots. Most of the early industrial robots were installed to take over the performance of hazardous and unpleasant work processes, such as welding, spray painting, pressing, and plastic molding. Such areas of application therefore have a greater degree of ownership than other application areas.

During the past decade, the manufacturing sector, exemplified by the auto and electrical machinery industries, has responded to slower economic growth, increased competition, and changes in consumer demand with a greater degree of small lot production and more frequent model changes. This trend has stimulated the demand for more sophisticated robots which, because of their re-programmability, can readily be adapted to new production requirements.

Demographic Factors

On a macroeconomic level, Japan's labor situation in recent years has contributed to the growing demand for factory automation, of which industrial robots are an important part. The 1970s saw general stagnation in the growth of the labor supply in the manufacturing sector, despite continued growth in the economy as a whole. The aging of the Japanese work force, coupled with the higher educational attainments of Japanese youth, have led to labor shortages, in particular of skilled labor. According to Japan's Ministry of Labor, in the early 1980s, the country had a shortage of over 600,000 skilled laborers. Labor shortages were particularly acute for small and medium-sized companies, which have a disadvantage in competing for scarce labor with large companies. Thus, the blue collar labor shortage is stimulating the demand for industrial robots in this sector of the economy.

Government Policies

Government policies to promote the introduction of industrial robots have been largely directed at small and medium-sized companies. They include JAROL, established on the initiative of MITI, the purpose of which is to lease robots to small and medium-sized companies at theoretically more advantageous rates. The Japan Development Bank provides at low cost 60% of the funds for JAROL; the remaining 40% comes from a syndicate of commercial banks. In 1980, industrial robots were designated by the government as eligible for financing offered by the Fund for the Modernization of Small/Medium-sized Enterprises and Equipment Leasing Plan. Also in 1980, the government launched the Program for Financing the Purchase of Industrial Robots for Occupational Safety, with funds for this program coming from the Small Business Finance Corporation. Finally, the government has allowed a special depreciation allowance for high-performance (with more than five degrees of freedom, and less than ±1 mm positioning repeatability), computer-controlled robots.

The Structure of the Industry

Japan's industrial robot industry is segmented by application areas. This segmentation of competition means that small and medium-sized companies are positioned to survive and grow in certain areas. Although the broad diversity of corporate participants which characterizes the industry is expected to continue, a process of consolidation will likely occur as the market grows.

Overview of Japan's Robotics Producers

In Japan, there are over 150 robotics producers, excluding suppliers of parts. The number of producers has increased steadily in recent years. Of these robot makers, over two-thirds are unlisted companies. Enterprises capitalized at less than ¥1 billion account for over half of Japan's robot producers.

Only a few companies specialize in industrial robot production; the majority branched into robotics from other fields. Thus, the dependence on robot sales is very low. The giants of the industry, such as Kawasaki Heavy Industries, Yaskawa Electrical Manufacturing, and Kobe Steel, have relatively low percentages of industrial robots in their total sales. The proportion is often higher for smaller producers.

Producer Matrix

Competition in Japan's industrial robot industry is segmented. The degree of competition varies according to product application. There is also a rough division of labor between the large and small to medium-sized robot producers in the markets they supply, or by product application.

The main application areas by which competition is segmented are assembly, cutting and grinding, pressing, spot welding, plastic molding, arc welding, and die casting. Again, the majority of these operations, with the exception of spot and arc welding, consist of simple material handling, where the robot supplies a workpiece to a processing machine and removes the finished piece. The largest and fastest growing application segment is assembly. While many of the larger companies have recently announced the development or sale of intelligent assembly robots, the assembly category as used by JIRA is very broad. The vast majority of assembly robots are lower-grade material handlers which merely supply parts to and remove the assembled workpiece from the assembly operation area.

Manufacturer-User Relations

The co-operation between Japanese industrial robot makers, regardless of size, and users, from feasibility studies through to installation and after-sales service, has been pointed out by industry sources as one of the main factors behind improvements in hardware and software quality; it has also contributed greatly to the increased demand for industrial robots. As a result, the emergence of independent robot-related engineering firms has been slow; only a handful exist in Japan.

Distribution

On balance, the industry is evenly divided between those companies which rely on outside agents, and those which sell directly. Most of the companies which rely on outside sales agents also handle varying proportions of sales themselves.

Agents selling industrial robots include both general and specialized trading companies. Most of the specialized trading companies are firms which handle machinery, since their existing sales channels can be used to market industrial robots. Other agents include regional producers of various types of machinery.

The role of trading companies is generally to offer their sales networks to the robot producer, and to assist by taking charge of instalment sales to users. That is, the trading company will purchase the robot from the producer and sell it to the user on an instalment basis. However, most trading companies are not in a position to take over the industrial robot maker's job of providing technical assistance or after-sales service to the user.

Large companies, and some small to medium-sized producers, often use affiliates, as well as independent agents, to sell their products. As a rule, smaller companies are more dependent on outside sales agents than large ones. These agents tend to be trading companies specializing in machinery. As the sales volume of smaller industrial robot producers increases, their dependence on outside agents also tends to rise. Or, from another point of view, in order to increase the geographical range of sales, smaller industrial robot companies must increase their dependence on outside agents with existing sales networks.

The Competitive Environment

What lies ahead for Japan's producers of industrial robots? What will their strategies be? What will be the determinants of survival and growth?

Market Environment

In the years ahead, those companies strong in technology, and positioned or moving into growth areas, will have better prospects for survival and expansion. There will also be some promising participants in industries peripheral to the industrial robot industry.

One determining factor is the continuing pressure to upgrade industrial robots. As discussed previously, the trend towards a growing demand for more sophisticated robots became apparent during the latter half of the 1970s, and has continued throughout the 1980s. Users, both large and small, are demanding higher-quality and more sophisticated industrial robots. There is still much room for improvement in robot speed, precision, and function, and reduction of robot weight and size. Improvements in robot intelligence are also necessary for more flexible and complex performance.

The pressure to upgrade robot products is being felt not only by the large companies, but also by the small and medium-sized producers. Even minor producers, in terms of sales and size of operations, are under pressure to upgrade their products.

All the major application areas are expected to show a growth in demand during the 1980s. Those areas showing relatively high growth and large potential market size are assembly and arc welding. Within the assembly application area, simple operations performed by material-handling robots will continue to account for the majority of assembly robot demand. Given the great diversity of product types, in response to the great diversity in user needs, this application area will remain highly segmented. The share of complex assembly performed by intelligent industrial robots in total assembly operations will gradually increase, with large enterprises such as NEC and Hitachi being the main beneficiaries. Arc welding is mainly the domain of large companies. Some technologically strong small and medium-sized companies have also entered the market in recent years. Arc welding, because of new entrants, is one of the application areas with the most intense competition. There have been some bankruptcies among the smaller robot producers.

Corporate Strategies

Large Japanese robotics producers are expected to increase their tie-ups with foreign companies for joint R & D and production in order to obtain an advantage in competition with other large domestic producers. Thus far, tie-ups between Japanese makers and foreign companies have centered on technology transfers or sales arrangements. In the future, tie-ups for joint R & D and production, ie more diverse and comprehensive co-operative arrangements, are likely to be the rule. An example is the Fanuc–GM agreement, which encompasses R & D, production, and sales. There have been 'divorces' as well, including the split-up of Kawasaki Heavy Industries and Westinghouse.

Up to now, Japan's industrial robot producers have largely concentrated on one area of expertise. However, some large producers are diversifying into high growth application areas with a large potential market size. Large companies will not be able to dominate every application area, nor necessarily be able to meet the demands of all customers within one application area.

The main strategy of small and medium-sized industrial robot producers is expected to be avoidance of direct competition with large companies through product specialization. Product specialization will take several forms. The first is by area of application. Smaller companies will specialize in producing robots for those application areas which large companies are not likely to enter, eg plastic injection molding. The second type of product specialization will be by product type. Smaller companies will continue to specialize in smaller robots, those which are largely custom-made, and robots in lower price ranges. A third type of specialization, mainly for medium-sized companies with particular technological strengths, will be in the production of certain intelligent robots (for complex assembly and other purposes) which are not amenable to large volume production, and thus are less attractive to large companies.

Small and medium-sized industrial companies are also expected to implement strategies to upgrade their product lines and to emphasize R & D. This will be a prerequisite if small and medium-sized producers are to compete among themselves, since the total market dictates higher performance robots at competitive prices.

Some small and medium-sized companies are expected to turn to participation in overseas industrial robot markets. Producers of plastic injection molding robots see the US and Southeast Asia as promising markets for exports of relatively simple robots. The higher degree of diffusion of these kinds of robots within Japan will be an added stimulus for exports. Thus, even among small producers of industrial robots, there will be those who give increasing emphasis to exports of either finished products or knockdown sets.

In conclusion, there exist a variety of options available to large and many small producers of industrial robots in Japan to maintain and expand market position in what will be a very rapidly growing industry. However, smaller participants face increasingly competitive conditions.

The Outlook for Japan's Robotics Industry

The basic dynamics of the industrial robot industry, including the growth factors of the past, are expected either to remain unchanged or to intensify. Robot-induced unemployment and labor transfers are not likely to be a serious hindrance to growth in industrial robot sales for the next several years.

Growth in the labor supply for the manufacturing industry has been stagnant throughout the 1980s. The Japanese work force will also continue to age. These factors point to continued shortages of skilled labor and labor for monotonous or heavy jobs, favoring an increase in the demand for further automation of production.

The demand for improved and consistent product quality, continued improvement in the economics of robot introduction, and further advances in robot technology will also continue to stimulate demand for industrial robots. Another impetus for growth will come from the changing composition of demand, in particular the growing use of industrial robots among small and medium-sized manufacturers. Some industry sources indicate that small and medium-sized companies are expected to account for half the total users of all types of robotics over time. Subsidiaries and subcontractors in the automobile and electrical machinery industries, which are under intense pressure to upgrade product quality while lowering costs, will lead the way. Government policies encouraging the introduction of industrial robots by small and medium-sized enterprises, as well as the fact that labor shortages affect smaller companies more than large ones, will also contribute substantially to the demand for robots.

The value of robots produced in Japan rose to ¥300 billion in 1985, then fell 7.6% in the next year due to the appreciation of the yen. Exports, which typically account for about 20% of Japanese robot production, were less affected by the strong yen in 1986 than sales to export-oriented domestic industries. In 1987, the stabilization of the yen and a resurgent economy boosted robot production to a new high.

The number of robots produced in Japan has been more than 40,000 each year since 1984. Between 1968 and 1987, over 290,000 robots were manufactured in Japan. Since the vast majority of these were destined for the domestic market, it should come as no surprise that Japanese factories are the largest robot owners in the world, accounting for approximately 60% of the total number of robots currently in use worldwide.

We estimate that productivity in the factory can be raised as much as 10-fold in the next 10 years if manufacturers take full advantage of the latest robot technology. The advancement of visual and touch-sensor technology will lead to increasing production of intelligent robots equipped with 32 bit central processing units (CPUs).

Consolidation in the robot business will likely proceed in the wake of the

Daikyu Kiko and Duck Engineering bankruptcies. The continued growth of OEM production for American companies also seems probable. As robots become more sophisticated, their applications will increase. A near doubling of annual robot production between 1987 and 1990 is well within the realm of possibility.

Japan's New Materials Industries

Japan's output of new materials has shown impressive growth, rising to the ¥3 trillion range in the late 1980s, placing it in number two position after the US. In most new materials fields, the US currently has the edge in technology levels, according to most observers. However, the Japanese new materials industry is mounting a broadly based effort to improve its international competitiveness in the main technology segments of fine ceramics, carbon fibers, engineering plastics, and amorphous metals. The continuing development of the new materials sector in Japan will likely have the effect of lessening the dependence of Japanese firms on imported technologies, reducing the share of foreign companies in the Japanese market, and increasing new materials exports from Japan. A corollary outcome will be to provide new competitive advantages to such primary consuming industries in Japan as automobiles/trucks, electronics, industrial machinery, and others. Approximately 300 Japanese companies are engaged in new materials R & D programs. However, the combination of the high cost of R & D, intensification of competition, and anticipated market size may result in an industry shakeout of considerable magnitude in such segments as fine ceramics, carbon fibers, and amorphous metals.

Technologies

'New materials' refers to a broad range of high polymers, fine ceramics, exotic metals and alloys, and composite materials usually containing carbon or ceramic fibers. Many of the basic production technologies for new materials were developed after World War II, and commercialization has largely been a phenomenon of the 1970s and early 1980s. The fine ceramics industry is examined below, as being representative of the achievements and problems of Japanese firms.

Fine ceramics are products made from highly pure ceramic powders sintered and treated under rigidly controlled conditions. Offering significantly improved heat-resistant, structural, and electrical properties, fine ceramics find a wide variety of applications in electrical and mechanical parts and components. Japanese companies dominate the world merchant markets for electro-ceramic products and rival the US in the development of engineering ceramics.

Industry Structure

Numerous Participants

Japanese companies are active in new materials development, and have entered the new materials field from the textile, chemical, ceramic and cement, steel, nonferrous metal, electric cable and machinery, and automobile industries.

Angles of Entry

The approach of Japanese firms to R & D in new materials is twofold. One approach is the attempt by suppliers of basic industrial materials, which have experienced slower growth and declining profitability since the first oil crisis, to diversify product lines and upgrade existing technologies. Typical examples are Toray's development of carbon fiber and Nippon Mining's R & D of amorphous metal alloys.

The other basic approach is R & D undertaken by such manufacturing industries as aircraft, automobile, and electronic/electric machinery, which are major consumers of basic materials. Japanese automobile and auto parts firms developing ceramic engine parts and fiber-reinforced body parts are typical examples of manufacturing sector participants. In many cases, manufacturers co-operate with basic materials suppliers in new material-related R & D.

New Specialist Firms

The share of new materials, or products made with new materials, in the total sales of most Japanese firms is still low. The main reason is that, in many cases, new material commercialization targets and prospects are still unclear. Furthermore, most Japanese R & D of new materials is undertaken by large, diversified firms with the requisite resources for intensive and long-term programs.

There are exceptions, however, and a few Japanese companies are already dependent on new material products for a significant proportion of sales. Examples include such ceramics companies as Kyocera, which is dependent on fine ceramics for about 70% of its total sales. There are also smaller companies, often privately held and in some cases joint ventures between Japanese and foreign corporations, which specialize in producing a particular new material, including Nippon Amorphous Metals Co (amorphous metals), Toho Beslon (carbon fiber), and Polyplastics (engineering plastics).

Government Support

Large Share of New Materials

More than half of all Japanese government support of high technology R & D is for new materials development (Table 5). In absolute terms, however, the amount of government financial resources going to new materials R & D is relatively small. The historical record is clear. For example, the Japanese government in 1983 budgeted about ¥3.2 billion for R & D related to all new materials, but during the same period the US government reportedly budgeted

Table 5   Government R & D Budgets for High-tech Areas

(¥ millions and %)

	FY 1981	FY 1982	FY 1983	FY 1984	FY 1985 (planned)	Average Annual Growth FY 1985/ 1981 (%)
New materials	1,356	2,596	3,191	3,258	3,611	28
Biotechnology	675	1,043	1,191	1,201	1,337	19
New function devices	673	1,128	1,451	1,478	1,585	24
Total (including other)	2,714	4,786	5,850	5,952	6,547	25

Source: MITI.

about ¥16 billion for R & D of fine ceramics alone. The difference is largely attributable to the absence of major military development programs in Japan. The size of Japanese government budgets for high technology R & D understates the importance of the government's role in allocating resources and setting research priorities for private industry.

MITI Support of New Materials R & D

MITI is seeking to increase the amount of government support for new materials R & D. As primary planner for Japan's future industrial structure, MITI's goals in promoting R & D in new materials are twofold. First, MITI is in favor of increasing the share of the so-called knowledge- and technology-intensive industries within Japan's economy. Secondly, it views new materials R & D as a means to revitalize declining basic industries, such as petrochemicals, chemicals, and cement.

A significant portion of MITI budgets for new materials is earmarked for a number of important basic R & D projects at the Government Industrial Research Institute laboratories. One project is concerned with the development of composite metal alloys using aluminum impregnated with ceramic particles. The goal of the project is to develop economic mass production technologies for such composite materials by 1988. In another project, MITI is planning to spend roughly ¥30 billion between 1985 and 1993 on the development of precision machining technologies for new materials, including the application of accelerated, high-density electron beam technology to the machining of fine ceramics. MITI also introduced a number of initiatives to expand government support by proposing that: (1) favorable tax and financing measures be made available to promote R & D in new materials; (2) increased subsidies for research be made available; and (3) MITI be permitted to increase expenditures on gathering technical information in order to assist public and private research organizations active in new materials R & D.

Japan's Strengths and Weaknesses

Lagging in Basic R & D

Perhaps the major disadvantages Japan faces in competing with the US in new materials development are a weakness in basic R & D, the lack of large military development programs and markets, and efforts by the Ministry of Finance to curb Japanese government spending programs. Most Japanese research on new materials is thus conducted by private industry.

Small Military Sector

The absence of a large military market, moreover, means that Japanese firms, in contrast with many of their US and European competitors, cannot easily recover initial development costs by supplying a new product on favorable terms to military users. As a result, there is a greater tendency to avoid risks, and much of the research conducted in Japan is relatively short-term and commercial applications oriented.

Japan's Competitive Position

For the above reasons, Japan lags in the development of such new materials as amorphous metal alloys and engineering ceramics, which are at a relatively early stage of the R & D cycle. Japanese firms are also dependent on US and European technology for engineering plastics.

On the other hand, the emphasis of Japanese R & D on application, economic production and early commercialization of promising new materials technologies does offer certain advantages. For example, Japanese companies have been able to dominate world markets for electroceramics on the basis of significant advances made in production and process technologies. Kyocera alone supplies an estimated 70% of world demand for ceramic packages for use in integrated circuits. Furthermore, Japanese firms pioneered superior production methods for PAN-based carbon fibers, and currently supply about 60% of the world carbon fiber demand.

Prospects

Rapid Growth in Production

As production, processing, and application bottlenecks are resolved, the growth in Japanese production of new materials will surpass by a wide margin that of conventional materials, such as steel, chemicals, and textiles. For example, Japanese production of amorphous metal products will likely amount to about ¥35 billion in 1990, compared to the 1983 level of about ¥3 billion. Despite rapid growth in production, by 1990 the ratio of new materials to conventional materials in production value terms is expected to be less than 5%.

Limited Impact until after 1990

High investment costs, relatively small markets, and intense competition will significantly limit the contribution of new materials products to sales growth and profitability for many Japanese companies. For example, there are already more than eight Japanese commercial producers of carbon fiber, and at least 15 more Japanese companies are planning to start, or have already started, production despite the fact that current production capacity exceeds world demand by almost 300%. It is estimated that there are more than 200 Japanese companies developing or marketing fine ceramic products. Almost 30 Japanese companies are conducting R & D in amorphous metals, although the main product commercialized thus far in Japan is relatively low value-added magnetic heads. Intense competition and declining margins characterize Japanese markets for certain engineering plastics.

The future growth and profitability of basic materials companies in the steel, petrochemical, chemical, cement, and other industries over the medium term will depend more on improving current operations than on the development of new materials-related products. Certain companies, including Kyocera, Toray, Asahi Chemical, Toho Rayon, NGK Insulators, NGK Spark Plug, Toshiba Ceramics, Engineering Plastics, Polyplastics and others are expected to record relatively high rates of growth based on superior technologies and active fielding of new materials products. The full-fledged development of most new materials markets, however, will come after 1990.

Fine Ceramics in Japan

Introduction

An analysis of the fine ceramics sector goes far in helping to understand Japan's overall effort in the broad field of new materials. The Japanese market for fine ceramics was roughly ¥858 billion in 1985 (Table 6). By segment, Japanese companies dominate the world market for electroceramic products and rival US companies in R & D of engineering ceramics. The demand from such initial consuming industries as electrical and mechanical components is rising as the performance characteristics of Japanese fine ceramics improve. Between 1984 and 1990, the growth in Japanese fine ceramics output is expected to average 20–25% annually, to reach ¥1.5 trillion by 1990. Such anticipated future market volumes are too small to support the 250 Japanese companies now active. A shakeout of considerable magnitude is almost certain to occur in the Japanese fine ceramics industry in the coming years, but the key players will survive.

Increasing Activity

Japanese activity in fine ceramics development became prominent in the 1970s, due to a combination of several factors, including:

- a growing demand after the first oil crisis for fuel-efficient engines and related components capable of operating at high temperatures;
- a rapid expansion in markets for electronic components using ceramics; and
- improvements in manufacturing, processing, and machining technologies,

Table 6   Japanese Fine Ceramics Market Size Forecast

(in ¥ billions)

Type of Material	1985	(1987)	(1990)	(1995)	(2000)	2000/1985
Electromagnetic	601	651	869	1,250	1,788	3.0 times
Mechanical	106	112	136	184	252	2.4 times
Thermal	58	58	110	205	42	7.3 times
Medical chemistry	60	59	70	94	177	3.0 times
Optical times	32	44	135	406	1,007	31.3
Superconductors and others	1	1	5	163	491	410 times
Total	858	925	1,325	2,302	4,137	4.8 times

Source: Japan Fine Ceramics Association.

Source: Japan Fine Ceramics Association.

which made the production of fine ceramics for a growing number of applications economically feasible.

Large Number of Entrants

There are over 170 corporate members of the Japan Fine Ceramics Association, and it is estimated that as many as 250 Japanese firms are involved in fine ceramics R & D. In terms of existing fine ceramic material and component products, the ceramic, cement, and glass industries are the most active, followed by a number of other industries, including electrical equipment/ electronics, chemical, machinery, and nonferrous metals industries. The Japanese electrical equipment manufacturing industry is the most active in terms of fine ceramic-related patent applications. Furthermore, the pace of fine ceramic-related patent applications in Japan has increased considerably since 1981.

The Market for Fine Ceramics

Market Segments

Major markets for fine ceramics include capacitors, IC packages, wave filters and sensors for electroceramics; spark plugs, tools used in semiconductor production, and ceramic fibers for engineering ceramics; and human tooth and bone implants for bioceramics.

Electroceramics

Japanese Lead in Proven Technology   Japanese production of ceramics for electronic component applications is well established, and Japanese companies have achieved a dominant position in world markets. Japanese electroceramics producers (such as Kyocera) often use the products in-house for electronic equipment product lines, or have secure markets among affiliated electronic equipment producers (such as Toshiba Ceramics with Toshiba Corporation). This access to large and rapidly growing markets, plus automation of production, improvement of processing technologies, and a policy of aggressive marketing worldwide, are the main factors behind the Japanese success in electroceramics.

Capacitors   Capacitors account for the largest share of electroceramic shipments in Japan. Murata Manufacturing is the largest supplier of ceramic capacitors, which are used extensively in a variety of consumer appliances and other electronic equipment. Murata controls an estimated 25% of world markets and 60% of the Japanese market.

IC Packages and Wafers   Electroceramics used in integrated and hybrid circuits, including ceramic packages, substrates, and wafers, together account for the second largest electroceramic market. Kyocera is the dominant firm in this area, supplying an estimated 60–70% of world ceramic package consumption and about 70% of the Japanese market. Other Japanese companies active in producing ceramic packages and wafers include NGK Spark Plug, Narumi China, Shinko, and Toshiba Ceramics.

Other Electroceramic Market Segments   Other important market segments for electroceramics include piezoelectric ceramics and ceramic sensors. Piezoelectric ceramics generate electricity when subjected to pressure; they find applications in buzzers used in watches and electronic games, and also in speakers and filters used in consumer electronics. Murata is a major world supplier, followed by Sumitomo Electric, Sumitomo Special Metals, and NGK Spark Plug. Ceramic sensors find a variety of uses, ranging from office automation equipment to thermostats in electrically heated toilet seats. Leading suppliers of ceramic sensors include Kyocera, Murata, Matsushita Electric, and Chichibu Cement.

Engineering Ceramics

Early Stage of Market Development   Engineering (also known as structural or industrial) ceramics is at an earlier stage of development and commercialization than electroceramics, and accounts for just over 30% of the total Japanese fine ceramic production. Engineering ceramics has been the focus of considerable Japanese R & D since the first oil crisis, as companies tried to find lighter, stronger, and more energy-efficient substitutes for steel to use in mechanical and other engine parts. Over the past decade, a number of promising application areas have emerged, including automotive engine parts, mechanical seals, valves, superhard cutters and grinding tools, and ceramic fibers for use in advanced composite materials.

Cutting Tools   Ceramic disposable cutting chips and ceramic-coated chips and grinders exceeded ¥1 billion in 1983, estimated at 30% of the Japanese market for disposable cutting chips. Ceramic chips and grinders, along with ceramic-coated and cermet chips and grinders, are gradually replacing tungsten carbide products. The leading companies in this field include Sumitomo Electric and Showa Denko.

Mechanical Seals   Engineering ceramics used as mechanical seals include silicon carbide and aluminum oxide ceramics. About 70% of this market is accounted for by automotive water pump applications.

Valves   With the appearance of all-ceramic valves, the Japanese market for ceramic valves has grown at an impressive pace. Fujikin, a valve-making firm, controls an estimated 70% of the Japanese market, followed by Yamatake-Honeywell and Motoyama Engineering Works. These companies reputedly procure ceramic materials from Kyocera, NGK Spark Plug, and Toray.

Japan Trails in Engineering Ceramics   Japanese companies believe that US and UK companies have an advantage in basic formula and process technologies in the engineering ceramics field. In many cases, Japanese companies have tried to overcome this gap through technology imports, and most of the major tie-ups with non-Japanese firms are in the area of engineering ceramics. Firms such as Carborundum – through its joint venture with Hitachi Chemical, Hitachi Carborundum – are expected to secure patent coverage in Japan for certain basic engineering ceramic technologies, such as those related to the sintering of silicon carbide ceramics.

On the other hand, the intensity of Japanese activity in engineering ceramics, and the strength of Japanese companies in commercializing new technologies, indicate that Japan will probably catch up to the levels of the US and certain Western European countries over the midterm. Japanese companies are already world leaders in providing ultra-pure powders necessary for the manufacture of engineering ceramics.

Government Support   The Japanese government has targeted the promotion of engineering ceramics technology in order to close the perceived gap between Japan and the US. Representative government-supported projects include R & D on:

- heat-resistant ceramics, funded as part of the Advanced Gas Turbine (Moonlight) project;
- basic research on sialon (SiAlON) ceramics, conducted at the Government Industrial Research Institute (GIRI, Kyushu); and
- research on the generation of micro-cracks during the machining of engineering ceramics, conducted at the Mechanical Engineering Laboratory.

Although MITI is the sponsor of most projects, the Science and Technology Agency and the Ministry of Transportation are also funding separate research on engineering ceramics.

Bioceramics

Kyocera ('Bioceram') and Asahi Optical ('Apaceram') are the leading Japanese developers of bioceramic teeth, bones, and joints. Kyocera's teeth and joints are made from chemically inert polycrystal and monocrystal alumina, and have the advantage of not being rejected by the body's immune system. Kyocera started sales using the 'Bioceram' brand name in 1979. Asahi Optical started sales of apatite-based bioceramic teeth implants in 1984, and is also developing applications for the repair of bones and joints. Apatite is similar to bone in chemical composition, and potentially can provide a medium for bone and joint regeneration. Another firm, Mitsubishi Mining & Cement, is also developing apatite teeth. Although the potential market for bioceramics, particularly for dental applications, is quite large, Japanese companies at present are concentrating on conducting clinical trials and educating Japanese dentists and orthopedic surgeons about the surgical techniques required.

Prospects for Japanese Fine Ceramics

The Japanese market for fine ceramic materials and parts is expected to grow on average by about 20% per year through 1990, totaling about ¥1.5 trillion by 1990. Fine ceramics are thus expected to constitute the largest new materials market in 1990, although ¥1.5 trillion is still considerably smaller than most markets for conventional materials. The share of engineering ceramics in

Japan's fine ceramics market will increase to just under half the total in 1990, with further expansion anticipated after 1990.

Electroceramics

Continued Growth   Growth in the Japanese demand for electroceramics has been impressive. The primary driving forces will be growth in Japanese integrated and hybrid circuit production, and growth in the production of other ceramic electronic components.

Continued Competition with Plastic   The impact of plastic packages and other housings on the market for ceramic IC packages has largely run its course, and an estimated 80% of all Japanese-produced ICs are currently housed in plastic. Plastic packages have the advantage over ceramics in terms of weight and cost, but are less resistant to heat and moisture. Over the medium term, Kyocera, NGK Spark Plug, Narumi China, and other firms will continue to enjoy strong demand for ceramic packages for devices operating at high speeds or under adverse (primarily high-temperature and high-moisture) conditions.

In the longer term, however, competition with plastics even for harsh-environment IC applications is expected to increase as Japanese firms continue to develop new plastics which promise to replace ceramic packages for all but the most severe operating conditions.

Engineering Ceramics

Importance of Engine Parts Development   Average annual growth in Japanese markets for engineering ceramics is forecast at 25–30% to 1990. The growth in engineering ceramics production will be influenced largely by continued success in the development and commercialization of ceramic parts for internal combustion engines. There are over 20 Japanese companies currently developing ceramic parts for diesel and gasoline engines. Most companies are concentrating on developing parts rather than an all-ceramic engine. This is because, in addition to technical problems, production costs in terms of energy consumed are greater than the reduction in fuel consumption realized through the higher operating temperatures of an all-ceramic engine.

With the development of zirconia (zirconium oxide) ceramics stabilized with yttrium, considerable progress is being reported in Japanese development of ceramic engine parts. Efforts are also being made to develop stabilized silicon nitride and silicon carbide ceramics, also for engine parts applications. Only a handful of ceramic parts have been commercialized, including hot plugs, glow plugs, fuel injection nozzles and piston ring inserts, as well as several ceramic fiber-reinforced metal parts. Major commercialization of ceramic engine parts is expected from 1987, starting with turbochargers, tappets, rocker arm pads, piston cylinder liners, and other parts subjected to intense heat during the operation of the engine. Commercialization of an all-ceramic engine before 1990, if at all, is not anticipated.

Prospects for Increasing International Competition   As Japanese companies intensify their efforts in basic and applied R & D in engineering ceramics, there is some potential for conflict with non-Japanese companies over technology and patent rights. For example, in 1980, Carborundum charged Kyocera with alleged violation of US patents for alpha silicon carbide pressureless sintering technology. On the other hand, Kyocera filed an objection with the Japanese Patent Agency over the patent application for silicon carbide sintering technology filed in Japan by the joint venture between Hitachi Chemical and Carborundum, Hitachi Carborundum. Japanese companies active in new ceramics development voiced their concern that Japan would remain at a considerable disadvantage in the commercialization of engineering ceramic products if Carborundum's patents were fully granted in Japan as well as in the US.

Original Japanese Developments Increasing   Original Japanese breakthroughs in engineering ceramics are occurring with increasing frequency. For example, one technology which may provide Japanese companies with the means to avoid infringing Carborundum patents was jointly developed by Osaka University and Sumitomo Electric. This technology involves the instantaneous synthesis of silicon carbide ceramics under high pressure (30,000 atmospheres). This technology reportedly requires only one-tenth the time of conventional (eg Carborundum's) pressureless production/sintering methods, and potentially can reduce production costs by 50–60%. Several patents have been filed as a result, and the two partners claim that the technology can also be applied to titanium boride and other engineering ceramics production.

In another development, Asahi Glass filed for patents in Japan and West Germany in 1984 to supplement coverage already obtained in the US, the UK, France, and Canada for the production of 'Ceraroi C' (marketed by Mitsubishi Corporation in the US as 'Roiceram'). Ceraroi C is a silicon carbide ceramic developed for engineering applications. The company is aiming to strengthen its patent coverage in Japan as activity in engineering ceramics increases. Ceraroi C uses alumina (aluminum oxide) as an auxiliary additive, and is more difficult to sinter and less resistant to initial impact than Carborundum's pressureless sintered alpha silicon carbide eramics. On the other hand, Ceraroi C is reportedly stronger under long-term stress and is being used in hot air control valves for blast furnaces by Nippon Kokan and other Japanese steel makers.

Conclusions

Major Market Expansion after 1990
Japan's fine ceramics market will average annual growth of at least 20% to 1990. Continued market expansion is expected during the 1990s as a number of basic technological bottlenecks are resolved, and as expertise in sintering/processing and the non-destructive testing of fine ceramics is accumulated. Most of this growth will occur in the area of engineering ceramics, which is

expected to account for more than 60% of the Japanese fine ceramics market in the year 2000, estimated at ¥3–4 trillion.

Impact on Firms Limited by Competition and Development Costs

A number of Japanese companies, including Kyocera, Toshiba Ceramics, Hitachi Corp., Hitachi Chemical, Asahi Glass, NGK Spark Plug, and NGK Insulators, are expected to benefit from the growth of Japanese fine ceramic markets, given their relatively high dependence on fine ceramic sales and their ability both to overcome technical deadlocks and to field new products effectively. On the minus side, however, fine ceramics production is characterized by increasing competition and high development costs. A gradual shakeout will be observed during the coming decade among the large number of Japanese companies currently involved in fine ceramics R & D.

The Japanese Push into Biotechnology

Introduction

The Potential of Biotechnology

The development overseas of recombinant DNA and cell fusion biotechnologies has stimulated considerable Japanese interest and activity since 1980. These new technologies are potentially applicable to a number of fields, including pharmaceuticals, chemicals, food processing, agriculture, environmental protection, and mining.

By the year 2000, Japan's markets for products incorporating biotechnology are expected to reach as high as ¥15 trillion, according to a perhaps overly optimistic forecast by Japan's Ferment Industry Association. A notable portion of these markets will be accounted for by pharmaceuticals produced through biotechniques, several of which will be commercialized during the late 1980s. On the other hand, the extensive use of biotechnology for the production of petrochemicals and basic chemicals will not be realized until the 21st century.

Strategies

Japan is several years behind the US in biotechnology. Developments overseas and a growing awareness of the long-term importance of biotechnology have stimulated Japanese government ministries to establish programs and guidelines for upgrading domestic technology levels. However, Japanese government support for biotechnology has not been prominent compared with the activities of foreign governments, or the support the Japanese government has given to other industries.

The main motive force behind Japanese activities in biotechnology is the private sector. Japanese participants in biotechnology are typically large firms in the pharmaceutical, chemical, food-processing, and textile industries. These firms are currently focusing most of their R & D activities in biotechnology on the development of new production techniques for pharmaceuticals. Pharmaceuticals are likely to be among the first substances for which biotechnology production techniques will be commercialized, and their high value-added nature allows for relatively rapid and easy recovery of investment. Japanese companies have been active in forming tie-ups with foreign companies, particularly venture businesses in the US which specialize in biotech-related R & D, in order to obtain the best technology available. Domestic tie-ups have also been important in gaining access to the technologies and marketing resources of companies in other industries.

Biotechnology and Japan's Drug and Chemical Industries

Drug and chemical companies have been the most active Japanese participants in biotechnology. Companies in both industries have concentrated largely on the development of biotechnical production processes for pharmaceuticals, and are dependent on foreign companies for the relevant biotechnologies. For drug companies, biotechnology provides the means to produce new and existing pharmaceuticals more efficiently and with greater purity. For chemical companies, it provides a means of diversifying into the fine chemical area of pharmaceuticals.

The contribution of biotechnology to Japanese drug and chemical companies during the 1980s will be marginal as most of the new pharmaceuticals or production processes currently being developed will not reach the commercialization stage until the late 1980s. Another factor is the large number of firms which are competing in the development of the most promising pharmaceutical products. After 1990, however, the Japanese drug industry stands to benefit from the growing number of biotechnologically produced drugs which will reach the market. Sales of these drugs will also benefit some chemical companies, but during the next 20 years biotechnology alone will not remedy such problems of Japan's chemical industry as high energy costs and low demand growth.

Prospects and Implications

Japan will be competitive in the commercialization of products produced through biotechnology as a result of its sophisticated level of expertise in fermentation technology, experience in the production of antibiotics, enzymes, and amino acids, its capabilities in immunology and strain preservation, and a large domestic drug market along with a well-established system of clinical trials. Another Japanese strength is that most biotech-related R & D is being undertaken by large companies which are capable of marshaling the capital and personnel resources necessary for the long-term investment required to commercialize biotechnological production.

On the other hand, it will be several years before Japan becomes a leading source of new developments in biotechnology, due to current weaknesses in such fundamental areas as recombinant DNA technology. In order to catch up with the levels of the US in biotechnology, Japanese firms will continue to increase investment in biotech-related R & D. In particular, investment levels will increase as Japanese firms approach the commercialization stage for various biotechnologically produced goods. It is also probable that Japanese biotech-related investments in the US will increase, as Japanese firms seek an operations base from which to monitor and participate in American developments in biotechnology. These developments will present lending and financial consulting opportunities over the long term.

Biotechnology: Working Definition

Biotechnology is a general term describing a variety of technologies which utilize the metabolic processes of living organisms to produce goods or process materials. Traditional biotechnology includes the use of micro-organisms to ferment the juice of grapes into wine, and the use of yeast to brew beer and raise dough for bread. Fermentation, the basic technology comprising traditional biotechnology, is also fundamental to the production of antibiotics used to fight diseases and enzymes used in the production of various foodstuffs, such as rennin for the production of cheese. Accordingly, the main industries which make the most extensive use of the traditional biotechnology of fermentation are the food and drug industries. Japan's current fermentation-related markets (largely food products and pharmaceuticals such as antibiotics) total well over ¥4 trillion.

The last decade has seen a number of dramatic developments in man's ability to modify and cultivate micro-organisms in order to produce new useful substances, and also to produce in greater volume and purity those substances which can presently be produced only in small amounts at great cost. These new technologies are often collectively referred to as *new biotechnology*. Potentially the most important new technology is recombinant DNA technology. Other key fields developed in recent years include cell fusion, mass cell culture, and bioreactor technologies.

Recombinant DNA

This technology involves cutting and joining deoxyribonucleic acid (DNA) molecules and implanting them into a host organism. By this process, micro-organisms with strong breeding capabilities can be programmed to produce a variety of useful substances. For example, a joint venture between the Swedish company Kabi Vitrum and Genentech of the USA, Kabigen, has introduced DNA for the production of human growth hormone into a strain of the common bacteria *Escherichia coli* by recombinant DNA methods. The volume of human growth hormone produced by several batches of such *E. coli* is reportedly equivalent to the amount supplied by several ten thousands of pituitary glands from human cadavers, the only other source. Growth hormone is essential for treating dwarfism, and may have other clinical uses which can be researched now that it can be produced more economically in much greater volume.

The State of Biotechnology in Japan

Japan has a long history of using micro-organisms and traditional biotech-niques for the production of a variety of foodstuffs, including *sake*, soy sauce, and *natto* (fermented soy beans). However, Japanese activity in new biotech areas, such as recombinant DNA and cell fusion, did not reach significant levels until the late 1970s; Japanese firms have been especially active in various areas of biotechnology since 1980. The technical level of Japanese activity in new biotech areas, especially genetic engineering and recombinant DNA technol-ogy, is currently about four to five years behind that of the US.

Government guidelines in response to increasing research activity in new biotechnologies have been established over the last decade. In 1979, the Ministry of Education issued guidelines regulating recombinant DNA research at Japanese universities, and in the same year the Science and Technology Agency issued essentially the same guidelines to govern such research at all research institutes, both public and private. This was three years after the National Institutes of Health issued their guidelines on recombinant DNA experiments in the US.

In 1981, a group of 14 Japanese companies active in biotechnology formed the Biotechnology Development Technical Association. The functions of this association are to negotiate with the government on such subjects as subsidies for biotech-related R & D and research guidelines. In 1982, MITI established a Bioindustry Office to promote the development of Japan's biotechnology-related industries, to monitor new developments and gather information, and to sponsor and co-ordinate research projects.

Industry Participants

A large number of Japanese companies in a wide variety of industries have launched R & D programs in biotechnology. Well over two-thirds of the leading Japanese companies in the drug, chemical, food, textile and paper/pulp industries have research and development projects in biotechnology. Many of these companies, particularly in the food and drug industries, started their activities in biotech prior to 1976 as a result of their dependence on fermenta-tion techniques for the production of enzymes, antibiotics, and other products. However, Japanese companies only became active in genetic engineering on a significant scale in 1979–80.

Japanese participants in biotechnology are not only characterized by their number and the variety of industries they represent, but also by their size. Until recently in the US, much of the activity in biotechnology has been undertaken by small venture-capital companies specializing in biotech R & D. However, in Japan, biotech activities are almost exclusively undertaken by large compa-nies in the existing industries of pharmaceuticals, chemicals, food processing, textiles, and paper/pulp.

A majority of Japanese companies are conducting research in such traditional biotechniques as fermentation, microbe and cell screening, and enzyme utilization. Among new biotechnologies, particular activity by Japanese companies is being seen in the areas of recombinant DNA, cell fusion, and bioreactors. It is interesting to note that, among companies surveyed by MITI, more Japanese companies active in biotech are conducting research in cell fusion than in recombinant DNA. This indicates that many companies have concluded that cell fusion technologies are likely to provide more practical gains than recombinant DNA technologies in the near future.

Reasons for Aggressiveness in Recent Years

A number of factors are behind the recent surge in Japanese interest in biotechnology. Foremost amongst these is the impact which foreign developments have had on many Japanese companies and bureaucrats, in creating an awareness of the potential importance of biotechnology and of Japan's weaknesses when compared to other countries. Another factor is the consensus reached within government and industrial circles that Japan must transform itself into a technology-intensive country for which biotechnology, along with other advanced technologies, is vital. Finally, the potential for growth of biotech-related areas and the wide range of potential applications are also important factors accounting for the recent Japanese activity in biotechnology, particularly new biotechnology. In surveys of leading listed Japanese companies, biotechnology is ranked among the highest potential growth areas.

In 1980, Stanford University and the University of California (Berkeley) made a patent application for the process for producing biologically functional chimeras (a chimera being an organism in which tissues are of varied genetic origin), developed by Dr Stanley Cohen and Dr Herbert Boyer. The broadness of the Cohen-Boyer patent, which covers the use of vectors (a self-replicating molecule of DNA which transmits genetic information from one cell or organism to another) for introducing recombinant DNA into a host cell or micro-organism, jolted Japan into an awareness of the gap between it and the US in the area of new biotechnology, particularly in genetic engineering. Because the process covered in the Cohen-Boyer patent had already been announced in an academic paper, application was not made in Japan or Europe. Nevertheless, given the fact that the US is the largest consumer market in the world, the patent has important implications for the competitive position of Japanese biotech companies which may eventually want to export to the US substances produced through recombinant DNA techniques.

The Level of Japanese Biotechnology

Japan is generally judged to be several years behind the US in genetic engineering, particularly in recombinant DNA technology; it is also considered to be behind certain Western European countries in this area. Significant contributions by Japan to recombinant DNA research date from only 1980, whereas the US has been the leading country in this field since the late 1960s. By and large, Japan is dependent on foreign technology in such important areas as recombinant DNA and cell fusion. This dependence was pronounced in the early 1980s, with two cases of biotechniques being introduced to Japan from abroad in 1980 to 12 cases in 1981. Also at that time, a majority of new entrants into biotechnology formed tie-ups with foreign companies. Another indication of the lower level of Japanese technology within recombinant DNA research is that the country as yet has no P4 facilities. P4 laboratories are the most secure for performing potentially dangerous experiments in recombinant DNA.

An analysis of genetic engineering patents filed in Japan also indicates that Japan lags considerably behind other countries, particularly the US. Between 1974 and 1981, almost 70% of the 102 patents relating to genetic engineering filed in Japan were filed by foreign entities. In terms of cumulative patents relating to recombinant DNA filed in Japan the Japanese record is even less impressive. The US alone accounts for about 50% of recombinant DNA-related patents filed in Japan; Japanese entities account for only about 20%.

While Japan does have a basic weakness in genetic engineering – and, specifically, recombinant DNA technology – it is strong in many other important aspects of biotechnology, particularly in the traditional biotech areas of fermentation and enzyme utilization. It is also fairly strong in such related areas as immunology and microbe strain preservation, although not up to the level of the US. These strengths are valuable as Japan works to build up its expertise in such new biotech areas as cell fusion and recombinant DNA, and they will be important as it moves from the basic research stage, which characterizes most biotech activities, to the commercialization stage.

Government Policies

During the 1980s, the Japanese government has taken on the task of overseeing the country's transformation from a net importer of foreign technology to a technology-innovative nation, dependent on high-technology areas for economic growth. Within this process, biotechnology has come to be regarded as one of several key technologies essential for Japan's future. The government is also looking to biotechnology as a means to aid certain structurally depressed industries, notably the petrochemical and other basic chemical industries. It is hoped that biotechnology will eventually enable these industries not only to reduce their energy and other production costs substantially, but also to come up with new products to revive lagging sales. Finally, the Japanese government expects that biotechnology will develop new energy sources, such as biomass for the production of methane, which will eventually provide the country with more energy resource options and a greater degree of energy independence.

While considered vital to the nation's future, the role of the government in promoting the domestic bioindustry has been limited to issuing guidelines, subsidizing various biotech-related R & D projects (especially those which are long-term in nature and entail considerable risk), and following technical and regulatory developments in other countries. The role of the government is not substantial when compared to other countries, or compared to its role in promoting other industries.

Guidelines

The *Guidelines on Recombinant DNA Experimentation* were first issued in 1979. While basically modeled after the guidelines issued by the National Institutes of Health (NIH) in 1976, the 1979 guidelines were the most severe issued by any nation for recombinant DNA experiments. Complaints by Japanese researchers that the severity of the guidelines were substantially hindering their efforts in recombinant DNA research led to a substantial relaxation of the guidelines in 1982.

Basically, the relaxations removed the requirement for registration of the detailed plans of each recombinant DNA experiment with the Ministry of Education or the Science and Technology Agency, lowered the security level (P level) by one or two levels for various grades of potentially dangerous recombinant DNA research, and allowed the use of disease-causing micro-organisms in research without the individual approval of the Ministry of Education, except for particularly dangerous micro-organisms. The revised guidelines are still stricter than those in force in the US or in Western European countries. Governments in these countries allow a wider range of micro-organisms to be used in recombinant DNA research, whereas Japanese researchers are still basically limited to two types of *E. coli*, yeast and *Bacillus subtilis* as hosts for the introduction of DNA.

On an individual basis, however, the Japanese government usually gives permission to conduct recombinant DNA experiments which fall outside the guidelines if they are considered to be particularly important. For example, Kyowa Hakko Kogyo has received government approval for the use of the world's largest fermentation tank (2,000 liters) for the mass culture of *E. coli* programmed to produce interferon. Kyowa Hakko has also recently developed a new recombinant DNA technique which utilizes *corynebacteria* as host. These bacteria are considered to be potentially more useful in avoiding problems associated with *E. coli*, such as difficulties in purifying the substances produced. However, the use of *corynebacteria* as host for introducing DNA-carrying vectors is not provided for in the present guidelines. Nevertheless, Kyowa Hakko as well as a number of other companies expect that the guidelines will be relaxed in this case. On the whole, Japanese companies active in biotechnology report that while Japan's official guidelines for recombinant DNA research are stricter than those in other countries, they are no longer a significant obstacle to research and development.

Government R & D Projects

A large number of Japanese government ministries and agencies are sponsoring their own independent research and development programs in biotechnology. These programs, while being long-term and involving a fairly large number of company participants, are not very large in terms of government funding. The reception of these programs by private companies active in biotechnology varies between industries, with chemical companies being basically positive about participation in government R & D projects in biotechnology and drug companies being basically negative.

Ministry of International Trade and Industry
MITI is the most active Japanese ministry in sponsoring biotech-related R & D projects. It is especially concerned with developing biotechnologies which will aid the structurally depressed basic chemical industry. This explains the fact that most of the participants in MITI's projects are chemical companies.

An industrial bioreactor development project is receiving the largest amount of funding and has the largest number of participants. This project is devoted to the development of energy and resource-saving processes for the manufacture of chemicals using enzymes and micro-organisms. A mass cell cultivation project is devoted to developing alternate media and methods for culturing animal cells which are capable of producing useful substances, such as human hormones. And a recombinant DNA project is developing new vectors and new host micro-organisms, with the ultimate goal of boosting Japan's technical and innovative capabilities in this area to the levels of the US.

Science and Technology Agency
This agency is involved in a variety of projects directly and indirectly related to biotechnology. Among those directly concerned with biotech are projects for (a) developing bioreactors for the synthesis of peptides; (b) promoting basic research on recombinant DNA and increasing the safety of recombinant DNA techniques, including the construction of Japan's first P4 facility in Tsukuba Science City in 1983; and (c) screening and preservation methods for developing Japan's stock of useful micro-organisms.

Ministry of Agriculture, Forestry and Fisheries
This ministry has three main projects: the Green Energy Project, which is concerned with agricultural applications of various biotechniques; the Biomass Conversion Project, which seeks to develop technologies for the effective utilization of untapped biological resources to supply food, animal feed, and energy needs; and a project for the development of new biological resources through cell fusion and nucleic transplant, with the aim of developing superior species of agricultural crops.

Ministry of Education
The activities of the Ministry of Education are limited largely to funding research projects conducted at universities. Projects being funded by the Ministry of Education include those concerned with recombinant DNA techniques, the molecular structure of eucaryotic cell control, the mechanism of biological energy conversion, basic research on the utilization of biochemical reactions for the manufacture of useful resources, and others. These examples indicate that the research funded by the Ministry of Education is mainly basic in nature.

It can be seen that a large number of government bodies are currently supporting research in biotechnology. The projects supported by the Science and Technology Agency and the Ministry of Education are mainly basic research-oriented. Those of MITI and the Ministry of Agriculture, Forestry and Fisheries are concerned more with meeting the needs of certain manufacturing industries and the agricultural sector.

Evaluation of the Government's Role

Despite the involvement in biotech R & D by a large number of government agencies, the overall role of the Japanese government in supporting biotechnology is comparatively small. Government support in terms of funding of biotechnology is not large when compared to that given to activities in other areas judged important for the future. In 1982, about ¥6 billion was allocated for biotech-related government expenditures. This is less than half the almost ¥13 billion budgeted by the government for computer and information industry-related research and development projects during the same period. The Japanese government accounts for only about 10% of total Japanese expenditures in biotechnology-related R & D. Compared to its policy towards such industries as steel and automobiles in the past, the direct role of the Japanese government in fostering the domestic bioindustry is not prominent.

The level of government support of biotech R & D is also poor compared to that of other countries. The Japanese government has yet to provide direct assistance in the setting up of venture businesses in biotechnology, as has been done by the governments of France and the UK. The level of US biotechnology-related expenditure is about three times that budgeted by Japan in 1982.

The evaluation of the government's role in biotech by individual companies varies. Not all companies are willing to participate in government-financed projects. Chemical companies are basically positive about such participation, which is understandable given the bias of MITI's projects, in particular, towards the interests and needs of the basic chemical industry. Drug companies, as a whole, have indicated that they are basically negative towards participating in government projects. This is most often due to the fact that the technologies involved, such as recombinant DNA or cell fusion, are often directly relevant to the competitive positions of drug companies due to their potential for developing new pharmaceutical products. As a general rule, companies do not participate in projects which involve their particular area of expertise. For example, Kyowa Hakko, which has particular strengths in recombinant DNA, does not participate in MITI's recombinant DNA project, but rather, in the cell fusion project. Two considerations are involved. One is a desire to protect one's own technological expertise in an area from being leaked to one's competitors; the other is a desire to gain useful skills and knowledge in an area where one is not so strong.

Strategies

R & D in Biotechnology

Since most Japanese companies have not reached the commercialization phase for the products they are planning to produce through biotechniques, the quality and size of biotech-related R & D are particularly important. At present, Japanese companies are making considerable efforts to catch up with the technical levels of biotech activity in other countries. At the same time, they are anxious not to lose any competitive advantages that may be gained from R & D in biotechnology. Thus, Japanese companies are making considerable efforts to upgrade and expand their biotech-related R & D programs. Growth in biotech-related R & D expenditures of various important industries has approached or exceeded 20% during the last two fiscal years – higher than that for other areas of research and development. As a result, the share of biotech-related R & D in total R & D is steadily rising for companies in various industries which are active in biotechnology.

Food companies are particularly aggressive in biotechnology. Biotech-related R & D account for almost one-third of total research and development expenditures, a much higher ratio than for companies surveyed in other industries. Drug companies, however, have a lower ratio. Differences between the two industries explain this variation in the share of biotech-related R & D. Food companies have had to devote a very high proportion of R & D to traditional biotech areas, in particular, fermentation and enzyme-use technology, for the production of foodstuffs and food additives. In recent years, food companies have increased their already high ratios of biotech-related R & D to total R & D by increasing their activities in such new biotech areas as recombinant DNA and cell fusion. On the other hand, new drug development is quite capital-intensive and competitive. At any one time, a drug company is undertaking a number of R & D projects for the development of new drugs. Thus, in terms of total R & D, Japanese drug companies are not able to apportion as great a percentage of their R & D expenditures for purely biotech-related R & D projects as are companies in other industries.

It is expected that the level of biotech-related R & D will expand in the future.

Personnel

The training and recruitment of qualified personnel for research and development in biotech is a major concern amongst Japanese companies due to the shortage of such personnel in Japan, particularly individuals with expertise in genetic engineering. In addition to in-house training, existing personnel are being sent to domestic and foreign research universities and research institutes, while Japanese researchers working and studying abroad, as well as experts from other Japanese companies, are being recruited. Suntory, for example, recently recruited Japanese researchers who previously worked for the National Institutes of Health in the US and at the textile firm Teijin.

Emphasis on Drugs

Japanese companies active in biotechnology are attempting to narrow the focus of their efforts as much as possible. Of the many products which potentially can be produced using biotechniques, the main focus at present is on the development of biotechnology for the production of pharmaceuticals. This is true not only of drug companies, but also of companies in the chemical and food industries. The basic reason behind this is the expectation that pharmaceuticals will be the first products manufactured through biotechnologies to reach the commercialization stage. Another consideration is that the comparatively high value-added nature of drugs allows easier and faster recovery of investment.

The risks associated with the development of drugs also encourage Japanese companies to narrow their target areas of activity in biotechnology as much as possible. Due to the long periods of time required for clinical testing and to apply for government approval for the manufacture and sale of new pharmaceuticals, including existing drugs produced by new methods, the correct timing of market entry is crucial, yet extremely difficult. There is considerable risk that a competitor will develop a biotechnique that will produce a given substance more efficiently and in a higher degree of purity before R & D investments can be recovered. Thus, most Japanese companies are concentrating their activities in a relatively small number of pharmaceutical areas judged potentially large in market size, or in which there is little competition. For example, about 15 companies are carrying R & D for the production of interferon, which, if it proves to be an effective antiviral/anticancer agent, will have large demand.

Tie-ups with Foreign Companies

Most Japanese companies active in biotechnology have concluded agreements with foreign enterprises in order to accumulate basic technology rapidly or to improve the level of technology. Many of these agreements are concerned with the transfer of recombinant DNA technology, this being the area where

Japanese companies are weakest. Many large and leading companies, such as Green Cross in the drug industry, Mitsubishi Chemical in the chemical industry, Meiji Seika in the food industry, and Teijin in the textile industry, have biotech-related tie-ups with foreign companies, especially US venture businesses specializing in the development and licensing of various biotechnologies. Foreign venture businesses are attracted to large Japanese companies because of their strength in applying technology commercially.

Tie-ups with foreign companies in biotechnology take many forms, including investment in foreign biotech companies and contracts for research. Examples include Green Cross's investment in Collaborative Research, Inc. (USA), investment in Genentech (USA) by Toray and Daiichi Seiyaku, and a contract for research on tissue plasminogen activator directed to Genex (USA) by Yamanouchi Pharmaceutical. Perhaps the most common form of foreign tie-up is technology transfer. Thus far, there have been few joint ventures between Japanese and non-Japanese companies in the area of biotechnology. One example is a joint venture between Nippon Reizo and Centennial Corporation (USA) called United Biotechnological Corporation. This joint venture was founded in 1982; its major business is the importing of calf serum used for research and development in cell fusion.

Sources of Technology

Japanese pharmaceutical companies are largely dependent on foreign companies for various biotechnologies. Most of the technology being received by Japanese drug companies from abroad is concerned with recombinant DNA, followed by cell fusion techniques. At least seven Japanese drug companies are dependent on foreign sources for recombinant DNA technology, mainly US venture businesses specializing in biotechnology, and at least three companies are dependent on foreign sources for cell fusion technology. Other tie-ups between Japanese drug companies and foreign entities cover a wide range of specific biotechniques.

Mochida Pharmaceutical and Otsuka Pharmaceutical are exceptions to the above generalization. These two companies receive technology for the production of interferon and monoclonal antibodies from the Japanese research company Hayashibara Biochemical Laboratories.

Prospects and Impact

Many of the pharmaceuticals produced through biotechnology which Japanese drug companies are currently developing will reach the commercialization stage by the late 1980s. However, despite the likely commercialization of a number of such drugs before 1990, the overall contribution of biotechnology to Japan's drug industry is likely to be marginal during this period. One reason for this is that drug companies are competing with a number of non-drug companies in the development of these pharmaceuticals. As many as 15 Japanese companies are developing interferon, and a large number of non-drug companies are developing other important pharmaceuticals. Thus, while the potential markets for some of these products may be large, it is probable that they will be shared by a number of non-drug company participants, thus limiting the potential impact of these markets on existing pharmaceutical companies. Another factor is that the efficacy of some of the substances being developed is still open to question, and may ultimately prove disappointing. The efficacy of alpha-and-beta interferons as anticancer drugs, in particular, seems doubtful according to a number of industry sources. Difficulties have also been noted in the clinical trials in Japan of human insulin produced through recombinant DNA techniques, and imported by Shionogi from Eli Lilly, although recent reports indicate that Shionogi has resolved these problems. Finally, there will be some time lag between the start of commercialization of a drug in the late 1980s and the recovery of investment.

Despite increasing competition, it is expected that over the long run, biotechnology will have a substantially beneficial impact on Japan's pharmaceutical industry. An increasing number of new biotechnologically produced drugs will reach the market during the 1990s. New drugs, along with the aging of Japanese society and a growing concern for health, will stimulate growth in the domestic drug markets. In addition to being the first important products produced by new biotechnologies to be commercialized, drugs are also expected to account for the largest share – as much as half – of future biotech-related markets. Furthermore, the production of new drugs and the development of new drug production techniques through biotechnology by companies outside the pharmaceutical industry will also provide marketing opportunities for Japanese drug companies.

The Outlook for Japan's Biotechnology Industry

Relaxation of government regulations is a positive factor promoting Japanese R & D of new biotechnologies and bringing these technologies to the market place. The year 1986 saw extensive relaxation of guidelines concerning the use of recombinant DNA, cultivation of micro-organisms, and participation of private companies in the development and marketing of seed grains.

The first biotechnologically produced drug approved for sale in Japan was Toray's Feron-brand beta-interferon (September 1985). The second was a human growth hormone manufactured by Sumitomo Pharmaceutical (March 1986). Despite this progress in getting drugs on to the market, indications are that the range of applications and markets for biotechnologically produced substances may be smaller than originally anticipated.

Interferons are a case in point. The market for alpha-interferon is currently estimated at about ¥5 billion annually, and Toray reports that monthly sales of beta-interferon averaged about ¥0.2 billion during 1986. Several companies suspended development of recombinant DNA-produced drugs during 1986, and additional suspensions are anticipated. Limited efficacy and severe side effects appear to be the main problems.

It is becoming increasingly clear that, with few exceptions, biotechnology will not result in blockbuster products making a tremendous contribution to corporate profits over the short term. In cases where potential market size is in the tens of billions of yen per year, as with erythropoietin (an anti-anemia drug), the number of Japanese participants is too large, often resulting in inefficient duplication of R & D efforts.

A number of Japanese companies are engaged in the biotech development of new rice varieties. Another cultivation receiving growing emphasis among Japanese researchers is a technique for increasing the number of useful plant mutations. As with biotechnology for the development of pharmaceuticals, however, plant biotech is characterized by long lead times before commercialization.

From Integrated Circuits to Computers: Japan's Vertically Integrated Information Industry

Introduction to Japan's Computer Industry

After the US, Japan has both the second largest computer industry and the second largest computer market in the world. In 1986, Japanese production of computers and related equipment reached the ¥3.9 trillion level (Table 7).

Domestic companies hold the greater share of the home market. Local computer makers have persistently won share from IBM-Japan, which for many years had been able to dominate the domestic market as a result of its technological and marketing strengths. For example, IBM-Japan's share of the domestic computer population had declined from about 50% in 1965 to somewhere near 25% in the mid-1980s.

In world markets, the industry's leading companies now offer a serious challenge to the position of US companies, and threaten to erode further the position of European makers. The most immediate challenge in the US market is in the peripheral product segment, and in Europe, and more recently the US, Japanese makers have emphasized increased microcomputer sales.

Government Policies

The government has played a vital role in the development of the Japanese computer industry. Unlike many industrialized nations, in Japan the government has a well-articulated industrial policy for increasing the contribution of the information industries within the macroeconomy. The distinctive element

Table 7   Computer Production

(in ¥ millions)

	1970	1975	1980	1985	1986	1987 (Jan.–Mar)
Computers	125,443	259,120	488,900			403,632
General-purpose				1,366,768	1,552,585	
Personal				833,747	987,288	
Mainframe				338,586	363,783	
				194,435	201,514	
Peripherals	126,419	163,400	351,002			406,600
External Storage				1,356,927	1,629,047	235,446
Input /Output Device				787,454	999,384	171,154
				569,473	629,663	
Terminal Equipment	17,913	74,855	279,209	520,991	598,401	176,718
Others	27,156	24,192	58,462	134,087	132,208	39,494
Total	296,931	521,567	1,177,573	3,378,773	3,912,241	1,026,444

Source: *Japan Electronics Almanac.*

of government support has not been the absolute amounts of the monies spent, as much as the quality of the direction and assistance provided to the industry's companies. For example, the government has sponsored four or five major R & D programs for key computer-related technologies, providing monies on a matching-fund basis.

The early period of the industry was characterized by strict controls. However, the general trend of government activities regarding the computer industry has been to rely less on outright subsidies and to avoid direct intervention, as has been the case in certain other nations. Instead, current policy focuses on fostering industry growth through such indirect measures as tax incentives.

Competitor Profiles

The leading companies in the Japanese computer industry are generally diversified electronics producers; only Fujitsu is primarily a computer maker. The top six domestic companies, excluding IBM-Japan, in terms of computer-related sales are Fujitsu, Hitachi, NEC, Toshiba, Oki, and Mitsubishi. Reliance on computer revenues by US makers is generally higher than in Japan. At the same time, Japanese computer companies are less 'profitable' than US computer makers. Furthermore, the Japanese computer industry is domestic market-oriented in terms of shipments. Only a small percentage of total computer production is exported, although export growth in certain product segments, such as peripherals, terminals, and personal computers, has been high (Table 8).

Prospects

The computer industry is a definite growth sector of the Japanese economy and will continue to exhibit high growth throughout the late 1980s and beyond. The domestic industry has effectively matched or surpassed foreign companies in computer hardware quality and technological competitiveness. Furthermore, a strong consensus exists within the industry to step up the development of software, an area in which the industry has been lagging far behind the foreign competition.

Domestic industry growth will match the worldwide average as foreign companies continue to lose their share in the Japanese market, and as computer-related exports from Japan and Japanese output overseas continue to rise and account for a higher percentage of production. Moreover, the industry will show increased international competitiveness in specific product segments. An interim growth product for the industry was the office computer, or small business computer. A new growth product is the personal computer, which entered the take-off stage in 1981. Peripherals and terminals will also show high growth.

Table 8 Computer Sales in Japan

(in ¥ millions)

Rank	1983 Company	Computer Sales	1984 Company	Computer Sales	1985 Company	Computer Sales	1986 Company	Computer Sales
1	Fujitsu	681,300	Fujitsu	867,300	Fujitsu	1,016,100	Fujitsu	1,064,000
2	IBM Japan	612,200	IBM Japan	768,700	IBM Japan	914,500	NEC	964,300
3	NEC	520,300	NEC	662,000	NEC	813,000	IBM Japan	878,500
4	Hitachi	443,000	Hitachi	532,000	Hitachi	600,000	Hitachi	702,000
5	Toshiba	183,000	Toshiba	231,500	Toshiba	293,000	Toshiba	341,000
6	Oki Electric	154,800	Oki Electric	185,000	Oki Electric	197,200	Oki Electric	184,500
7	Mitsubishi E.	136,000	Mitsubishi E.	165,000	Mitsubishi E.	163,900	Nippon Univac	148,800
8	Nippon Univac	107,600	Nippon Univac	121,500	Nippon Univac	135,200	Mitsubishi E.	142,000
9	Burroughs	66,800	Burroughs	80,700	Burroughs	81,800	NCR Japan	86,900
10	NCR Japan	61,200	NCR Japan	69,600	NCR Japan	80,300	Burroughs	65,800

Source: Japan Electronics Almanac.

Computer Industry Structure

The computer industry has emerged as one of Japan's leading growth industries, with total production growing at a high compound annual rate. The industry will continue to increase its international competitiveness in specific product segments over the mid- to long-term. In contrast to the US, the number of new entrants into the industry is extremely limited. Significant changes in market shares occur as individual companies compete with each other for position in specific market segments. The industry leaders continue to exhibit strength in their ability to adjust strategies quickly according to changing market conditions.

Industry Concentration

The Japanese computer industry is more highly concentrated than in the US or Europe. With reference to only the number of companies, Japan's computer industry is dominated by six large electronics companies, whereas hundreds of companies have been active in the computer industry in the US. In general, the second tier of the computer industry is somewhat undeveloped in Japan. However, while the top six Japanese computer makers account for around half of total domestic industry revenues, both domestic and foreign companies compete in an international market wherein IBM accounts for approximately 60% of total computer hardware revenues.

The degree of risk to the companies in the Japanese computer industry is lower than for corresponding US companies. The total corporate performance of the industry's companies is far less dependent on computer sales because the leading Japanese computer makers are mainly well-diversified electronics manufacturers. In the domestic market, a limited number of new entrants also reduces risk; potential foreign entrants face considerable market constraints and strongly entrenched domestic companies.

Domestic companies are competing aggressively with each other and with foreign companies for position in the domestic market. Competition takes the form of price, hardware quality, and service. However, the general stability of the computer industry's structure in Japan substantially lowers the chances of major exits from the marketplace.

By international standards, Japanese makers earn low rates of return from computer operations. While it is a complex issue, a look at roughly comparable operating margins shows that Japan's computer makers have consistently recorded lower margins than US computer companies. The ability to accept lower margins allows domestic companies to compete aggressively on the basis of price, both in Japan and overseas.

Several factors account for the low profitability of Japanese computer makers relative to the operations of foreign companies outside Japan: differences in national accounting standards, intense price competition in the domestic market, close relationships with domestic banks which permit high levels of interest-bearing debt, a general tendency among Japanese companies to stress their cash (as opposed to profit) positions, as well as the fact that domestic companies have higher levels of taxable income vis-à-vis foreign computer companies in the local market.

The vast majority of the industry's shipments are to the domestic market. Only about 10% of total production is exported, whereas IBM-Japan's export ratio has been roughly 25%. More specifically, the exports of the domestic makers are concentrated at the low end of the product spectrum, with IBM-Japan accounting for much of the general-purpose computer exports from Japan.

Overseas, the industry's strategy has been to rely on original equipment manufacturer (OEM) relationships to market both peripherals and terminals, as well as a widening range of computers. Own-brand marketing is utilized in certain overseas markets, and while the stated policy of industry participants is to stress own-brand marketing overseas as a longer-term goal, the feasibility of this strategy becomes more difficult as they try to market complex, high-end computer products.

Factors of Industry Growth

No single factor, such as massive government aid, has been the decisive cause of the rise of the industry. The combination of factors that have contributed to the growth of Japan's computer industry includes: technological strength, various economies of scale as diversified electronics companies, a relatively large domestic market, and strong government support. Finally, the structural characteristics of the Japanese computer industry show important differences compared to the industry in the US.

Technological Strengths

A major advantage of the Japanese computer industry has been its capacity for technological innovation. At the macro level, the industry has been able to draw on the technical training of the Japanese labor force, an advanced educational system, and in-house training of employees who usually work for the same company for the full span of their careers.

In addition, unlike the specialized computer producers in the US, most Japanese computer makers began their operations as telephone equipment manufacturers. Japanese computer makers have been able to utilize this experience as the technologies for communications and computer equipment have converged.

Again in contrast to the US, most Japanese computer companies have substantial semiconductor production operations. In addition to strong free market demand, Japan's computer makers have achieved high-volume production efficiencies for semiconductors due to the strong in-house demand from their computer and consumer electronics operations. Domestic computer makers can thus produce semiconductor devices used in computers on a cost-effective basis and, by staying at the forefront of semiconductor technology, they can improve the capacity of their computer-related products.

Economies of Scale

As large and diversified electronics companies, Japan's computer makers can realize economies of scale for production. Japanese companies are using their experience as volume producers of consumer electronics and communications products to mass produce semiconductors, peripherals, and terminals, which are essentially commodity businesses. The major implication for foreign competitors involves the strength of the Japanese industry in these commodity businesses.

Given the sharp cost reductions in semiconductor devices and the ability to source components on an OEM basis, software development is beginning to account for an increasing percentage of the total cost of bringing computers to market. As a result, the domestic computer makers are attempting to create economies of scale for software development. Major companies are investing heavily in software factories employing literally thousands of people, as well as establishing software subsidiaries.

In contrast to these mass production policies, the domestic makers have held production of large mainframes at a medium level in order to attain the standards each has set internally for minimum acceptable rates of return. As already mentioned, these profit standards have been lower than those for US companies.

Investment

A related factor accounting for the growth of the domestic computer industry is its commitment to strategic capital investment. The investment trends of the top six computer makers demonstrate a strong commitment from senior management over the long term.

The domestic makers have consistently invested in new plant and equipment, and at the same time have held constant, or in some cases reduced, their labor force through automating production processes. This is indicated by the steady gains made in sales per employee, and the rising trend of gross capital expenditure per employee. It should also be noted that since the domestic makers have emphasized the automation of production of advanced computer-related products, they have not sought to take advantage of lower labor costs overseas. As a result, the level of direct foreign investment by the industry's participants has remained relatively low, with the bulk of direct foreign investment aimed at the largest and most sophisticated computer market, the US.

While investment in R & D by domestic computer companies has been relatively low compared to the amounts spent by such giant computer companies as IBM, the absolute amounts have been supplemented by the synergies available from various government programs. In general, companies in the computer industry are not cash-flow constrained, due to their well-diversified product and business portfolios, sound financial management, close relationships with banks, and their acquired experience in raising funds in world capital markets. Much of the actual R & D spending is hidden from scrutiny since it takes place at the plant level. Finally, Japanese companies are able to realize significant commercial returns on investments in R & D in part because employees rarely spin out to establish competing companies. Even where this does occur, the spin-outs typically maintain close relationships, financial and otherwise, with the original parent corporation.

Marketing Networks

Japanese computer makers have their domestic marketing networks already firmly in place, and emphasize superior service to users. With improved price performance and semiconductor performance, marketing costs, including the high cost of service and support organizations, account for a rising percentage of the total cost of computers. Marketing constraints are therefore a major barrier to new companies entering the domestic computer market.

Domestic Market Demand

The domestic computer makers have benefited from the demand-pull of a large, and still growing, domestic market. Another competitive strength of the Japanese makers is the high degree of captive customers in the domestic market due to the predominance of industrial groups in Japan. In simple terms, this means that a particular computer buyer affiliated via an industrial group with a particular computer maker will tend to buy the products of that maker almost exclusively. In turn, the maker is committed to providing preferential service to that buyer.

Group affiliations are one reason why user loyalty to specific makers is stronger in Japan than in other national markets. Other factors are the extensive support by makers of the users' installations, thorough maintenance, dispatch of systems engineers to work on the sites of important users, and little differentiation in hardware reliability or price, which makes the initial penetration of a market segment crucial. As a result of these practices, Japanese makers have gained a strong hold on their domestic customer base.

Development of Strategies

The major business strategies of Japan's computer industry fall into three main phases of development. After an early period of avoiding head-on competition with IBM, the domestic companies now constitute a credible threat to IBM and leading US makers in both domestic and overseas markets:

- Formative phase, 1956–71
- PCM strategy, 1971–77
- Diversification and segmentation, 1977–81
- Post-'Japan sting', 1981–.

Formative Phase, 1956–71

During the early years of the industry, a top priority of the domestic computer companies was to import foreign computer technology due to the technological lag of the industry's participants. In this period, the domestic industry was tightly controlled by the government via strict import quotas and prohibition on inward foreign direct investment. However, the government also recognized that it was necessary to have IBM, the world computer technology leader, active in Japan both to develop the market and to allow domestic companies to access IBM's technology.

The government's solution was to permit IBM-Japan to begin the first foreign production of computers in Japan in 1960 with its 7000 series computer, in return for selling its patents to domestic Japanese computer companies at a fair market price. IBM has had an important role in the evolution of the Japanese industry by contributing to the development of emerging Japanese computer markets, and in influencing the strategies of domestic computer companies.

Due to its long technological lead over domestic companies, IBM-Japan had superior hardware, software, and support services, which amounted to a strong competitive advantage in meeting domestic market requirements. As a result, until 1974 the strategy of the domestic industry's companies was to avoid head-on competition with IBM-Japan.

One reason the above approach was possible was that the domestic market was growing at a high rate, which meant that domestic companies could compete in the low-end computer market segment, where IBM-Japan was less active. Accordingly, the more sophisticated and high value-added market segments were in effect conceded to IBM-Japan. These segments included bank and insurance company on-line computer systems, computer systems for steel and automobile production, and on-line reservation systems. IBM-Japan's significance in the growth of the domestic computer market was to develop the high end virtually alone.

In the early years of the industry's development, domestic companies did not simply price below IBM-Japan; rather, they targeted different customer groups at the lower end of the market. In fact, a direct move by Japanese makers against IBM-Japan's markets in around 1970 might have resulted in high-risk price competition with IBM-Japan. The major emphasis of domestic companies was to prepare for non-price competition with IBM-Japan by building their own service organizations and reputation for hardware quality. This preparation took the form of heavy investment in both plant and R & D, as well as attainment of the needed production volumes. Success in these basic areas enabled the Japanese makers later to compete on the basis of price.

The government also encouraged the development of indigenous computer technologies during this early period. In practice, Japanese companies were forced by marketing and technology constraints to concentrate virtually all marketing activities, and therefore product development, on meeting the needs of the emerging domestic markets. Due to technological factors and the trends in computer usage – specifically, centralized computer processing and batch processing systems which limited the use of peripherals – the major domestic product segments in value and volume terms during the period were small- and medium-sized general-purpose computers. During this period, the contribution of Japan's computer makers was to develop the lower end of the domestic computer market.

PCM Strategy, 1971–77

The industry's major strategies underwent significant changes between 1971 and 1974 when two domestic makers adopted IBM/PCM (plug-compatible) strategies. By the early 1970s, IBM had begun to win high diffusion worldwide for its 360/370 series mainframe computers, and as a result was gradually becoming an architectural standard for computer systems. Historically, the PCM marketing opportunity was created when Amdahl Corporation of the US was established in 1971. Amdahl's business objective was to sell PCMs that would outperform the IBM 370 computer, which had certain technological shortcomings.

The production of PCM computers in Japan resulted from developments in the computer industry overseas and the actions of the Japanese government. Before it became clear that IBM would become the standard in computer architecture, the policy of the Japanese government was in essence to hedge the risks that confronted the domestic industry. On the one hand, MITI established a government-backed program in which Hitachi and Fujitsu joined together to develop a family of computers, the M-series, that would compete directly against the IBM 370 series computer. At the same time, the government sponsored two other maker groups, NEC/Toshiba and Mitsubishi/Oki, to promote the development of indigenous non-PCM general-purpose computers.

After 1974, the decision to compete in PCM markets was given new impetus by the slight slowdown in the growth of the general-purpose computer market in Japan, where the diffusion rate had reached a relatively high level. Japanese makers intensified their attack on IBM-Japan's markets via add-on sales and product substitution sales. The strategy of the domestic makers was, in one sense, the classic PCM approach: to supply equipment and computers compatible with IBM software and hardware. One major advantage of this strategy was that domestic companies could save on software development costs via the ability to run IBM's extensive program library on domestic-made computers.

Another marketing opportunity arose as a result of the increased diffusion rate of general-purpose computers in Japan. Domestic makers could begin to attack IBM's traditional high-end markets, such as the banking sector, by first making add-on sales of PCM peripherals, terminals, and other equipment to already installed IBM computer systems. This strategy of stressing add-on sales to IBM computer systems led Japanese makers to expand the production of peripherals and, particularly, terminals, at increasing rates from around 1975. Product segment diversification in the domestic market thereby began at around this time.

With continued product upgrading, Japanese companies also began to compete in the domestic market on a product basis with IBM's larger general-purpose mainframes since such a family of computers was now available. Accordingly, the competitive trends in the domestic computer market began to be characterized by more intense product and price competition, since PCM makers usually compete by selling mainframes at low prices, as well as peripherals and other components that can be installed alongside the user's IBM equipment.

IBM's Response

Japan's PCM makers suffered a temporary setback in 1977 when IBM announced a substantial price reduction for the 370 series and the development of a new high-end mainframe, the 3033, which was introduced at a lower price than the 370. IBM had taken these measures in Japan and other countries primarily to defend its position against PCM makers who had reduced IBM's world market share from roughly 70% to 60% between 1971 and 1977.

The 3033 was a strong new mainframe entry by IBM, with internal operating speeds 1.6 to 1.8 times faster than those of the IBM system 370 series computer. In addition, IBM 3033 was initially priced at about 6% less for rental and 26% less for purchase than the IBM 370.

Before the IBM price cut, Japanese-made mainframes had list prices approximately 30% lower than the IBM 370 series, but the price cut effectively eliminated this differential. After IBM's price cut, the domestic makers responded to the IBM action by offering even larger discounts to prospective customers.

The ability of the domestic industry to respond successfully to IBM's price reductions marked a critical juncture in the industry's development, demonstrating that the industry could defend its market position in Japan against foreign competition under liberalized conditions. The domestic makers have in fact gradually eroded the share of IBM-Japan in the Japanese market. Furthermore, Fujitsu has surpassed IBM-Japan in terms of computer sales volume to become the number 1 computer company in Japan. In more general terms, IBM-Japan's yearly sales growth has fallen below the gains recorded by domestic companies.

Diversification and Segmentation, 1977–81

The industry finished the 1970s with an emphasis on product proliferation strategies for computers, as well as for related information-based systems.

Peripherals and terminals occupied an increasing percentage of total industry production since demand for these products continued to expand at a fast rate. In addition, an increasing number of companies from several industries, including the computer industry, diversified into the production of office automation equipment. Japanese computer vendors also diversified the end markets for these products by increasing exports.

The strategy of Japanese makers in the domestic market was to emphasize computers with proprietary operating systems in order to maximize add-on sales and to expand the captive customer base. Since the large mainframe market is relatively mature in Japan, companies continued to stress sales of lower-end products such as office computers to lower-end users such as small businesses and divisions of large companies. These computer systems were differentiated from most foreign competition by Japanese-language ability, lower prices, strong sales networks, and established service and support organizations.

The industry's participants did not follow a simple PCM strategy for the domestic mainframe market. Since the domestic mainframe market is relatively small and saturated, there is no ongoing demand/supply shortfall for these large mainframes. In addition, there are fewer product gaps in Japan that could become PCM marketing opportunities. For example, Fujitsu has developed the capability to produce all the necessary components of any system it sells in the domestic market, and need not rely upon components from other computer makers. (In addition, the domestic non-compatible makers, NEC and Toshiba, have adapted some of their non-compatible computer systems so that they can be used alongside components of certain other computer systems.) The interim goal of Hitachi and Fujitsu was to sell mainframes that emulate IBM in order to take advantage of IBM's mainframe software library until these domestic makers have further improved their increasingly extensive software offerings.

The Japanese makers placed added emphasis on market diversification through exports, and export growth exceeded the rate of production growth for the industry as a whole. This trend can be expected to continue as Japanese makers increase exports of peripherals and terminals, mainframes on an OEM basis, and most recently, personal computers.

In IBM-compatible mainframes, the PCM approach by around 1980 was viewed as increasingly important as an export strategy. This was in contrast to the earlier period when the PCM approach was used to attack IBM-Japan in the domestic Japanese market. Both OEM relationships and own-brand sales were utilized in export markets. However, it must be noted that the OEM approach was inherently risky, and would not guarantee market penetration. OEM agreements can be abrogated, meaning that the surest way of improving earnings performance and market share is own-brand marketing. But this avenue presents problems in terms of setting up sales networks and service organizations. The other major obstacle was, of course, the potential of a 'counter-attack' or some other defensive move by IBM.

The problems cited above constitute a major dilemma to Japanese makers across a range of product segments from mainframes to microcomputers. In the general case, domestic makers targeted OEM relationships as the initial strategy for entry into foreign markets with their mainframes, third-party dealers for microcomputers, and a degree of own-brand marketing for office computers.

Post -'Japan Sting', 1981–

In 1982, the FBI carried out a sting operation which led to allegations that both Hitachi and Mitsubishi had obtained proprietary IBM documents in questionable ways. The aftershocks of this case were considerable, particularly in the Japanese press, which was almost uniformly sympathetic towards the wrong-doers.

About one year later, Fujitsu, a major producer of IBM-compatible computers, and IBM became involved in a dispute over the use of proprietary computer technologies. The dispute continued for the next five years, with the American Arbitration Association acting as mediator. An agreement was finally reached in late 1987. According to published reports, the agreement compels IBM to make information available to Fujitsu that will allow the Japanese company to develop and maintain IBM-compatible operating systems for five to ten years. Fujitsu was reportedly absolved of improperly accessing trade secrets, but will have to pay IBM an undisclosed sum of money for past and future use of its technical information. This agreement was ratified by both parties in early 1988.

A further issue facing the industry has been retaliatory trade measures enacted by the US.

Government Role

The Japanese government contributes to the viability of the domestic computer industry mainly through indirect means, including co-ordination of research and development activities and partial subsidization of these programs, a variety of preferential tax measures, and provision of low-cost finance for mainframe computer rentals. However, the Japanese government has not intervened directly to reorganize the industry through nationalization, as has been done in Europe. Furthermore, the amounts of the subsidies have not been excessive by international standards.

MITI Policies

The Japanese government's support of the computer industry should be understood within the context of the government's wider role in the nation's economic and industrial planning. The government's articulated policy or vision has been to encourage high-technology industries in order to develop a more knowledge-intensive industrial structure for the nation. The computer industry is regarded as occupying a major place in this new industrial structure.

Since 1971, MITI has formulated its ideal vision of Japan's industrial structure and has concurrently established policies to implement these goals. According to *The Vision of MITI's Policies in the 1970s* of 1971, Japan's industrial structure should become more advanced due to the growth of technology- and knowledge-intensive industries, in contrast to the 1960s which were a period of heavy and chemical industrialization. After the 1973 oil crisis, MITI further adopted the view that the importance of energy-intensive industrial sectors to the macro-economy should be reduced. In particular, the production of higher value-added products will be emphasized through the enhancement of technology focusing on software and knowledge intensification. New technologies will be stressed in all industrial sectors, with key target industries being computers, microelectronics, biotechnology, new basic materials, and robotics.

Period of Controls, to 1974

During this early stage, the government adopted a protective infant-industry approach that was in line with its policies towards certain other industries at that time. (A chronological outline of the government's policies for the computer industry is shown in Table 9.) The government's strong control over the industry took three major forms:
- Controls and quotas on imports of computer equipment;
- Screening of applications to import computer technology; and
- Controls on computer-related foreign investment in Japan.

Although difficult to quantify, another early, and critical, role of the government was to encourage a 'buy Japanese' policy. In practice, this meant that government agencies would buy domestic equipment whenever possible, and that private companies would attempt to do the same based on an inclination to adhere to the perceived policy. It must be emphasized that this policy was never indicated as a formal directive.

Impact

Taken together, the policies outlined above served to promote the development of, and provide a market for, the domestic computer industry. This is quite different from the strategy of various European governments which have tried to defend and develop their own computer industries by supervising the consolidation of computer companies or establishing government-owned computer companies. The effect of the European solution has been to decrease competition for their computer companies, while the effect of the Japanese solution has been to allow the continued presence of the six makers in the industry and to give these companies an opportunity to compete with each other and, after liberalization, with foreign companies.

Even though the early controls were stringent, imports accounted for a very high percentage of installed computers in Japan until around 1965. Foreign companies were effectively excluded from establishing production bases in Japan until investment controls were finally lifted. The case of IBM-Japan was an exception, since it had a prewar presence in Japan. Subject to the government condition that ownership be shared 50% with Oki Denki, only Sperry Rand was able to make a direct investment in Japan during the period of controlled inward foreign direct investment. (The company thus formed was Nippon-Univac.)

IBM's Special Position

IBM had a wholly owned subsidiary in Japan prior to the liberalization of the domestic computer industry. In 1960, it sought approval from the Japanese government to import IBM computer technology into Japan and to begin local production of system 1440 IBM computers. The government agreed to the request, but on the condition that IBM make its major patents available to domestic firms at fair market prices. This development had two important effects: (a) IBM was able substantially to increase its position in the Japanese market; and (b) domestic companies, who were far behind technologically, could access the technology of the world computer leader.

The role of the government was gradually reduced as the domestic industry became stronger and Japan came under international criticism for its restrictive trade practices. In 1972, import controls on computers were lifted. Full liberalization of the industry, including the introduction of technology and capital, was completed by 1975.

Government Support and Financial Aid

Since around 1961, government support for the computer industry has emphasized partial subsidization of R & D, tax incentives, and the creation of a rental agency for mainframe computers (Table 9). These policies were thought necessary due to the previously limited financial resources of domestic makers compared to IBM. As a rough measure of this historical gap, IBM's research budget in around 1976 was approximately US$1 billion, while total Japanese government R & D grants for the computer industry were only about $65 million (¥19.6 billion). Clearly, Japanese computer firms have improved their financial positions considerably in recent years.

Governmental financial support of the industry has been rather modest; in fact, the subsidies supplied to the industry have not been excessively large by international standards. Table 10 shows, for example, that the subsidies provided by the Japanese government for VLSI development were roughly equivalent to the subsidies provided in the US, the UK, West Germany, and

Table 9   Government Role in the Computer Industry

Year	Policy	Feature	Matching Fund Subsidy
		Strong government role	
Early years	Controlled industry • Import quotas • No inward FDI	Direct intervention	
1960	IBM-Japanese computer makers licensing agreement	Direct intervention (MITI)	
1961	JECC Informal policy to buy Japanese computers	Financial support, guidance	
1972	IBM 370/3.5 generation computer program • LSI program • Peripherals and terminals	Co-ordination maker groups, subsidies	¥57.5 billion, 5-years ¥3.5 billion, 2-years ¥3.1 billion, 5-years
		Weaker government role	
1974	Liberalization of computer industry	'End' direct intervention	
1976	VLSI R & D program with five makers	Co-ordination, subsidies	¥29.1 billion, 4-years
	Japanese government may buy US computers		
1979	Next generation 'Operating Systems' development program	Co-ordination, subsidies	¥23.5 billion, 5-years
1980	Fifth-generation computer program	International co-operation sought; subsidies continue	(¥10.5 billion, 3-years)
1980	Superfast computer and semiconductor programs		
1972–79 Total actual subsidies	Software development	Co-ordination, subsidies	¥18 billion (¥9.2 billion)* ¥125.5 billion

Sources: IBI and JECC.
Note: * Indirect funding.

France. Furthermore, the US computer industry has benefited variously from government aid associated with substantial military and aerospace R & D programs.

Government-supported Rental Company: JECC

A large category of aid to the domestic computer industry has consisted of the loans made to the JECC (Japan Electronic Computer Co, Ltd), the government-sponsored computer rental agency, by the Japan Development Bank (JDB). In practice, the function of JECC is to buy computers from the domestic makers, and then to rent them to users. The amount of funding provided by the JDB has been gradually diminishing, with the required funds being supplied more and more by private banks.

Impact

The establishment of this semi-government agency allowed domestic companies to recover investment spending in R & D of computer technology through stimulating the demand for computers in Japan. Most companies simply did not have the resources, or strongly preferred not to risk those resources, to fund both R & D and computer rental finance.

Several factors suggest that the above 'cash flow' argument is plausible. For example, a major reason that Hitachi's computer division has traditionally been more profitable compared to the competition is that it has had the internal ability to fund and earn the profits from its own computer leasing and rental activities. Most other makers apparently lack this funding ability. In addition, certain clauses in the agreements for the 3.5 Generation Computer Program had called for repayment to the government if the makers earned certain levels of profits from those computers. However, domestic firms reported an inability to make these payments due to low profitability.

JECC provided users with a relatively cost-effective way to install computers, thereby stimulating demand for the industry's mainframes. Additionally, the government's role was important because a strong rental/finance ability was needed by domestic firms to counter IBM's own aggressive leasing and rental practices. Hitachi has been able to finance its own leasing activities from its profitable consumer electronics business and other diversified lines, while NEC and Fujitsu have relied more on JECC.

One outcome of the availability of JECC rental financing had been to discourage foreign and domestic leasing companies from entering the mainframe leasing business. After IBM initiated an aggressive price reduction policy for its 370 series computer, impetus was given to leasing companies, and a considerable number today provide such leases.

Government-sponsored R & D Programs

The government has provided indirect assistance to the industry by coordinating a number of R & D projects and partially subsidizing them on a matching-fund basis. The direction and partial subsidization of the computer industry's research and development has been carried out both by MITI and the Science and Technology Agency. During the time it was a public corporation, NTT conducted computer-related research in its own laboratory, such as the development of VLSI technology appropriate for telecommunications, and also undertook several joint research projects with domestic computer companies.

Typically, MITI holds talks with makers to decide priorities, organizes companies into groups for specific R & D purposes, sets up the organizational framework for the exchange of information and the sharing of results, and establishes joint laboratories such as NTTs. However, the bulk of the actual R & D work is conducted by the makers themselves. As an example of these general functions, Figure 14 shows the organizational framework of the VLSI program.

While several government-sponsored programs have been merged with others, a number of programs, listed in Table 9, can be identified as having had a significant impact on the domestic industry:

LSI Program, 1972–74

This project was implemented for the development of various large-scale integration (LSI) semiconductor technologies and funded on a matching-fund basis by about ¥3.5 billion from the government over a two-year period. The government-sponsored LSI program resulted in about 120 new IC-related patents. A corollary research program focused on the development of peripherals and terminals, and was funded with ¥3.1 billion over five years.

3.5 Generation Computer Program, 1972–75

In 1972, MITI established a subsidized program mainly for R & D of 3.5 generation computers, defined as those utilizing LSI semiconductor technology. This program was designed to counter IBM's 370 series computer by developing the basic technologies required for comparable domestic offerings. Five firms were organized into three groups for the project, and shared the costs and the resultant technologies of the developmental program. The total government matching-fund subsidy for this program was approximately ¥57.5 billion over a five-year period.

VLSI Development Program, 1976–79

This program was basically an outgrowth of the 3.5 generation program. The VLSI development undertaking was a four-year plan comprised of five companies organized into two groups. Micro-level decisions were left to industry participants, with the government providing broad direction and co-ordination (Figure 14). The government provided ¥29.1 billion on a matching-fund basis between 1976 and 1979.

Next-generation Operating Systems Development, 1979–83

This program focused on the development of advanced software operating

Table 10 Comparison of National VLSI Development Programs

(billions)

	Japan 1976–79	US 1979–84	France 1977–82	West Germany 1979–81	UK 1979–83
Subsidized amounts (government subsidy as percentage of total spending)	$0.13 (50%)	$0.15	F0.6 (50%)	$0.1 (Up to 40%)	$0.14 (20–50%)
Type of development organization	Joint research association NTIS, CDL	Defense Dept. and major makers	Co-operation among three makers	Government research center and three makers	various

Source: The Journal of the Institute of Electronics and Communication Engineers of Japan, August 1979.

Figure 14 Organization of Japanese VLSI Research and Development Program

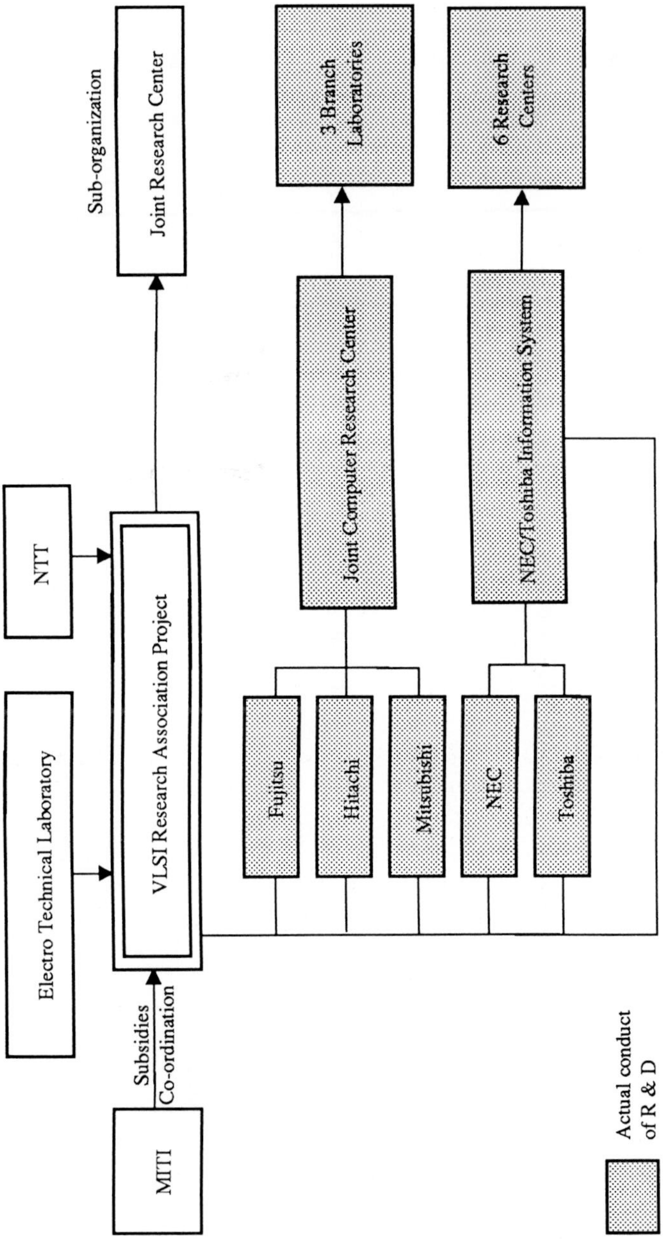

Sub-organization

Joint Research Center

3 Branch Laboratories

6 Research Centers

Joint Computer Research Center

NEC/Toshiba Information System

NTT

VLSI Research Association Project

Electro Technical Laboratory

Fujitsu

Hitachi

Mitsubishi

NEC

Toshiba

MITI

Subsidies
Co-ordination

Actual conduct
of R & D

Source: JECC.

systems for fourth-generation computers which use VLSIs. Spending on this program is expected to reach about ¥23.5 billion over the course of five years, with the bulk of this amount earmarked for the development of new operating systems. Additional target technologies include new terminal systems, Japanese-language information processing systems and terminal and peripheral equipment, and control programs for data network communications, data base management, and virtual machine systems.

Fifth-generation Computer Program, 1981–

Fifth-generation computers are as yet not completely defined, but MITI's working definition centers on architecture enhancement as opposed to improvements in semiconductor component technology. Fifth-generation computers would thus integrate into simplified architecture configurations such currently hardware-diverse functions as: logic, content-addressed storage, arithmetic, memory, and character and text recognition. In terms of functions, the fifth-generation computers, which will be in use in the 1990s, will incorporate artificial intelligence enabling the computer to perform such tasks as knowledge acquisition, inference by analogy, hypothetical logic, and deduction.

The fifth-generation computer program differs from previous programs in that the government originally invited the participation of foreign entities. This strategy was a recognition on the part of the government that the cost of future R & D will be substantial and that the most rational course would be to share the costs internationally. An additional impetus for inviting foreign companies to participate was to defuse international criticism about the government's support of the industry. However, over time, the role of foreign participants in the program proved to be minimal.

Impact of Government-sponsored R & D

The various government-sponsored R & D programs have enabled Japanese companies to catch up with US computer technology relatively quickly and to compete against the high levels of both private and public computer-related spending in the US and Europe.

Furthermore, the element of interchange of technology provided by the programs takes on added significance in Japan's low job mobility society. This situation contrasts with the US, where technology frequently travels from company to company via employee job changes and the establishment of spin-off companies.

Tax Incentives

Tax incentives for the computer industry are designed to provide preferential treatment to domestic makers and computer users. These tax advantages are outlined briefly in Table 11.

The most important tax feature is the reserve fund to allow makers to offset losses from computer repurchases. Specifically, JECC provides rental service

Table 11   1980 Revised Special Tax Measures for the Computer Industry

Measure	Feature
1. Tax deduction for increased expense of experimental research	Two-year extension
2. Special amortization for advanced machinery and equipment	Special amortization treatment – industrial robots (1/4→13/100)
3. Reserve fund for losses from computer repurchases	Legal reserve (5→2.5%)
4. Software program reserve fund	Grant-in-aid reserve provision (0.5→0.25%)
5. Reserve fund for foreign investment losses	• Reserve provision for large-scale projects (25%) • Two-year extension of reserve provision recycled nuclear fuel (100%), exploration and development of raw materials (40%) • General foreign investment reserve (15→12%)
6. Special deduction for profit on foreign transactions	Two-year extension basic income deduction rates (manufacturing ownership 35→28%, copyrights 10→8%, technology services 20→16%); basic income exclusion (50→40%)
7. Special amortization system for certain mining- and manufacturing-related R & D projects	Until 3/31/85

Source: *1980 Computer White Paper.*

computers on an operating basis, and requires makers to buy back returned computers which have not been fully depreciated. Previously, makers had minimized the impact of these expenses simply by increasing sales, so that any payments to JECC for returned computers were a relatively small percentage of payments received from JECC for new computers. However, the relatively high diffusion rate of mainframes has offset the sales expansion strategy to a certain extent.

In addition, the technological lifecycle of mainframes has shortened, resulting in increased returns by users of non-depreciated computers. As a result, payments to JECC by makers would be burdensome without the tax advantages.

Impact

The government has been effective in creating a variety of measures to benefit makers and users, and the scope of these measures has been expanded over recent years. In general, the current role of the government is best understood as emphasizing such indirect means as tax incentives, leaving complex decisions to industry companies, and the formulation of broad industrial policies.

Epilogue on Government Role

After strong controls during the early period, the government will continue to support the domestic computer industry via indirect means, while at the same time MITI subsidies on a matching-fund basis will also be provided. As the decisions required in computer business strategy and technology become even more complex, the ongoing trend of leaving day-to-day decision-making to the companies themselves will continue. Government assistance will become even more indirect and focus on tax incentives. These general governmental measures will benefit all industry participants, including domestic second-tier companies, while the results of R & D programs will accrue mainly to the specific program's participants, namely the top six computer makers. The viability of including foreign companies, other than perhaps IBM-Japan, in the fifth-generation computer program is still unclear. Viewed from this perspective, the paradox of the seeming dominance of MITI over the industry and the apparent supremacy of the top six computer companies becomes clear. That is, the top six makers will continue to dominate the industry, and will be aided by favorable government programs.

Outlook for Japan's Computer Industry

The scale of production in Japan's computer industry rose to ¥3,912 billion in 1986 on the basis of 14.1% growth in 1985 and 15.8% growth in 1986. Production growth stayed at a similarly high level in 1987 because of the strong market for mainframe computers.

A significant base of mainframes is installed in Japan. Japanese banks are in the midst of projects to install so-called third-generation, on-line banking computer systems, which have stimulated demand. Furthermore, mid-size mainframe computers showed a fairly high elasticity of demand due to their attractive price-performance characteristics. Overall, Japanese production of mainframes, supercomputers and superminicomputers increased by a healthy 18.2% to ¥985.4 billion in 1986.

Japanese personal computer output increased by 7.4% to ¥363.8 billion in 1986, a slower rate of growth than that of the larger-computer segment. Japanese personal computers were placed in a difficult position in 1987, due mainly to the retaliatory trade sanctions imposed on April 18, 1987 by the US. As a result of this measure, Japanese personal computers were made subject to a tariff of 100%, and Japanese personal computer makers suspended exports to the US. As a defense against this harsh measure, Japanese computer companies have begun production in the US and are also concentrating on expanding domestic demand. NEC began production in the US in May 1987.

Computer exports from Japan grew by only 4.9% to ¥1,383 billion in 1985, but picked up again with 11.4% growth in 1986. The US was the biggest overseas market for Japanese computers in 1986, taking just over half of Japan's exports in this category. About 28% of Japanese computer exports went to Europe.

Japan imported computers valued at ¥358 billion in 1985, but this amount fell by 23% to ¥276 billion in 1986. The appreciation of the yen was largely responsible for pushing down the value of imported computers. The US was the biggest overseas supplier of computers to Japan in 1986, accounting for 75% of all the computers shipped to Japan in that year. The second and third largest exporters to Japan were Brazil and Taiwan, each of which had less than a 5% share.

The outlook for the computer industry is mixed. Domestic market conditions are favorable due to the relatively high elasticity of demand based on continuing improvement in the price-performance ratios of computer products. On the other hand, exports will be hurt by the high yen and the sanctions on personal computer exports to the US. In 1987 and 1988, computer production in Japan is likely to continue rising at double-digit rates, with production outside Japan also growing.

Japan's Semiconductor Industry: World Leader

Introduction

With a production value on the order of ¥3.2 trillion in the fiscal year ending March 1989, Japan's semiconductor industry is in the number 1 position worldwide, ahead of the US. Its record consumption of over US$14 billion accounted for the largest share of the world market total. Clearly dominated by the Japanese and US industries, the semiconductor producers of all other countries continue to see their share of world output falling.

Market Conditions

Japan is the largest national market for semiconductors. Domestic demand is supported by such large consuming industries as consumer electronics, computers, communications, instrumentation, and factory automation systems. Integrated circuit exports have been concentrated within a gradually expanding range of the fastest growing high-end memory devices, which has contributed to trade frictions with Japan's trading partners. The share of foreign semiconductors in the Japanese market has remained low due to a long-term process of import substitution and discontinuation of production of key products by foreign companies. While, for a variety of reasons, Japanese producers are stepping up offshore production of integrated circuits, most of the value-added water fabrication process is likely to remain in Japan. Japan's semiconductor industry is destined to become increasingly international in terms of both production and sales (Table 12).

Product Segments: Strategic Victories

Integrated circuits account for the lion's share of Japan's semiconductor industry growth (Tables 13 and 14). In 1986, the output of integrated circuits was about ¥1,611 billion. In contrast, the output of discrete semiconductors, the other main product category, is growing at a relatively slower rate.

The key products for the industry are integrated circuits which utilize metal oxide semiconductor (MOS) process technology, which account for almost half of Japan's semiconductor output and are recording the fastest growth. By the early to mid-1980s, Japan had achieved a comparative advantage over the US in revenues per MOS wafer, but the US led in bipolar integrated circuits. The Japanese gains in MOS integrated circuits stem directly from its success in perfecting mass-production techniques. While the US maintains its lead in revenues per bipolar wafer, Japan is closing the gap as its production volumes increase. In key product segments, the Japanese industry has changed the rules of the game, making the experience curve steeper at the beginning with a quick increase in production volumes, and causing fast progression down the production–cost curve.

In the mid-1980s, the star product in the Japanese semiconductor industry was the 64K dynamic random access memory (DRAM). The mix of MOS products, such as the 64K DRAM, reflects a fast-paced shift to higher levels of integration and an aggressive push by Japanese vendors to establish themselves at the leading edge of MOS memory technology. Having achieved high production volumes for the 64K DRAM, Japan moved strongly into exports, capturing the major share of the US merchant market for these devices in the mid-1980s.

Table 12 Forecast of Worldwide Semiconductor Consumption

(US$ millions)

Region	1986	1987	1988	1989	1990	1990/1986 annual growth rate
Japan	10,451	12,183	14,124	15,091	16,976	12.9%
US	8,509	10,219	12,270	13,078	14,544	14.3%
W. Europe	5,344	6,254	7,098	7,578	8,303	11.6%
Others	2,052	3,447	4,358	4,946	5,423	27.5%
Total	26,355	32,102	37,850	40,693	45,247	14.5%

Source: World Semiconductor Trade Statistics.
Note: Exchange rate in 1986 = ¥167/$1; in 1987 = ¥146/$1; in 1988–1990 = ¥143/$1 (projected).

Table 13 Production Value of Integrated Circuits in Japan

(in million units)

	1980	% change	1981	% change	1982	% change	1983	% change	1984	% change	1985	% change	1986	% change	1st half 1987	% change
Semiconductor ICs	2,543	150.1	3,334	131.1	4,163	125.2	5,951	142.6	9,179	154.2	8,991	98.0	10,711	119.1	5,247	102.0
Linear ICs	1,164	136.9	1,558	133.8	1,641	106.0	2,252	136.4	3,463	153.7	3,624	104.6	3,959	109.3	1,996	105.3
Bipolar ICs	515	140.3	614	119.2	963	165.9	1,386	144.0	2,229	160.8	1,882	84.4	2,379	126.4	1,017	84.0
MOSs	864	181.1	1,163	134.6	1,558	134.1	2,311	148.0	3,486	150.8	3,485	100.0	4,373	125.5	2,234	109.8

Source: Ministry of International Trade and Industry.
Note: Above figures do not include hybrid ICs.

Table 14 Production Volume of Integrated Circuits in Japan

(Value in ¥ billions)

	1980	% change	1981	% change	1982	% change	1983	% change	1984	% change	1985	% change	1986	% change	1st half 1987	% change
Semiconductor ICs	516	150.2	622	120.6	744	119.6	1,039	139.7	1,828	175.9	1,677	91.8	1,611	96.1	783	100.8
Linear ICs	133	139.1	188	140.9	176	94.1	222	125.8	331	149.1	350	105.7	337	96.2	160	97.4
Bipolar ICs	73	142.1	94	129.8	131	138.4	153	117.5	261	170.2	256	98.1	273	106.8	122	89.9
MOSs	310	157.8	340	109.8	437	128.5	664	152.0	1,236	186.2	1,071	86.7	1,001	93.5	502	105.1

Source: Ministry of International Trade and Industry.
Note: Above figures do not include hybrid ICs.

Japanese success in the 64K DRAM market was followed by steep increases in 256K DRAM production volumes. Industry leaders such as NEC, Hitachi, and Fujitsu were able to stay roughly six months ahead of US vendors in raising production volumes of the 256K DRAM. Production increases reached the real take-off stage in 1985, and Japanese semiconductor producers were able to capture the major share of the US merchant market for the 256K DRAM.

At the time of writing, the 256K DRAM is still the leading product on the memory-device market. However, a MITI forecast indicates that production of 256K DRAMs has already peaked and could fall by 1% in the third quarter of 1988. In sharp contrast, production of the 1 M DRAM is expanding by 30% or more each quarter. In 1988, 1 M DRAMs are likely to account for 15% or more of all Japanese DRAM production. The six major semiconductor makers – NEC, Hitachi, Toshiba, Fujitsu, Mitsubishi Electric, and Matsushita Electronics – will start shipping 4 M DRAM samples in 1988, with mass production slated for 1990. A 16 M DRAM was test-manufactured by three of these companies in February 1988. With all but one or two US producers having exited the field, we foresee no serious challenge to Japanese domination of the markets for any of these sizes of semiconductors.

With an industry-wide strategy in force to target MOS DRAMs, Japanese vendors are diversifying the range of products manufactured in volume quantities. Japanese companies have broadened their presence in the worldwide MOS memory market beyond DRAMs into such other fast-growing MOS segments as 16K and 64K static random access memory (SRAM) devices, and 64K and 128K erasable-programmable read-only memory (EPROM) devices. Japanese pressure on US firms supplying these products has been intense.

Japanese companies have also stepped up their participation in the large digital bipolar integrated circuit market. The digital bipolar logic segment, traditionally dominated by Texas Instruments (US), has a total manufacturing presence in Japan. Japanese companies have been accelerating investment in order to make up for logic device shortages.

Despite high-volume output, linear integrated circuits account for a relatively low percentage of semiconductor production value due to extensive use in consumer equipment. While Japan's consumer electronics industry constitutes a high-volume market, consumer-grade linear integrated circuits are traditionally the lowest priced segment due to the saturation of, and price competition in, the consumer electronics markets.

Discrete devices represent a slow growth segment of the Japanese semiconductor industry. This situation is due to the maturity of the technology, the size of the production base, and the tendency to design out discretes in favor of integrated circuits wherever possible. The growth in the value of total domestic output started to decline in the late 1970s. Correspondingly, the share of discrete devices in total semiconductor output has dropped over time. Optoelectronics devices are recording by far the fastest growth amongst discrete semiconductors, with new applications opening up in communications.

Microprocessors

As of 1986, NEC was the only Japanese company with an independently developed design for microprocessors, although other companies publicly stated that they intended to enter the market. Among the new entrants are Hitachi and Fujitsu, which have started a joint venture to make use of real-time operating system nucleus (TRON) microprocessing architecture developed at the University of Tokyo. We expect to see the Japanese pour R & D resources into this field in an effort to dominate it as they dominate the overall integrated circuit market.

Semiconductor Companies

The list of the top 10 semiconductor vendors worldwide is dominated by the Japanese. The Japanese semiconductor industry is more concentrated than its US counterpart. While there are at least 31 Japanese merchant market vendors, and only a few other companies which produce semiconductors for captive use, the US has had many more vendors. Foreign semiconductor companies in Japan have relatively low market shares, but some are stepping up their activities to take advantage of new price competitiveness brought on by a weak dollar and to slow down the Japanese competition in the home market.

The vertically integrated electronics companies that dominate the Japanese industry enjoy a number of comparative advantages. The integrated operations of the vendors provide a captive market, shielding a proportion of production from the wider fluctuations in merchant market demand. Depending on the product mix, captive production also offers advantages at the equipment level.

The cost of capital advantage is one factor supporting sustained, heavy investment programs. In addition to the cost of capital differential enjoyed by Japan, which results in lower costs for strategic capital services, Japanese companies are considered low risks by Japanese lenders. Japanese companies seek funds outside Japan when these are available at low cost.

Growth of the Japanese semiconductor industry in the mid-1980s has been fueled by demand for very large-scale integration (VLSI) MOS memory, and competition with foreign companies centered on the 256K DRAM. Virtually no change in the structure of the Japanese industry is expected in the near future. Japanese companies will increase exports of VLSI MOS memory, winning share points from foreign enterprises in the process, and forcing foreign competition to make strategic adjustments.

Semiconductor Exports and Trade Frictions

The Japanese semiconductor industry, particularly the integrated circuit seg-

Table 15   Japanese Exports and Imports of Integrated Circuits (including hybrid ICs)

(Value in ¥ billions)

		1980	% change	1981	% change	1982	% change	1983	% change	1984	% change	1985	% change	1986	% change	1st half 1987	% change
Total	Exports	183	169.3	197	108.9	285	142.8	424	148.6	777	183.3	582	74.9	523	89.9	276	112.9
	Imports	109	110.6	111	105.0	127	111.5	153	119.8	222	145.6	165	74.4	146	88.3	72	100.2
To/from US	Exports	72	173.0	71	98.4	117	164.0	184	157.9	372	202.0	220	59.0	164	74.7	90	111.2
	Imports	70	93.9	71	101.3	84	118.5	108	128.9	164	152.0	125	76.7	110	87.8	54	96.9
To/from EC	Exports	32	253.4	28	88.6	42	149.5	55	131.8	119	215.0	109	91.6	92	82.7	39	81.2
	Imports	15	164.1	14	94.3	12	86.8	12	102.6	14	113.1	14	100.7	17	125.9	8	107.4

Source: Ministry of Finance.

ment, is export-dependent; as a result, industry performance has become strongly influenced by conditions overseas. While Japanese companies began integrated circuit exports in the early 1970s, until the end of the decade these companies had insufficient production capacity to supply both local and foreign markets. Japanese production of integrated circuits first exceeded domestic consumption in 1979. This gap has continued to widen, and in 1983 the value of Japanese integrated circuit production was equivalent to 135% of domestic consumption. The actual export ratio becomes higher when semiconductors exported in finished equipment are included. These export data reflect the ability of Japanese companies to meet user requirements overseas, as well as an industry-wide strategy of focusing on specific semiconductor product segments – particularly commodity, high-density memory integrated circuits that have strong market demand and require relatively low levels of applications support. The implication for foreign semiconductor companies has been intense competition with Japanese manufacturers in markets outside Japan.

Integrated Circuit Exports by Region

By geographical region, North America and Asia are the largest markets for Japanese integrated circuit exports (Table 15), with the US the most important market. High-end MOS memory devices account for most Japanese exports of integrated circuits to the US.

Successful penetration of the US integrated circuit memory market by Japanese-controlled companies resulted from a combination of factors. First, Japanese companies such as NEC, Fujitsu, Hitachi, and Toshiba established volume production capabilities in high-end, commodity memory devices through steady increases in capital investment. Secondly, US integrated circuit makers have periodically experienced difficulty in meeting domestic demand, providing opening wedges for offshore suppliers. For example, sharp increases in Japanese MOS memory exports in 1978 and 1979 resulted from a supply shortage in the US, with a similar situation occurring in bipolar logic devices in 1983. Following concern over Japanese exports of the 64K random access memory (RAM) during 1984 and 1985, trade-related friction concerning the next generation VLSI, the 256K DRAM, also rose.

In the early 1970s, Japan imported more semiconductors than it exported, but the situation has changed drastically since then. The industry's import ratio in 1987 was 10%, compared to an export ratio of 29%. If one were to include semiconductors installed in electronic equipment destined for export from Japan, the export ratio would likely rise to 60%. In recent years, Japan's export market in semiconductors has been characterized by much more rapid growth in Southeast Asia than in the US. In 1986, the value of semiconductors exported to Southeast Asia exceeded the value of those bound for the US for the first time.

In comparison, integrated circuits shipped to Asia are generally less advanced parts. Another characteristic of integrated circuit exports to Asia is the inclusion of semi-finished (wafer level) integrated circuits for final assembly there.

Japanese semiconductor producers made the first large-scale penetration of the US semiconductor market in 1979–80 with the 16K DRAM. This was in response to the demand generated by IBM's decision to buy 16K RAMs on the open market, and was compounded by yield problems which Texas Instrument reportedly suffered at the time. Japanese efforts to fill this gap in the US market were largely successful, and by the end of 1980 Japanese integrated circuit manufacturers reportedly had captured about 40% of the US 16K DRAM market. This was accompanied by prices which dropped from about US$6 in early 1980 to the $2 level at the end of the year (three power supply parts).

The US Semiconductor Industry Association (SIA) claimed at the time that Japanese producers were dumping their 16K DRAM integrated circuits in the US to gain market share and to prevent US vendors from selling sufficient 16K DRAM volumes to recover investments in R & D and production facilities. Formal charges were never made, and by 1981 US companies had rebounded, at least temporarily, increasing production and lowering prices to the extent that Japanese companies, again at least temporarily, scaled down their export targets.

A second round of trade friction occurred in 1982 over Japanese penetration of the 64K DRAM market in the US. Concern arose because the achievement of a strong position in the 64K DRAM – the first generation VLSI – was thought to be critical to success in more advanced VLSI devices, such as 256K DRAMs. Partly due to the Japanese government's sponsorship of the VLSI development program, in 1982 there were over four Japanese manufacturers of 64K DRAMs, as opposed to only two in the US. The SIA charged that Japanese government sponsorship of the program resulted in major R & D savings for the participating Japanese companies, and a rapid dissemination of the technologies developed, thereby giving Japanese companies an unfair advantage over US vendors. In 1982, Japanese producers held an estimated 65% share of the 64K DRAM merchant market in the US.

Trade friction issues continued to fester in the mid-1980s. Japanese dominance in the 64K DRAM market contributed to charges both of dumping and artificially high pricing. Japanese control of the US market for CMOS static RAMs represented another area for potential conflict. The actions taken by Intel and Zilog against NEC, though settled out of court, show that the microprocessor area too was to become a focus of tension. One effect of this trend, however, was reflected in NEC's decision to build a Californian facility. The move propelled other Japanese vendors also to establish US-based facilities, in part to reduce conflict over imports with local production. As a result, over the next several years the Japanese semiconductor industry became much more international in production as well as sales.

US trade policy will have a continuing effect on the Japanese semiconductor industry over the coming years. The Japanese government first entered into a semiconductor trade pact with the US in July 1986. In return for reducing semiconductor production in Japan, raising the prices of semiconductors exported to the US, and opening the Japanese market to US semiconductor makers, the Japanese were able to defuse a US dumping investigation that seemed unlikely to be settled in their favor. The trade pact became effective in September 1986 for a period of five years.

In response to later evidence which seemed to show that Japan was continuing to dump semiconductors in third countries, the US government instituted a 100% tariff on a broad range of Japanese electronic equipment in April 1987. The sanctions were partially lifted in June of the same year.

As a result of US pressure, Japan's semiconductor makers are now subject to strict administrative guidance. MITI has effectively frozen export shares at existing levels, which works to the advantage of market leaders. In the US, a floor price for Japanese semiconductors is being enforced. The floor price undoubtedly creates a more favorable environment for US producers, but ironically the Japanese may be benefiting even more from the creation of a stable market place and the replacement of price competition with competition based on technology and quality.

Overseas Production

Japanese companies have been engaged in overseas production of electronic components since the 1960s. However, offshore production of semiconductors, particularly integrated circuits, is a relatively recent phenomenon.

Japanese discrete device makers, faced with a tight labor supply and rising labor costs in the domestic market, actively sought inexpensive and abundant labor in Southeast Asia in the late 1960s. These makers included not only large electronics companies, but also small and medium-sized component makers which felt the labor crunch more seriously. At the same time, local governments in Southeast Asia encouraged investment by foreign companies in order to foster indigenous electronic component industries.

From the mid-1970s, Japanese component companies shifted the emphasis from investing in local production of discretes in Southeast Asian countries to investing in the production of integrated circuits in North America and Western Europe, where serious trade conflicts had arisen over Japanese exports. This move was also a response to increased investments in local production in North America and Western Europe by Japan's leading consumer electronics manufacturers.

Japanese Investment in the US

Most cases of Japanese investment in US-based integrated circuit production have occurred since 1978. Rather than establish joint ventures, Japanese companies have started US manufacturing operations through the acquisition of local integrated circuit makers, as in the case of NEC, or by setting up wholly owned manufacturing subsidiaries, as was first done by Hitachi and Fujitsu. In the mid-1980s, Japanese integrated circuit production facilities in the US assembled devices after front-end wafer fabrication steps were carried out in

Japan. Integrated circuit devices assembled first included mainly MOS memory 16K and 64K DRAMs, both of which have been at the center of US-Japan trade conflicts over semiconductors.

Several Japanese producers targeted front-end wafer fabrication of VLSIs in the US. NEC, for example, had plans to start fully integrated production, including front-end fabrication, of 64K DRAMs in early 1984. Management's aim was to have about 50% of the devices sold in the US produced locally within several years. Fujitsu would follow NEC.

Japanese Investment in Europe

Japanese semiconductor manufacturers began local production in Western Europe for reasons similar to their investment in the US. Additional factors have included high tariffs and the rapid increase in integrated circuit consumption by Western European industry. An additional impetus will likely come as companies position themselves for the EC integrated market of 1992. Japanese integrated circuit manufacturers compete mainly with American companies, since, with the exception of companies such as Philips and Siemens, there are no major Western European producers of integrated circuits.

Government Role

Government programs have been important in reducing the burden on individual Japanese semiconductor producers of basic R & D of integrated circuit technologies, allowing them to concentrate more on efficient methods for mass producing integrated circuits. MITI's role in guaranteeing that no one producer has been able to monopolize critical technologies developed in Japan, or imported from abroad, has been crucial to the market success of a number of Japanese semiconductor vendors. This has lessened the risk to the Japanese semiconductor industry overall. Imagine the impact on the US computer industry, in comparison, if IBM were somehow to stumble.

Government Controls

Restrictions on the imports of semiconductors into Japan, particularly integrated circuits with more than 100 circuit elements, were not lifted until the early 1970s. Liberalization of these restrictions occurred as a result of the pressure applied by the US government on the Japanese government. Integrated circuit import liberalization occurred in three stages during the early 1970s. By late 1974, importers with more than 200 circuit elements were freed from the obligation to obtain special permission from MITI for such imports. However, tariffs on integrated circuit imports into Japan remained quite high, at about 12%. These tariffs were lowered significantly in 1983.

MITI Intervention and Guidance

The case of Texas Instruments (TI) is illustrative of how MITI has sought to direct the growth of the local semiconductor industry. It is also reminiscent of IBM's experience in Japan. In 1964, TI applied to MITI for the establishment of a wholly owned subsidiary for semiconductor production. MITI initially refused the request on the grounds that its participation would hamper the development of the Japanese semiconductor industry. Texas Instruments in turn refused to license its patented technology to Japanese companies. MITI eventually proposed that in return for permission to establish a production subsidiary in Japan, TI should agree to the following conditions: (a) the subsidiary to be a 50–50 joint venture with a Japanese company; (b) the market share of TI's Japanese subsidiary to be limited to 10% of the total domestic market for semiconductors; and (c) Texas Instruments to agree to license its technology to other Japanese companies. After agreeing to these conditions in 1968, TI formed a 50–50 joint venture with Sony, and licensed its integrated circuit patents to NEC, Hitachi, Mitsubishi Electric, Toshiba, and Sony.

MITI guidance of the industry continued, but in ways more concerned with easing trade frictions than in protecting the local industry. MITI intervened, for example, in influencing the 64K DRAM export pricing policies of Japanese companies in order to attempt to circumvent dumping allegations. It also unofficially, according to reports, instructed Japanese companies to restrain publicity surrounding the 256K DRAM integrated circuit in order to avoid charges of product targeting. MITI also reportedly undertook an investigation regarding past supply shortfalls in the Japanese semiconductor market. On the other hand, it has introduced a number of schemes designed to increase imports of foreign integrated circuits into Japan.

Government R & D Programs

As we have seen, after the first oil crisis in 1973, MITI adopted the long-term goal of making the Japanese economy less dependent on energy-intensive heavy industries and more dependent on the knowledge-intensive, high-technology sector, particularly the computer and other information processing industries. Since the early 1970s, MITI has co-ordinated a number of government-sponsored R & D programs in the computer and microelectronics-related areas.

LSI Program, 1972–75 The goals of this project were to standardize basic integrated circuit structures and packages, develop test equipment, and raise the general level of Japanese semiconductor companies in large-scale integration (LSI) technology. The six participants from private industry were NEC, Hitachi, Toshiba, Fujitsu, Mitsubishi Electric, and Oki. The program was funded on a matching-fund basis by about ¥3.5 billion in government funds over a two-year period. About 120 new integrated circuit-related patents resulted from the program.

VLSI Development Program, 1976–79 This project was concerned with addressing the gap between US and Japanese technology in the area of VLSI technology, the next step upward in circuit complexity. Participants from private industry included all the members of the LSI project, except for Oki Electric. The government provided ¥29.1 billion on a matching fund basis during the program's duration. This program also concentrated on analyzing trends in US production and testing equipment, with the aim of strengthening the domestic semiconductor fabricating equipment industry. It is important to note that aside from the specific project goals achieved by the program, it also served as a focus for disseminating advanced integrated circuit technology through the top Japanese integrated circuit suppliers.

New Function Semiconductor Elements This program is being conducted under the rubric of the Next Generation Industries Basic Technologies R & D Program, which was initially scheduled to be provided with ¥25 billion in government funding between fiscal 1981 and 1990. This broad-reaching project actually covers a number of areas: new materials, biotechnology, and new semiconductor function elements. Ten Japanese companies, including the six large computer makers, have been organized into an Association for R &D of Advanced Semiconductor Devices. The patents resulting from the project may be licensed from the government. Furthermore, the project is fully government funded, with no repayment requirements.

The Role of NTT

Nippon Telephone and Telegraph (NTT), recently privatized, has performed an important role in basic research in integrated circuit technologies. NTT is also a major consumer of semiconductors produced in Japan, since its role is largely R & D and it mass-produces no parts on its own. At least four major NTT labs are involved in R & D of semiconductors, and upon occasion joint R & D work with Japanese electronics manufacturers is undertaken. While itself engaged in a number of basic research projects centering on such new materials as gallium arsenide, indium phosphate, and others, NTT reportedly also turns to Japanese electronics manufacturers to develop pilot lines in order to evaluate whether experimental semiconductor devices can be efficiently mass-produced.

Consumer Electronics: Japan's Victory over the US

Japanese production of consumer electronics products, including household appliances, total over ¥7 trillion, which makes it by far the largest consumer electronics industry in the world. Japan's consumer electronics industry has played a leading role in establishing Japan's position in the postwar world economy, and in establishing its reputation for reliable and innovative products. In terms of worldwide market shares, some estimates for 1986 put total Japanese consumer electronics output at US$26.1 billion, the US at $6.5 billion, and Europe at $7.4 billion (Table 16).

Japan's electronics industry as a whole, including consumer and industrial electronics and electronic components, is just about on par with or ahead of the US, depending on the definitions used. In Japan, the electronics industry is more or less evenly composed of the consumer, industrial, and component electronics segments, in terms of production value. In the US and Western Europe, on the other hand, industrial electronics account for the largest share. Over the past decade, both the US and Japan have recorded increases in the

Table 16   Production of Electronics Industries in Major Countries

(in US$ million)

	1981	1982	1983	1984	1985	1986	5-year average growth rate
Japan							
Total value	47,266	44,077	53,741	71,304	74,248	104,464	17.2%
Household appliances	16,765	14,187	16,141	19,915	20,537	26,109	9.3%
US							
Total value	116,839	127,464	147,297	176,572	198,872	209,753	12.5%
Household appliances	11,670	11,827	14,575	17,758	5,682	6,500	−10.9%
Europe							
Total value	47,480	53,421	76,686	70,185	86,526	94,442	14.8%
Household appliances	12,814	13,551	7,975	7,112	7,110	7,444	−10.3%

Source: Electronic Industries Association of Japan.
Note: Statistical data base for Europe changed from 1984 onward.

share of electronic components in total electronics production. Much of this increase is accounted for by the growing production of integrated circuits.

The definition of the consumer electronics industry is perhaps too limiting in the case of Japan because the leading companies have diversified business portfolios extending well beyond consumer electronics products. Japanese consumer electronics companies also often manufacture electronic components and office automation systems. Given the increasing applications of integrated circuits in consumer electronics products, the capabilities of Japanese companies in electronic components will make a significant contribution to the future growth and competitiveness of Japan's consumer electronics industry.

Transition to Lower Growth

After several years of extremely rapid growth, annual increases in the value of consumer electronics production first began to decline during the 1970s. Compound annual growth rates for Japanese consumer electronics production as a whole, and for many major products, have been sluggish for some time. As a result, companies have found themselves burdened with maturing products that offer little opportunity for the development of new domestic market demand. An additional effect of this situation has been greatly increased competition in a domestic market characterized by fewer first-time buyers. The most recent response has been a plethora of new products, which have successfully stimulated new demand both in Japan and overseas.

Market Trends in Japanese Consumer Electronics

In addition to favorable export demand, growth of the Japanese consumer electronics industry has also been driven by domestic demand – the first or second largest national market for consumer electronics. In fact, given the anticipated decline in export dependence, Japanese consumer electronics producers will have to place greater emphasis on the domestic market if they are to maintain present levels of domestic production. In addition, Japanese consumer electronics makers utilize the domestic market as a source of information for future trends in consumer needs, and as a testing ground for future products and concepts.

Domestic Japanese Market

One key issue confronting the Japanese consumer electronics industry in the domestic market has been a slow-down in overall demand stemming from the high ownership rates of most key products (Table 17). Thus, demand has come to center around replacement demand or second-unit purchases. In order to stimulate replacement demand and second-unit purchases, consumer electronics firms have developed new models of existing product types with new and improved functions, or which are smaller and lighter in size. For example, in

Table17 Japanese Diffusion Rates for Principal Consumer Electronics Products

(in %)

	1977	1978	1979	1980	1981	1982	1983	1984	1985	1986	1987
Color television	95	98	98	98	99	99	99	99	99	99	99
Video-tape recorder	–	1	2	2	5	8	12	19	28	34	43
Stereo	55	57	57	57	59	62	59	58	60	61	59
Tape recorder	56	60	61	62	63	65	70	70	74	74	75
Refrigerator	96	100	99	99	99	100	99	99	99	98	98
Washing machine	98	99	99	99	99	99	98	98	98	99	99
Vacuum cleaner	94	95	96	96	95	97	96	97	97	98	98
Microwave oven	23	27	31	34	37	40	37	41	41	45	52
Airconditioner	26	30	36	39	41	42	50	49	49	55	57

Source: Economic Planning Agency.

the mid-1980s, color TV manufacturers started marketing 14-inch color TV sets to stimulate household demand for a second color TV. In order to stimulate replacement demand, color TV manufacturers also equipped TV sets with built-in multiplex broadcasting receivers and other new functions.

Structure of Supply and Demand

The international competitiveness of Japan's consumer electronics industry is demonstrated by its low import dependence and high export ratios. In this sense, the Japanese consumer electronics industry has been a classic example of an export-driven industry. Furthermore, the majority of Japanese consumer electronic exports have been to industrially advanced countries. The strong position of Japanese consumer electronics firms in foreign markets is being further strengthened by the industry's growing production presence overseas.

Japan's dependence on consumer electronic imports has historically been very low. The consumer electronics market is characterized by fierce competition between domestic firms, which has in part prevented any significant market penetration by foreign-made products. In addition, in the period until 1970, the government maintained relatively high import tariffs in order to protect the domestic consumer electronics industry from foreign competition. Another factor impeding imports in earlier periods was the system of foreign exchange controls governing the yen rate. By any measure, however, it must be concluded that the current low import dependence of Japan for consumer electronic products provides a good indication of the level of international competitiveness achieved by Japanese consumer electronics companies. Differences in import dependence can be explained by the fact that such products as radios and tape recorders, which have had a higher import dependence (Table 18), are technologically unsophisticated and more easily produced overseas by Japanese firms.

Exports of Japanese Consumer Electronics

Japanese exports of consumer electronics stand at about ¥1.9 trillion, equivalent to over 74% of total production (Table 18). The most dramatic rise in exports occurred in 1976, when the value of exports jumped 74% over the level of 1975, as Japanese firms tried to make up for the stagnation in domestic demand by aggressively expanding exports. A by-product of this aggressive expansion, however, has been conflict with Japan's major trading partners. Japan's consumer electronics industry has responded by diversifying export markets and the types of products exported, and increasing investment in overseas production.

Trade Friction

The sudden rise in exports in 1976, and the continued high levels of exports thereafter, has led to an increasingly hostile international climate for Japanese

Table 18 Japanese Production/Export/Import Trends of Consumer Electronics

(in ¥ billions)

	1976	1980	1984	1985	1986	1987 (Jan – July)
Production	2,225	2,932	4,719	4,912	4,436	2,130
Export	1,403	2,047	3,306	3,519	2,601	1,287
Import	29	38	23	24	32	31
Exports as % of production	63.1%	69.8%	70.1%	71.6%	58.6%	60.4%

Sources: Ministry of International Trade and Industry and Ministry of Finance.

consumer electronics exports. The sharp rise in exports of color TVs to the US in 1976 resulted in three years of 'voluntary' export restrictions on Japanese color TV exports to that country. Similar voluntary restrictions were enacted in response to the criticisms of EC nations concerning the flood of Japanese video-tape recorder (VTR) exports to Europe during 1982.

Diversifying Export Product Mix

Faced by the increasing ownership rates of existing key products, and restrictions on exports of such important products as color TVs, Japanese firms have concentrated on increasing VTR exports. On balance, VTRs have achieved a dramatic rise in exports in both value and volume terms. VTRs became the largest export item in 1982, accounting for about 43% of total exports. Tape recorders are the second most important export item for the industry. Tape recorders, however, have seen a steady decline in their share of total exports since the early 1970s, when they accounted for over 45% of exports. The share of color TVs in total exports peaked in 1976, and has declined steadily since then, reflecting the increased production of color TV sets offshore by Japanese firms.

Diversifying Export Markets

The industrially advanced countries of North America and Western Europe previously accounted for over 60% of Japanese consumer electronics exports. In recent years, the proportion of exports destined for Europe has increased in relative importance, reflecting strategic moves towards market diversification on the part of Japanese producers. Export market diversification, made necessary by mounting friction over consumer electronics exports between Japan and its industrially advanced trading partners in North America and Western Europe, is also shown by the rise in importance of Asian markets for Japan's consumer electronics industry.

Decline in Importance of the North American Market

The share of the US market in total Japanese consumer electronics exports has declined significantly over time. Nevertheless, despite a long-term decline in relative importance, the US continues to be the largest single national market for Japanese consumer electronics exports. For example, the US alone has accounted for the largest share of total Japanese VTR exports in value terms. The share of color TVs in total consumer electronics exports to the US declined from the 15–20% range to about 8% after voluntary restrictions on exports to the US by Japanese companies were enacted in 1977. These facts mean that US trade policies vis-à-vis Japan will continue to be of concern to the Japanese consumer electronics industry.

Growth of the European Market

Western Europe became the most important regional market for Japan's consumer electronics exports in 1979, when the region accounted for one-third of total exports. Exports to Western Europe continued to rise, in yen terms, during the latter half of the 1970s. In the face of color TV export restrictions and other trade-related problems with the US, Japanese companies intensified their efforts to export to European markets during the latter half of the 1970s.

The rise in the relative importance of Western Europe among Japanese export markets can be attributed primarily to the rapid increase in VTR exports to this region, despite the presence of indigenous VTR makers, such as Grundig and Philips.

Overseas Production of Japanese Consumer Electronics

Several main trends have characterized overseas production by Japan's consumer electronics industry. One is that the volume and variety of products produced overseas has increased steadily in recent years. Another trend through the early 1980s was the shift in emphasis from investment in local production in developing countries, to investment in production in the advanced countries of North America and Western Europe. Most recently, the sharp appreciation of the yen has set off an explosion in production growth in Asia.

Japan's consumer electronics industry has steadily increased its offshore production (Table 19). With the exception of tape recorders and VTRs (there being no overseas production of VTRs by Japanese firms prior to 1981), most important consumer electronic products have shown higher growth rates in overseas production than in domestic production. More radios and monochrome TVs were manufactured by Japanese companies abroad than in Japan, and offshore production of color TVs equaled half the domestic production.

Southeast Asia

During the early phases of Japanese investment in consumer electronics production abroad, one of the main goals was to remedy the tight labor supply conditions and rising labor costs in Japan by taking advantage of the relatively low labor costs in Southeast Asia. This was important given the labor-intensive nature of consumer electronics product assembly during the 1960s. As Southeast Asian countries enacted protectionist policies to foster indigenous consumer electronics industries, Japanese investment in local production served to maintain its share in protected markets. Another factor promoting investment in Southeast Asia was the challenge presented by the growing production of local consumer electronics industries in such countries as South Korea and Taiwan. Japanese companies sought to forge links with potential competitors in this region at an early stage in their development, in a largely successful attempt to confine them to their home markets. And since the yen shock of 1985, the sharp rise of Japanese investment and production levels in Asia has been nothing short of breathtaking.

North America and Europe

From the mid-1970s, a major goal of overseas production by Japanese consumer electronics companies was to remedy the rising trade frictions between Japan and its North American and European trading partners over the Japanese consumer electronics industry's high export levels. As a result, the share of

Table 19   Japanese Domestic and Offshore Production of Consumer Electronics

(in 1,000 units)

		Production in Japan		Offshore Production		OEM Production	
		1986	1987	1986	1987	1986	1987
Video	Production quantity	35,253	35,238	2,714	5,694	870	930
	% of total Japanese production	90.8%	84.2%	7.0%	13.6%	2.2%	2.2%
	1986/1987		100.0%		209.8%		106.9%
Color TV	Production quantity	15,019	11,700	18,680	23,478	160	280
	% of total Japanese production	44.4%	33.0%	55.2%	66.2%	0.4%	0.8%
	1986/1987		77.9%		125.8%		175.0%
Audio	Production quantity	33,070	18,895	22,118	38,352	4,825	7,790
	% of total Japanese production	55.1%	29.0%	36.9%	59.0%	8.0%	12.0%
	1986/1987		57.1%		173.4%		161.5%

Source: Japan Electronic Industry Development Association.

Japanese investment in consumer electronics production in developed countries such as the US, the UK, West Germany, Belgium, and France was dramatically increased during the 1970s in order to circumvent voluntary export restraints and other existing or impending restrictions on the industry's sales in these markets. In most cases, investment in overseas production was a direct result of import restrictions, such as those implemented by the US in 1977 on Japanese color TV imports. This is shown by the fact that most Japanese color TV production overseas started operations in around 1978. Furthermore, the Japanese consumer electronics industry sought to take advantage of the rapid appreciation of the yen during the latter half of the 1970s, and the many favorable tax and other terms offered by governments in advanced nations eager to recruit Japanese investment.

In 1972, Sony was the first Japanese consumer electronics company to invest in color TV production in the US. Matsushita followed Sony, starting US-based color TV production in 1974. After the establishment of voluntary restrictions on color TV exports to the US in 1977, other firms, including Sanyo, Mitsubishi Electric, Toshiba, Sharp, and Hitachi, also began manufacturing color TVs in the US and Western Europe. Japanese penetration of the US market has been so successful that the largest single share of total US color TV production is manufactured by eight Japanese-owned companies.

In recent years, Japanese investment in consumer electronics production in North America and Western Europe has been characterized by diversification and increasing sophistication of the types of products produced. Japanese companies also launched production of VTRs in Europe, mostly as the direct result of EC protests and action taken by such countries as France against the rapid increase in Japanese imports. Another key factor is the desire by Japanese companies to establish production bases prior to the start of the EC integrated market in 1992.

Factors Affecting the Growth of Japan's Consumer Electronics Industry

Private Sector

In its drive towards world leadership in consumer electronics, the Japanese industry has developed a number of important relative strengths. While government assistance has played a role, factors contributing to industry growth originate with the individual companies themselves. The private-sector elements of industry growth include price competitiveness, quality control, well-established distribution strategies, and emphasis on R & D and advanced electronics componentry.

Price

Japanese manufacturers have been able to keep prices generally level since around 1970 by absorbing shifts in foreign exchange rates. Among the factors underlying this are: (a) many of the manufacturers anticipated that foreign exchange fluctuations would be a long-term problem and implemented special pricing policies for overseas sales; (b) prices have been co-ordinated with model changes, which have usually been frequent enough to allow price adjustments associated with new models rather than raising the prices of currently marketed models; (c) the establishment, by some companies, of production facilities in countries where the increases in labor costs have been less than in developed nations; and (d) a policy throughout the industry of working to absorb increased costs through rationalization and automation, which has largely been concerned with reducing the unit costs of components and reducing the time necessary for assembling parts.

The impact of cost reductions resulting from decreases in componentry and the increased automation of assembly lines achieved through the introduction of integrated circuits can be seen in the decline in prices of major consumer electronics products over time. By contrast, the average price index for all commodities has consistently risen in comparable periods. Consumer electronics makers have always been under competitive pressure to lower their prices, and the declines in price for most product categories were largely made possible through the utilization of integrated circuits in end products and experience curve effects associated with rising output volumes.

Quality

Along with the rationalization of operations has been a concern with strict quality control and recognition of the importance of a reputation for reliability and craftsmanship. For example, in 1979, the ratio of defective sets to total color TV production was only 0.4% in Japan, compared to 5% in the US. Japanese companies do not have the extensive service networks overseas that some foreign manufacturers do, a point which underscores the importance of a low defect rate, and which also feeds back into costs. With a low defect rate, Japanese companies are under less pressure to invest in extensive service networks.

Maintaining a low defect rate is the primary concern of Japanese manufacturers with regard to production in advanced industrial nations. Japanese companies express concern at not having sufficient control over the quality of locally produced parts, should their use be necessary, and at the effects of labor disputes on quality standards.

Distribution and Delivery

The Japanese consumer electronics industry has traditionally stressed meeting delivery times promptly and most companies have developed reputations as steady and stable suppliers, a point that has also aided manufacturers in developing and maintaining distribution and marketing networks in overseas markets. In addition, manufacturers work to keep distribution costs down, taking such measures as using ships going to several countries to which products are destined, especially from production facilities in third countries, and finalizing production schedules well in advance in order to meet promised deliveries.

Investment and R & D

While Japan's investment in consumer electronics appears to be lower than investment in electronic components, it should be remembered that there is a general identity between the systems and components industries in Japan. As a result, investment in components divisions serves to benefit directly consumer electronics divisions as well, since such components as integrated circuits are used to upgrade consumer electronics products. The growth in investment levels in electronic components reflects the rapid increase from the late 1970s of the range of integrated circuit applications. Much of the growth in investment in consumer electronics is related to increasing VTR production capacity and increasing exports of consumer electronics, particularly VTRs.

The emphasis of research and development activity in Japan's consumer electronics industry is less on basic research, and weighted more toward application and product development. The result is that while the industry has been responsible for few major breakthroughs, it excels at applying new developments and adapting them for mass-production techniques.

Specifically, Japanese consumer electronics companies have devoted most of their R & D to developing and improving production processes, product design, and commercialization. While varying from company to company, 50–70% of R & D expenditure is devoted to production process development. The larger half of the remaining 30–50% of R & D expenditure goes to product design and commercialization. The share of basic research in R & D undertaken by Japanese consumer electronics companies is low.

Another important strength is the speed of development. Applied research is not only undertaken well, it is also undertaken quickly, resulting in a minimal length of time between development and commercialization. This orientation is unlikely to change in the near future, nor is it likely that the importance of R & D will lessen, given the need to maintain sales within an increasingly competitive environment and the search for new product areas.

Electronic Components

One of the main competitive strengths of Japanese consumer electronics companies is that they have led the world in applying electronic component and integrated circuit technologies to consumer electronics applications. Unlike the US, for example, most leading consumer electronics companies in Japan are also major producers of integrated circuits. The utilization of integrated circuit technology has resulted in per unit reductions in the number of components used, enhanced end-product quality, and lower unit production costs. Combined with generally low internal profit objectives, these factors have allowed Japanese consumer electronics companies to implement aggressive pricing strategies.

Reduction in Components

Color TVs provide a good example of the efforts of Japanese consumer electronics companies to reduce unit componentry. Japanese companies started to phase out vacuum tubes in favor of transistors from 1970. From 1971, they led the world in applying integrated circuits to color TV sets. In this regard, the strength of Japanese consumer electronics companies in linear integrated circuit production technology has been particularly important, linear integrated circuits being the type most suited to consumer electronics applications.

Reductions achieved in the number of color TV components during the 1970s were substantial. For example, by the late 1970s, Sanyo was able to reduce the number of components used in its 19-inch models by 65% after a decade of effort. The adaptability of integrated circuits to automatic insertion into a color TV chassis, as well as the smaller number of components, enabled Sanyo to make considerable progress in automating what had been a labor-intensive assembly process.

Commonality of Components

Not only do Japanese consumer electronics manufacturers strive to reduce the absolute number of components required for a particular product, but they also attempt to use the same components for a wide variety of products. The goal is to lower unit costs of component manufacture through volume production, and also to achieve cost reductions by using the same machinery for a wider variety of manufacturing processes.

Internal Production of Integrated Circuits

The most important technology for the consumer electronics industry in recent years has been that for integrated circuits and semiconductors. In this regard, it is significant that Hitachi, Matsushita, and Toshiba are among the leading five Japanese producers of semiconductors, while Sanyo, Sharp, and Sony are among the top 10.

Internal production of semiconductors by major consumer electronics companies has important implications for the competitiveness of Japan's consumer electronics industry. Japanese consumer electronics companies have ready access to high-quality semiconductor components designed to meet the specific requirements of their consumer electronics products. Japanese companies have a significant advantage in that their consumer electronics product design divisions and integrated circuit production divisions are closely integrated. US electronics producers, however, must procure integrated circuits and other components from a semiconductor industry primarily geared to meet the needs of the computer and telecommunications industries.

The result of these factors is that Japan's consumer electronics industry can be expected to remain internationally competitive and that the major restrictions on its activities are more likely to be political. In this sense, the situation surrounding the industry echoes some of the major concerns facing the Japanese economy as a whole, particularly regarding an increasingly restrictive international climate for exports.

Government Role

While the Japanese government has consistently lent its support to the development of the consumer electronics industry, the level of support has been considerably lower than that given to industries such as the computer industry. The main role of the government with regard to consumer electronics has been to protect the industry from import competition at an early stage, to co-ordinate a limited number of R & D programs, to promote exports, and finally to manage exports via orderly marketing agreements and industry-wide directives. Today, the main activity of the government regarding consumer electronics is to regulate exports.

Import Regulation

In the early period until 1970, the Japanese government sought to protect the consumer electronics industry via high tariffs. This policy was in line with the government's 'infant industry' approach in its policies for consumer electronics and other industries. In 1970, the import tariff on consumer electronics products was lowered from 30% to 7.5%, with the tariff being eliminated completely in 1974.

There were several motivations for the elimination of tariff protection: (a) it was recognized that the industry had become sufficiently developed so as not to require such protection; (b) criticism from Japan's trading partners had begun to increase; and (c) Japanese companies themselves were beginning to account for a growing percentage of imports into Japan as a result of increased offshore production.

It is important to note that, unlike the case of the computer industry, consumer electronics imports were never subject to special import regulations. Instead, they have been subject to general quota regulations which applied to a wide range of products. The quota system limiting the importation of consumer electronics products into Japan was relatively lenient, and was ultimately abolished in 1972.

In summary, during the crucial formative years, the Japanese government played an important role in protecting the domestic industry from imports. As discussed below, the government's attention then shifted dramatically to export regulation in the mid-1970s.

Government R & D Programs and Other Aid

The Japanese government's support of the broadcasting industry has contributed to the expansion of domestic demand for consumer electronics products. In the early 1950s, for example, the government enacted a series of laws concerning radio and TV broadcasting, and also reorganized the semi-governmental broadcasting company, NHK. Equally important was the development of a strong private broadcasting industry. By the mid-1950s, approximately 60 radio stations provided a service covering all of Japan, and color TV broadcasting was begun in around 1960; by 1971, all television programming in Japan was in color.

Prospects for Japan's Consumer Electronics Industry

Data on Japan's consumer electronics industry suggest some important changes in the structure of supply and demand. The value of Japanese consumer electronics production in 1987 was 12.1% lower than in the previous year. Production values for all consumer electronics, excluding color TVs and tape recorders, registered declines. In the same period, the value of exports recorded a 25.4% decrease from a year earlier. The adverse effect of the strong yen was the primary factor behind the declines in production and export values.

VTR production value in the first 10 months of 1987 fell 13.9% from the corresponding period of 1986. Exports were down by an even greater 19.5%, due primarily to a drop in exports to the US. In contrast, domestic shipments of VTRs and VTR cameras grew at annual rates of 30% and 55% respectively.

Production of color televisions in Japan rose 5.7% in value and 3.5% in volume terms in 1987, supported by a sudden boom in the popularity of large-screen models. Exports continued to decline in 1987, reflecting the appreciation of the yen and the shift to overseas production. In 1987, offshore production of Japanese color televisions was twice as high in unit terms as domestic production.

The production value of stereo sets and stereo components in 1987 fell 2.2% and 14.9% respectively. Once again, the strong yen was the main culprit. One bright spot has been the market for compact disk-radio-cassette players. Domestic sales of this type of machine were up 450% in the first quarter of 1988 compared to the same period of 1987.

In 1988, Japan's consumer electronics industry expects another decrease in exports due to the adverse effect of the strong yen. In particular, exports to the US will likely drop to three-fourths of the previous year's level. Japanese consumer electronics companies are expected to combat the high value of the yen by purchasing more parts and components produced by foreign manufacturers and by shifting production offshore. The domestic market will continue to gain in importance for Japanese makers.

Epilogue: US Strategic Mistakes in the Consumer Electronics Sector

The experience of the US consumer electronics industry over the past 25 years, culminating most recently in its rejuvenation by Japanese investment, seems to point to the absence of sound long-term business strategies among US corporations. Although there have been extenuating circumstances, such as the often irrelevant and perverse short-term pressures exerted by capital markets on the decisions of US management, the fact remains that the US consumer electronics industry is now being reincarnated by Japanese manufacturers. If the industry is still in fact economically viable, why did it experience a decline as imports into the US increased and then come to life again under Japanese management? Aside from oft-repeated arguments about the superiority of Japanese factory automation techniques, these alone probably cannot explain the peculiar scenario over the past 25 years, under which US management has been replaced by Japanese management, essentially running the same industry.

A review of the history of the US consumer electronics industry suggests that the developments in the industry in the US have been significantly influenced by the absence of a long-term strategy on the part of management.

Management strategies have what appear to be relatively short-term horizons. The underlying assumption in the consumer electronics industry seems to have been that the industry would probably always remain on top internationally and that any inroads made by foreign companies would be the result of low wages or unfair trade practices.

Because of this emphasis in their thinking, US companies appear to have made some clear strategic errors. For example, US companies sold their technology in the late 1950s and '60s, and even into the 1970s, at relatively low prices to Japanese companies, which later became their competitors. There was no underlying anxiety or concern at that time about Japan becoming a serious competitor in a broad range of high-volume products. That Japan might become the world leader was unthinkable.

The prevailing management theory in the 1960s was that competitiveness could be preserved principally by moving production to low-wage areas of the world. The possibilities for automation were not explored as fully as they were later by Japanese companies. Cost comparisons and feasibility studies of setting up assembly facilities in the developing nations versus investing large sums in the development of automated production facilities at home showed that setting up overseas had the more immediate impact. The results of investments in fully automated facilities were uncertain. In addition, problems arising from opposition by labor unions, which feared extensive layoffs at existing plants, were judged to be potentially more serious than adding new production facilities in Southeast Asia. Any movement of existing production capacity to developing nations could also be justified to unions by pointing to unfair foreign competition such as that from Japan, which was a lower-wage nation at that time.

Over the years, the US consumer electronics industry conceded more and more, apparently not having the resources or enthusiasm to try to take the initiative. Japanese manufacturers made very substantial inroads through exports under their own brands and through supplying large retailers with low-cost television sets to sell under their brands. The latter OEM strategy put a strong ally on their side in the US. Although charges of dumping, ie selling below prices in the Japanese domestic market, were brought on numerous occasions, this proved to be exceptionally difficult to prove, so that US manufacturers obtained no legal protection. By the early 1970s, they were facing competition from low-cost Japanese producers which had attained sufficient scale and accumulated experience to undercut even the most efficient of US manufacturers, even those using offshore production centers in order to reduce costs.

By the mid-1970s, the latest fad in management thinking in the US was that the US economy should be moving into higher and higher value-added sectors. The manufacture of television sets could be left to the Japanese; the US would now become a post-industrial, highly service-oriented economy. As a result, the remaining US manufacturers were reluctant or unable to develop and market VTRs and other new products.

Japanese Strategy Long-term

In contrast to the US, Japanese consumer electronics manufacturers adopted a long-term strategy, emphasizing the development of a world market for their products. They clearly enjoyed certain advantages, such as relatively cheap access to technology, labor relations that at least did not retard the introduction of highly automated production processes, somewhat lower wages during the late 1970s, and essentially open access to the two largest markets in the world – Japan and the US – access which allowed them to develop the scale necessary to become the lowest cost-integrated producers in the world.

Perhaps the strongest element of the Japanese strategy, however, was the tenacious adherence to the objective that they had to be major competitors in high-volume markets for manufactured products. Their aim was, and still is, to be world-class suppliers of the major high-volume items in the largest international markets. This focus on middle- to lower-end volume markets made increased efficiency essential. Japanese manufacturers therefore obtained existing automation technology from the US in the 1970s, where it had found a relatively limited market, and adapted it so as to maintain their competitive advantage.

As a result of this long-term, steady strategy, made possible in part by the equally long-term views of financial institutions supporting Japan's leading consumer electronics companies, Japanese companies have in effect been able to drive US companies almost out of their home market. Now that the yen has appreciated, Japanese companies are faced with the need to manufacture in the

US. In other words, manufacturing in the US is once again a viable economic and business proposition. But oddly enough, instead of US companies seizing the initiative, it is Japanese companies that are resurrecting the US consumer electronics industry.

Although many factors have led to this peculiar train of events, one fact remains: if US companies had maintained a long-term strategy of maintaining and expanding their position as world-class suppliers, had monitored developments in Japan very carefully, and seized the initiative in product development and automation, they would probably still be in existence today.

Tokyo as a Key Financial Center

Once described as a 'fragile blossom', following the first oil crisis, Japan has shown a strong ability to adapt to severe shocks and to continue to build its position as an industrial and financial power. Since the early 1980s, Japan has moved from having a deficit in its current account to become the world's largest exporter of capital. Barring stoppages of raw material supplies, Japan's position as a supplier of capital and Tokyo's standing as a financial center will continue to rise. Only four or five years ago, talk of the possibility of Tokyo becoming a *leading* financial center would have met with some scepticism, and any suggestion of Tokyo being the world's leading financial center would have been regarded as quite optimistic. After all, as recently as 1980, Japan was running a deficit in its current account as it struggled to pay for oil costing more than US$30 a barrel.

Since the early 1980s, Japan has shown a strong ability not only to adapt, but also to move out in front in many areas. If one considers the current account balance alone, Japan moved from a deficit of US$10.7 billion in calendar 1980 to a surplus of $86 billion in calendar 1986 and $87 billion in 1987. Over the same period, the long-term capital balance moved from a net inflow of $2.3 billion to a net outflow of US$131.8 billion in 1986 and $137 billion in 1987 – more money than any country has ever placed overseas in a single year.

Assisted by a strong dollar and a weak yen during the first half of the 1980s, many Japanese industries moved to consolidate their international positions in strategic industrial sectors, particularly in electrical and electronic equipment. Drawing on the strengths of a business system that encourages long-term planning and the acquisition of a leading market share internationally, and on the advantages of co-operative business and government relationships, many Japanese industries have taken internationally dominant shares in strategic markets. Moreover, until the sharp appreciation of the yen at the beginning of 1985, many Japanese companies remained virtually unchallenged by foreign competition in the home market.

By 1984, it had become clear that the Japanese industrial establishment had developed a money-generator likely to be more powerful and long-lasting than OPEC. Japan's trade balance exceeded US$44 billion in 1984, and the net capital outflow rose to almost $50 billion.

An equally important development, of far-reaching significance, was the emergence of signs that Japan's invisible trade balance deficit was beginning to decline. During the postwar period, Japan had usually run a deficit in its invisibles account because Japanese companies paid more to foreigners for insurance and shipping services than was received in income from overseas investments and other sources. But the rise in overseas investments, both in plant and equipment and in securities, began to bring a higher inflow of earnings to offset payments for insurance and freight. The invisibles deficit dropped from US$13.6 billion in calendar 1981 to $7.7 billion in 1984, and then to $4.6 billion in calendar 1986.

As forecasts of the OECD and international banking institutions suggest, even with a strong yen, Japan's current account surplus in US dollar terms will decline more slowly than hoped for. At the same time, the outflow of long-term capital will continue, leading to a further reduction in the invisibles deficit.

In contrast, the US is on a course to become a debtor nation of unheard-of proportions. Even strong measures in the US to reduce fiscal and current account deficits are likely to take four to five years to succeed. Japan will be the principal foreign financier of this external debt of the US.

Forecasts of where these trends will lead differ in detail, but the magnitude and implications are similar. By the early 1990s, Japan may have net external assets of US$500 billion, while the US may well have net external liabilities of between $700 billion and $1 trillion. The attitudes and apparent strategies of Japanese securities companies and institutional investors are already having a significant effect on the placement of US treasury bonds and on dollar interest rates. This influence could increase significantly by the early 1990s.

In addition, a very rough calculation suggests that, by the late 1980s, the US may be paying over US$60 billion a year in interest charges to foreigners holding its debt. Thus, if Japanese investors hold only half the external debt of the US, Japan's current account may still be in surplus, even if Japanese industry loses some of its ability to compete and if the trade surplus is eliminated.

The Potential

A comparison of the world's three major financial centers suggests that Tokyo has some important strengths that may enable it to move into a leading position. These include a large and growing base of domestic savings, a basically strong domestic economy that is likely to adapt to the effects of a stronger yen, and important social underpinnings that will support the development of a sophisticated financial center.

One of Tokyo's principal strengths is the large volume of monetary assets in the economy. Recent estimates put total monetary assets at more than ¥600 trillion, growing at about 8% annually. One of the principal factors leading to this large volume of liquidity has been the consistently high rate of personal savings in Japan. Despite a decline from more than 20% in the 1970s, the savings rate from household incomes remains well above 15%.

Other indicators of the size of Tokyo's financial muscle include the total outstandings in the financial markets. According to estimates made in late 1986, Tokyo's financial market size stood at the equivalent of US$1.5 trillion, compared with $2 trillion in the US. The figure for Japan was about three times that of West Germany. The Japan offshore market, which began in late 1986, has expanded to US$130 billion as at the end of March 1987, already rivalling Hong Kong and Singapore in size.

The large volume of liquidity in Tokyo is in part responsible for some remarkable statistics. For example:

- The average price/earnings ratio on the Tokyo Stock Exchange in late 1986 was 60, and in mid-1988 it was about 70, despite the temporarily adverse effects of Black Monday.
- The total market valuation of Tokyo Electric exceeds that of the exchanges of Hong Kong, Singapore, and Sydney combined.
- The total market value of NTT exceeds that of IBM, AT&T, Exxon, General Electric, and General Motors combined.

There are no changes in the offing which appear likely to reduce the savings rate in Japan or to lower significantly the available volume of monetary resources. If the yen continues to strengthen, the overseas purchasing power of Japan's monetary assets will rise, contributing to Japan's potential as a capital exporter.

Some discussions as to the future of Tokyo as a financial center link its eventual position to Japan's current account surplus. The argument goes that the current account surplus enables Japan to export its liquidity. If Japan became less competitive, this would place a limit on its role in providing financial resources to the rest of the world. In fact, this linkage appears to be weaker than many suppose. From 1984 to 1987, Japan reported large trade and current account surpluses, but exports of net long-term capital have far exceeded those surpluses. In 1986, Japan's overall balance, after net long-term and short-term outflows, was US$44.8 billion in deficit and $29.5 billion in the red in 1987. This means that foreigners have a willingness to accept yen assets. Until the early 1990s, the US will be occupied with the task of regaining its international competitiveness and its ability to pay its way internationally. The yen may very well remain attractive to international investors and even become more so as the US moves further into debt. At least in the medium term, yen assets seem likely to be in demand, and Japan can continue to run an overall balance of payments deficit, providing the world with liquidity.

Tokyo Compared with London and New York

As the center of the Euromarket, London handles a massive volume of international transactions. The focus of operations of large UK institutions and foreign institutions in London is the provision of international services. The domestic market for financial services in the UK is much smaller than in the US and Japan, but London has a secure position because of the drawing power of international banks and securities houses either based there or with substantial operations there. The institutions, personnel, communications infrastructure, and the location of London in the highly industrialized European time zones all attract business to London and make it, by most indications at present, the largest international financial center.

What would happen if another major city in Europe offered similar advantages? Ignoring the costs of relocation, there is really no reason why most of the transactions now carried out in London might not be carried out in another equally well-equipped center in the European region. Although this is not likely to happen, the point is that the economy of the UK and sterling alone are not sufficient reasons for locating the world's largest international financial center in London.

New York is in some ways the reverse of London. The domestic market in the US is very large, and the US dollar is still the principal international currency. The provision of financial services to corporations operating in the US and the financing of the US government fully justify the existence of New York as a financial center. However, compared with London, the international component of business in New York is a smaller percentage of the total. New York is the leading domestic financial center for the world's largest economy. International activities take place on a large scale, but are secondary to domestic activities.

Tokyo at present is rather more similar to New York than to London. Japan has a large domestic market for financial services. The largest part of the operations of leading Japanese financial institutions is still domestic, despite the fact that they have built up substantial international banking and securities businesses. If anything, the emergence of large volumes of liquidity in Tokyo has shifted the attention of Japanese financial institutions back to their domestic market and promoted the links between their domestic and overseas offices.

Another important difference between New York and London on the one hand and Tokyo on the other is the extent and pace of deregulation. New York, and the US market in general, is highly deregulated compared with Tokyo. The US has already experienced and made adjustments to the deregulation of interest rates, equity commissions, and other measures that Japan has yet to adopt to the same extent.

In part, as a result of deregulation, the role of foreign financial institutions in the US economy is substantially larger than in Tokyo. In the US, foreign banks and securities companies, some of them Japanese, own major US institutions. Leasing Japanese commercial banks, for example, have operations in California that rank among the top 20 institutions in that state. Two Japanese institutions are already primary dealers in US government securities – one directly, and the other through the acquisition of a US primary dealer.

In both London and New York, foreign financial institutions play a major role in the market. In contrast, in Japan, foreign commercial banks account for less than 3% of loans, and as of mid-1988, for a variety of reasons, no foreign commercial bank had acquired a Japanese institution. Foreign securities companies appear to have been more successful in making inroads into the Japanese market, particularly in market niches such as brokerage services for foreign investors in Japanese equities. However, for the majority of activities, their overall position is not comparable with the role of foreign institutions in the London and New York markets.

Another important advantage which will contribute to the growth of Tokyo as a financial center is Japan's location in the Pacific Basin. Tokyo is geographically well-positioned to be the leading banking and securities center for the Asian and Pacific regions. The countries in these regions, particularly in Asia, are expected to achieve higher rates of growth as a group than any other major area of the world until the year 2000. Tokyo has strong historical ties to these regions, and its financial institutions have considerable experience in evaluating projects, in providing financial resources, and in dealing in the markets of the region.

Strategies for Long-term Growth

Despite these strengths, one of the question marks about Japan at present is the extent to which the stronger yen will weaken the industrial base and detract from the long-term growth potential of the Japanese economy. The principal issue for export-oriented industries in Japan in the closing years of the 1980s and into the 1990s will be adaptation to the strength of the currency. Options include:

- the movement of production offshore to the US, Europe and Asia;
- the upgrading of existing product lines manufactured domestically in order to remain competitive in more specialized and sophisticated market segments; and
- diversification into related, or in some cases unrelated, product areas, particularly those with close links to domestic rather than export demand.

Although the impact of the stronger yen on many export industries has been serious, Japanese corporations appear to have a number of economic advantages that will make the exercise of one or more of the above options easier. For example, there is no problem of inflation, with the exception of a probable medium-term increase in rents arising from the sharp rise in real estate costs. Wage increases in Japan remain low and well under control.

Japanese corporations are also benefiting from historically low interest rates, as well as highly favorable funding terms and conditions in overseas capital markets. The leading Japanese corporations appear likely to obtain funding readily for such restructuring measures as:

- closing plants near urban areas and developing income-earning properties;
- setting up facilities in the US or other overseas markets;
- acquiring companies overseas; and

- buying income-generating properties overseas.

Because of the availability of funds, Japanese corporations, with their strong banking ties, seem to be well-positioned to obtain financing for restructuring.

But will strategies for corporate survival, such as moving plants overseas, erode the production base in Japan? The answer appears to be that it will not, judging from the process that has already been going on in certain industries since the 1960s. The strategy is likely to be to reduce production capacity in noncompetitive products and to move a portion of this production capacity offshore so as to remain competitive and retain market share, but wherever possible to keep the production of top-of-the-line items in Japan. In some industries, corporations may invest overseas in the US and elsewhere in order to retain the market share they have already carved out, while maintaining product development, assembly, marketing, and distribution capabilities in Japan. The rationale for this approach will be to retain a closeness to the Japanese market, which in many areas is one of the world's most demanding and sophisticated.

Nevertheless, in some export industries, 'hollowing out' is bound to take place. However, tax and other measures are already stimulating more consumer spending and housing construction, so GNP growth of at least 2–3% is likely to be sustained into the 1990s. Japan's industrial base is very likely to retain much of its strength despite some 'hollowing out', because Japanese corporations are determined not to make the same mistake as US corporations which exported key manufacturing skills to other nations in the 1960s and 1970s.

From the point of view of foreign and domestic financial institutions, the presence of Japanese corporations which are leaders in their respective fields and which have increasingly diverse international operations will provide many business opportunities. Therefore, even with some 'hollowing out', the domestic economic base and potential customer base will provide a strong basis on which Tokyo can become a leading financial center.

Tokyo's Social and Political Environment

Tokyo's other strengths – more difficult to quantify, but equally as important – are the social underpinnings necessary in order to maintain a leading position as a financial center. Some of these strengths are:

- A well-educated and internationally aware group of financial professionals and individuals with the potential to become professionals. One of the bottlenecks in Tokyo's growth will be the training of sufficient personnel. However, the human resources are available for training, even though the investment to be made will be substantial.
- A population that is willing to accept change when it appears to be in the Japanese interest and when a consensus has been properly hammered out. Japan has been very reluctant to change in many areas because one or other of these conditions was not satisfied.

- A politically and socially stable environment where individuals for the most part feel secure, where financial institutions are regarded as being very sound (with not one bank failure during the postwar period), where individuals save a substantial portion of their earnings in order to attain their own goals and for their financial needs after retirement, and where more than half the population regards itself as being part of the 'middle-middle' class and nearly 90% regard themselves as being at a level somewhere within the middle classes.

All things considered, Tokyo appears likely to be the fastest-growing and most attractive of the three major centers from the point of view of business opportunities. In summary, some of the reasons for this are:

- Japanese corporations based largely in Tokyo will increasingly require sophisticated international services as their operations become more international and complex.
- Leading foreign corporations will find a presence in Japan more and more important. This will lead to a continuing increase in the number of foreign companies entering Japan and the expansion of the operations of many corporations already in the market. The number of foreign corporations listed on the Tokyo Stock Exchange, for example, exceeds that of the New York Stock Exchange, and is expected to rise to several hundred by the end of the 1980s.
- Japan has substantial room for further deregulation, which will make it easier for both Japanese and foreign financial institutions to do business.

The Requirements

In order to realize the full potential of the market, Japanese and foreign financial institutions, governments, and other interested parties should be aware of some of the requirements for furthering the development of the market. These include continued, and preferably bolder, deregulation, a better awareness of the potential of the Tokyo market, training of the necessary personnel, and a larger investment in infrastructure in order to curb runaway real estate costs.

Continued deregulation appears to be one of the central requirements for further development of the market. Some of the main areas for consideration are:

- Expansion of the types and volume of short-term financial instruments available to domestic and foreign investors.
- Increased availability of futures and options instruments. The bond futures market, which began operations in late 1985, has shown explosive growth because it plays an important role in helping investors to hedge the risks of their large portfolios of government bonds.
- Further deregulation of interest rates.

As Paul Hofer, Chairman of the Institute of Foreign Bankers in Tokyo, stated in a speech in February 1987: 'I have watched the process of deregulation in Tokyo now for more than five years. I think the monetary authorities have taken major strides toward deregulation. But one deference I detect in the process of deregulation is greater emphasis on survival and soundness of even smaller institutions in Japan. The two Samurai principles, "Work for long-term survival" and "Co-operate with the authorities," seem to come into play here. The process of liberalization in Japan has been, in my view, a brilliant job of defending and protecting the interests of Japanese financial institutions. Every change has been made carefully and orchestrated to prevent disruption and to nurture Japanese institutions into strong domestic and international players.'

This is another clear example of the private and government sectors working together in Japan. If we refrain from making any value judgements, we can at least say that the approach to deregulation in Japan is different from the emphasis in Europe and the US. There, the thrust of deregulation has been to use competitive forces to increase market efficiency and stimulate market growth. In Japan, domestic interests are very carefully weighed and the final decision need not represent a victory for efficiency in the short to medium term. The fact that Japanese corporations have issued more bonds in international capital markets in recent years than in the domestic market is eloquent testimony to the rigidity of the rules in Japan. Also reflecting the priority placed on domestic interests is the fact that Euroyen financial instruments have been deregulated far more rapidly than domestic yen instruments.

At present, many foreign banks are reducing their loans outstanding to Japanese corporations and are emphasizing the marketing of fee-based services. This is in strong contrast to the strategies of Japanese banks in the US as they continue to build strong relationships, including credit exposure. Foreign banks in Japan would be in a stronger position to expand their loan portfolios if they had access to yen funding at rates competitive with Japanese banks.

In addition to further deregulation, another requirement appears to be the generation of a stronger consensus on the potential of the market. Numerous instances can be cited where decisions on deregulation could probably have been speeded up significantly if the development of Tokyo as an international financial center had received higher priority over purely domestic concerns.

The Pitfalls

The rise of Tokyo to the position of the world's premier financial center in the coming years will also not be without pitfalls for Japan. Two of the most significant of these problems will be the accompanying rise in Japan's international political position and overseas reactions to Japan's success, not only in the strategic industrial sectors, but also now in the financial services.

With Tokyo as the leading financial center by the early 1990s and the leading creditor of the US – which has become the world's largest debtor – the potential for friction appears likely to rise rather than diminish. As C. Fred Bergsten pointed out in 'Economic Imbalances and World Politics', *Foreign*

Affairs, Spring 1987:

> '...with America as massive debtor and Japan as massive creditor, [this] will pose major challenges to global management in both the economic and political spheres. In both areas a newly pluralistic world power structure must be arranged, with a revised leadership role for America – perhaps using its security position to pursue economic goals – and an increasing leadership role for Japan. The only precedent dates from the 1920s, when Anglo-American co-operation attempted but ultimately failed to reconcile the decline of Britain and the rise of the United States, due to the unwillingness of both countries to understand and adapt to their new positions. The new [US] Administration in 1989 will have to address these matters with highest urgency.'

It is to be hoped, however, that Japan can direct its capabilities for adaptation to assume its new responsibilities in the world economy.

Another pitfall may be a phenomenon observed in recent years, but which with each incidence seems to become more intense. The emergence of Tokyo as the leading financial center is bound to create resentment. This resentment will be all the sharper because of the basic difference between government and business interaction in Japan and elsewhere. In Japan, business and government generally co-operate to attain economic objectives and, particularly in the financial sector, the government has taken special pains to look after the interests of private financial institutions. In the US and Europe, considerations of competition and efficiency have often taken precedence over the careful supervision and nurturing of individual financial institutions. As Japan and Japanese financial institutions have risen to pre-eminence internationally, the feeling has grown that these two systems may be incompatible. Other countries may therefore adopt a more protective role to ensure that competition is conducted on a more-or-less level playing field. From the Japanese point of view, this may imply the need to examine and reconsider the ambitions of Japan as a country and the ambitions of Japanese corporations so as to permit a smoother adjustment to Japan's growing role.

When the newness of Japan as number 1 in finance begins to wear off, it is to be hoped that Japan will realize that it has a massive responsibility to revitalize not only its own economy, but also the economies of Europe and the US, as well as a responsibility to promote the continued development of the industrializing nations. The challenge for Tokyo will be enormous. The co-operation and assistance of financial institutions, governments, and other interests around the world will be essential for Tokyo's continued success.

The Growing Role of Japanese Banks

Deregulation in Japan and other markets, along with the appreciation of the yen, have catapulted Japan's leading banks into the front ranks of the world's financial institutions. Most of the top 10 banks, outside the US, in terms of assets are now Japanese, and, barring any sudden drop in the value of the yen or other disruptive developments, Japanese banks seem very likely to hold this position for some time to come. Some of the reasons for this view include Japan's rising status as a creditor nation, the growing use of the yen as an international currency, and the relatively solid position of leading Japanese banks, despite the controversy over capital ratios.

Rise to Prominence

The latest rankings of banking institutions show continued gains for the international standing of Japanese banks. The top five banks in the world, as measured by total assets, are now all Japanese. The list of leading international banks, including US banking institutions, now reads: Dai-Ichi Kangyo Bank, with in the order of US$251 billion in assets; Fuji Bank, with $219 billion; Sumitomo Bank, with $214 billion; Mitsubishi Bank, with $209 billion; and Sanwa Bank, with $200 billion.

Among the leading banks outside the US, Japanese banks account for eight of the top 10. In assets, the Sanwa Bank is followed by the Industrial Bank of Japan, with $167 billion. The seventh and eighth positions are occupied by two French institutions, Caisse Nationale de Crédit Agricole and Banque Nationale de Paris, and in ninth and tenth place are Tokai Bank and Mitsui Bank.

Among the top 50 institutions, Japanese banks hold 22 positions; between 51st and 100th, they hold 11 positions. Thus, Japanese banks account for one-third of the leading 100 financial institutions outside the US.

Other indications of the rising position of Japan's banking institutions include data published by the Bank for International Settlements (BIS). According to BIS data, Japanese banking assets rose to the US dollar equivalent of $1,117.7 billion, or 32.8% of all international bank assets, at the end of 1986. This compares to only 23.0%, or $517.9 billion, in 1984. At the same time, the share of US banks dropped to 17.6%, from 26.4% in 1984. The other major group of banks gaining share internationally were the West German institutions, which showed an increase to 7.9% of international bank assets in 1986, versus 6.4% in 1984.

The Growing Role of the Yen

Factors leading to this marked rise in the international role of Japanese banks have included the increased role that Japan has begun to play as a creditor nation. Japan's net external assets rose to US$180 billion at the end of calendar 1987, while those of the US plunged to a net deficit of more than $200 billion. The building of this large international asset position, however, has not depended heavily to date on exporting capital from Japan. Instead, a high percentage of the international assets of Japanese banks have been funded in overseas markets. The days of the so-called 'Japan rate' following the first oil crisis, when Japanese banks were charged a premium for dollar funding, are long gone. More Japanese banks have triple-A ratings for their debt issues than US banks, so Japanese banks are able to raise funds and to act as intermediaries in all the major markets.

It seems clear, however, that Japan's rising status as a creditor nation will enhance the position of Japanese banks, as they, along with other leading institutional investors such as the life insurance companies, play a growing role in recycling Japan's current account surpluses back to the US and the rest of the world.

In view of the limited progress to date in reducing the trade and fiscal deficits in the US, it appears likely that Japan will continue to play a major role in funding the US in the years to come. Some are even forecasting that the net external deficit of the US will exceed $1 trillion in the early 1990s and may exceed $1.5 trillion in the mid- to late-1990s before it begins to decline.

Although many commentators in the US are quick to argue that the US external deficit will probably not rise as a percentage of the GNP, this argument appears to be somewhat lacking in appreciation of the underlying realities involved if the US goes that far into debt. The division of almost any number by the GNP produces a small percentage since, after all, it is one of the largest numbers to be found.

Two of the most important implications appear to be that the growing reliance of the US on finance from Japan will provide the impetus for internationalization of the yen and further enhance the status of Japan's financial institutions.

According to BIS data, total Euroyen and external positions in domestic yen amounted to the equivalent of US$173 billion at the end of calendar 1986. This puts the yen second only to the German mark after the dollar. At current rates of growth, international yen positions may very well overtake mark positions in 1987 or early 1988, making the yen the second most important currency after the US dollar. At recent rates of growth, however, it may take until the end of the century to catch up with the dollar.

Challenge of Internationalization

Japanese banking institutions seem very likely to retain their strong international positions for some time to come, in view of the growing role Japan will play as a creditor nation and the expanding usage of the yen in international transactions. Attainment of this status is the crowning achievement of intense efforts over the last century.

As for other Japanese industries, the next barriers appear to be cultural: becoming a closely integrated part of the international community.

Japan's Position in World Capital Markets

Stock Crashes in Japan versus the US

The effects of the drop in stock-market prices in Japan have been very different from those in the US. Holdings of equities by households in Japan are far lower than in the US, measured as a percentage of total financial assets. In addition, the economy in Japan entered a period of domestic-led expansion in 1987, after a prolonged slump in industrial output following the upward revaluation of the yen in late 1985 and 1986. Barring a severe downturn in the US economy, Japan appears likely to continue to show real GNP growth of around 3%, following real expansion of 4.9% in fiscal 1987, led primarily by the domestic sector. Prospects for the US are much less certain. Analyses suggest that the principal casualty of the stock-market drop will ultimately be the dollar, since the US no longer has the option of keeping interest rates high in order to attract foreign capital to finance the fiscal deficit. Instead, the US must use monetary policy as a means of sustaining momentum in the economy.

Differences in Household Assets

The impact of the drop in stock prices in October 1987 on Japanese households is in the final analysis likely to be much less severe than in the US. Bank of Japan data on the holdings of financial assets show that Japanese households had only 1.4% of their assets in stocks at the end of 1985, compared to nearly 25% for households in the US. Total holdings of securities, including stocks, bonds, investment trusts, and other instruments, accounted for 12.8% of household assets in Japan, versus 39.1% in the US.

Japanese households have slightly more than 70% of their financial assets in the form of currency or deposits, compared to only 33.8% for the US. Money in insurance and pension funds accounted for about 17% of individual assets in Japan, versus 25% in the US. Thus, the percentage of personal assets subject to fluctuations in value is under 15% in Japan, but around 40% in the United States.

Corporations Also Less Vulnerable

Similar data on corporations show that about 6% of monetary assets are held in securities, versus 10% in the US. Japanese corporations have also availed themselves of such investment instruments as fund trusts and specified money trusts which are accounted for only on the maturity of the trust (for most types of companies), which is typically five years.

Because of the option of greater leverage through bank borrowings in Japan and less underlying concern with short-term fluctuations in stock valuations, the corporate sector was under less pressure to alter its plans of expanding capital investments in 1987 and 1988. Most corporations in the US, however, faced substantially lower price-earnings multiples in 1988 than before Black Monday.

Different Economic Fundamentals

Another factor which may lessen the impact of lower stock prices in Japan is the difference in economic fundamentals. With the exception of 1982, the US economy showed moderate to strong expansion from 1981 to 1987, sustained by a rising government deficit and growing borrowings in the household sector. These trends have continued virtually unchanged in 1988. In part because of a low household savings rate in the US – only 4% in 1986 – external borrowings have expanded rapidly. The drop in stock prices appears to have been linked in part to concern about the ability of the US to continue to borrow externally in order to sustain economic momentum. The rise in US interest rates just prior to the stock-market drop appears to have reawakened concern about the medium- to long-term implications of rising external borrowings. Another problem in the US is that inflation in consumer prices has moved up from just under 2% in 1986 to around 4% in 1987 and 1988.

In contrast, since early 1987, the Japanese economy has been on an upward trend, following the slump in industrial output which followed the massive upward revaluation of the yen beginning in September 1985. The most recent GNP data show a strong upward trend in domestic demand, led by moderate growth in consumer spending, high levels of investment in private housing and office building construction, and expansion in private capital investment. Also in Japan's favor is a continued high rate of savings, of about 16%, and inflation in consumer prices of less than 1% thus far in 1987.

The Internationalization of the Yen

A Working Definition

The word 'internationalization' is used very frequently in commentaries on Japan without explanation of its specific meaning. For the purpose of this analysis, in the most general terms, full internationalization of the yen would mean that there were no impediments to the use of the yen by non-residents in monetary transactions, including all types of trade and capital transactions.

Specifically, useful measures of the extent of yen internationalization are:
- The percentage of Japan's exports and imports that are denominated and ultimately paid for in yen currency.
- The liabilities of non-residents that are generated originally from yen sources within Japan and are scheduled for payment in yen, including yen-

denominated foreign bond issues, yen-denominated external loans, and yen-denominated syndicated loans.
- The level of foreign investment in Japanese securities, including all types of bonds, other debt instruments, and equities.
- The volume of yen deposits held by non-residents.
- The liabilities of non-residents and residents generated from Euroyen sources, including Euroyen bond issues and loans.
- The outstanding volume of Euroyen CDs.
- The overall value of the Euroyen market, as computed by the BIS.

Advantages of Yen Internationalization

Increased use of the yen offers important and clear advantages for Japanese trading interests, institutional investors, and financial institutions. For exporters, importers, and institutional investors, the principal advantage of increased use of the yen as an international currency is the reduced foreign exchange risk. For financial institutions, increased use of the yen will also imply a substantial enhancement of their position as financial intermediaries.

Any significant growth in overseas holdings of yen assets, however, will restrict Japan's domestic monetary and fiscal policy options. Stabilization and maintenance of the value of the yen will have an important impact on what policy decisions can be made.

Overall, rapid progress has been made towards increased use of the yen in international transactions. The sharp rise in capital exports from Japan, combined with the gradual deregulation of interest rates and the relaxation of restrictions on the use of domestic yen and Euroyen, have contributed to a marked increase in the use of the yen as an international currency.

At the end of 1987, the yen stood third as an international currency, following the US dollar and the German mark. Total Euro- and domestic external liabilities positions in yen amounted to the equivalent of US$361 billion at the end of 1987, versus $1,855 billion for the US dollar and $420 billion for the mark. At recent rates of increase, the yen may overtake the mark in the early 1990s, but barring any wholesale movement out of the dollar, it will be 15–20 years before the yen can achieve a position on a par with the dollar.

Measures of Internationalization

Various measures show the yen to be rising rapidly in prominence. The main contributors to yen internationalization in recent years have been associated with capital flows rather than trade transactions, namely:
- Growth in yen-denominated medium- and long-term loans made to foreign borrowers;
- Inflows of funds into Japan's securities markets; and
- Outstanding short-term Euroyen loans.

Other contributors include trade transactions and Euroyen bonds. The appreciation of the yen has reduced the bargaining power of Japanese exporters and resulted in a decline in yen-denominated exports. As the yen appreciated, the percentage of exports invoiced in yen declined from 37% in 1986 to 35%

in 1987. The preference for dollar payments on the part of countries supplying raw materials to Japan is also expected to continue to restrain denomination of imports in yen.

Euroyen bond issues appear to have made a contribution to yen internationalization, but since proceeds of these issues are generally swapped into other currencies, it is not certain how much Euroyen bond issues are in fact increasing the yen liabilities of non-residents.

Yen-denominated foreign bonds have contributed to yen internationalization, but the freeing of restrictions and the removal of inflexibilities involved in issuing these bonds will be necessary in order to prevent cannibalization of the market by Euroyen issues.

The greatest potential in the years ahead for further internationalization of the yen appears to be from outflows of capital from Japan. As Japanese investors work to recycle Japan's large current account surpluses, pressures are very likely to grow to denominate a growing percentage of these overseas investments in yen. For example, Japan's investors will very likely finance a growing portion of the external indebtedness of the US, which is forecast to exceed $1 trillion by the early 1990s. The foreign exchange risks involved in investing large sums seems likely to generate strong pressures for the denomination of more liabilities in yen.

The Dollar and the Yen

In evaluating the progress towards internationalization of the yen and prospects for its increased use, it is also useful to review the reasons behind the dollar's status as the key international currency.

- *A stable political environment.* Despite the fact that economic goals and methods in the US change more frequently than in Japan, the US has a consistently stable political and legal environment which has gained the confidence of investors. Japan is also highly regarded for the stability and orderliness of its political processes.
- *A large base of high-quality assets.* The ultimate indication of the value of a currency is what it will purchase. The US has a wealth of valuable assets, including real estate, a wide range of securities, and companies available for acquisition, in addition to its services and products. These are the ultimate backing of the currency. Japan, too, has a wealth of assets, even though at the present time, surplus domestic liquidity appears to have inflated asset prices and reduced yields on most investments. Also, as noted below, although instruments in the Euroyen market are increasing in scope, the variety of financial instruments in Japan is narrower than in the US.
- *Availability of resources.* The US has extensive raw material resources, even though it is not self-sufficient. Japan, as is well known, is highly vulnerable to disruptions of its raw material supplies.
- *The ability to protect its assets.* The US has a large and powerful military,

whereas Japan is limited by its constitution to having only defensive forces. This implies that Japan is dependent on the US to keep the international sea lanes open so that it can import raw materials and, ultimately, to provide a military deterrent in the event of aggression by a foreign country.

Conclusions about the Present Position of the Yen

Although some of the measures of the internationalization of the yen are ambiguous, a number of facts stand out clearly:

- In terms of combined Eurocurrency and domestic currency liabilities, the volume of the international yen market was about US$361 billion in 1987. This was far less than the $1,855 billion for the total international position of the dollar (Eurocurrency positions plus external positions in domestic currency), but it exceeded that of the Swiss franc, which was $207 billion, and was about 86% of that of the German mark, which amounted to $420 billion in 1987.
- In recent years, the yen's international position has grown faster than that of the US dollar, the Swiss franc, and the German mark. If this trend continues, its international position may exceed that of the mark, but it will take 15–20 years to exceed the present position of the dollar.
- The position of the yen is very sensitive to deregulatory measures. Changes in regulations have brought a very rapid response in virtually all cases. In part, this appears to be a result of the growing international position of Japanese banks and other financial institutions. Because they are clearly best positioned to access and supply yen to the international market, Japanese banks and institutional investors have much to gain from expansion of the scope of their operations, especially since corporate lending has become less profitable.

This last point is particularly obvious when one examines the relative position of Japanese and foreign institutions in terms of being bookrunners for Euromarket issuers and lead managers. Japanese securities companies and banks are the dominant bookrunners, both to Japanese Eurobond issuers (accounting for a 91% share of the market) and non-Japanese yen international bond issuers (accounting for a 95% share). As managers of Euroyen and Samurai issues, where full credit is given only to the lead manager, Japanese institutions hold a 94% market share. Only if full credit were given to each manager do non-Japanese institutions become significantly involved, handling 45% of the issues.

Prospects for Yen Internationalization

Effects of Likely Regulatory Changes

Following the agreements reached between Japan and the US in May 1984,

Japan has undertaken a wide range of deregulatory measures, including:
- The reduction of minimum denominations for CDs, money market certificates, and large deposits with negotiated rates;
- Establishment of an offshore market;
- Introduction of a bidding system for short-term government debt;
- Liberalization of Euroyen bond issues;
- Granting of permission for foreign banks to enter the trust business; and
- Granting of licenses to a growing number of foreign securities companies to open branch operations.

It is beyond the scope of this book to review and evaluate these measures in detail, but for a more detailed discussion see *Financial Liberalization and Internationalization in Japan*, prepared by the Federation of Bankers' Associations of Japan. Listed below are those regulatory measures that appear likely to be adopted in the near future and their implications for the internationalization of the yen.

- *Further liberalization of interest rates.* Although deregulation of interest rates has come at a measured pace, deposits have grown markedly with each decrease in the minimum allowed deposit. In the 12 months ended February 1988, the outstanding balance in negotiable rate time deposits alone rose from ¥18 trillion to ¥50 trillion, increasing ¥1 trillion in February 1988. It is estimated that market-rate funds now make up 50% or more of the funding sources of the Bank of Tokyo, Mitsui Bank, Mitsubishi Bank, and Sanwa Bank. All other Japanese city banks are thought to be in the range of 32–40%. Another decrease in the minimum deposit of negotiable rate time deposits is set for the autumn of 1988. Further reductions in the minimum size of deregulated deposits and minimum holding periods will result in a broadening of the short-term investments available to non-residents.

- *Further expansion in government short-term debt and continued growth in spot and future bond market transactions.* Japan's government debt, which stood at approximately ¥150 trillion in 1986, is expected to continue to rise steadily, and possibly at a faster pace than expected, through to the early 1990s. Government paper outstanding will therefore continue to expand, providing a convenient investment instrument for yen funds.

- *Continued lowering of the barriers between commercial banks and securities companies.* The securities companies and trust banks in particular have been in an advantageous position as Japan has become the world's largest exporter of capital, and as the inflow and outflow of capital has expanded. Although no specific measures have been announced, steps will probably be taken to increase the scope of securities-related operations of city and larger regional banks, thus expanding the number of institutional players in the markets and facilitating capital exports and non-resident liability creation.

- *Continued growth in the participation of foreign financial institutions, particularly investment and merchant banks.* In the spring of 1988, the number of foreign securities companies with branches in Tokyo reached 45, and the number of foreign securities companies with seats on the Tokyo Stock Exchange increased from eight to 24. These developments will contribute to increased non-resident liabilities as these institutions place Japanese funds overseas, a growing portion of which may be denominated in yen. They will also promote growth in yen assets of non-residents as they become better positioned to place foreigners' investments in yen bonds and equities.

• *Development of new markets.* The introduction of stock index futures and a broader range of other futures instruments will also contribute to expansion in capital inflows and outflows, thus leading to expanded use of the yen.

Non-resident Liabilities Likely to Propel Yen Internationalization

The internationalization of the yen was previously defined in four contexts:

• Use of the yen in trade;
• Liabilities of non-residents denominated in yen;
• Assets of non-residents denominated in yen; and
• Liabilities and assets of residents and non-residents denominated in Euroyen.

The principal impetus for greater international use of the yen through to the early 1990s is very likely to emanate from the second item: liabilities of non-residents denominated in yen. The reasons for this are as follows:

• *Use of the yen in trade may not show major changes from present levels.* With the yen remaining strong through to the early 1990s, Japanese exporters will not be in a strong bargaining position and therefore will have difficulty in raising the percentage of exports denominated in yen. Importers will not be strongly motivated to shift to yen payments because of prospects for a stronger yen and the continuing preference of overseas suppliers of raw materials for dollar payments – although this may begin to change. The rise in overseas direct investments by Japanese corporations may lead to increased purchases of foreign parts from overseas affiliates and this, in turn, may lead to more yen payments since overseas subsidiaries are likely to accept the terms of parent companies in Japan.

• *Investments in Japanese stocks and bonds by non-residents are expected to continue to grow.* The driving forces behind this prospective growth are (a) the strength of the yen, (b) the rising role of Japanese companies internationally (for equity investments), and (c) the diversification of portfolios of overseas pension funds and other investors. By their nature, however, these capital inflows will be very sensitive to interest rates, currency fluctuations, and trends in the market.

• *The principal impetus for yen internationalization appears likely to be the growing role that Japanese institutional investors will have in recycling Japan's trade and savings surpluses.* With continuing growth in overseas investments, Japan's income from overseas will continue to rise, eventually leading to a steady inflow of profits, as well as interest and dividend income by the early 1990s. This income alone will result in a large continuing current account surplus, whether or not the trade surplus diminishes. Although investors may be driven principally by yields, particularly as corporations become more yield-conscious and demanding of their pension fund managers, the prospects for a gradual decline in the value of the dollar are likely to bring a shift to denominate more of the liabilities being created in yen, rather than in dollars. The foreign-exchange risk will otherwise be substantial and daunting, for instance, if Japanese investors were to continue to invest in a significant portion of the expanding debt of the US government, which is expected to climb to $1 trillion in the mid-1990s.

- *The Euroyen markets are expected to continue to grow*, although faster expansion in external positions in domestic yen may continue, as Japan continues to export funds from its trade surplus and excess domestic savings.

Measures to Promote Yen Internationalization

In simplest terms, the measures needed to promote the increased use of the yen in international transactions are all a continuation of the measures taken since the release of its reports by the Japan-US Yen-Dollar Ad Hoc Committee in May 1984. Several of the most important of these measures are listed here.

- *Promotion of the development of short-term money markets in Japan and in Euroyen markets* in order to provide a greater range of low-risk, attractive financial instruments for investment of yen funds. Some of these measures might include: (1) removal of stamp duties and other restrictions to make the yen bankers' acceptance (BA) market a viable, working market; (2) further reductions in minimum denominations for deposit instruments with deregulated rates and an expansion of available maturities; (3) further expansion of the short-term government securities markets; and (4) introduction of broader futures markets. Many of these steps are now being taken.

- *Removal of remaining restrictions on the creation of non-resident yen liabilities.* This implies full liberalization of all types of bond and equity issues by non-residents.

- *Continued opening of the Japanese financial markets to foreign financial institutions.* For commercial banking institutions, this means allowing fully competitive access to yen funding so that these institutions can play a role in recycling liquidity. For investment banking institutions, it means continuing along the current course of permitting more institutions to have branch status and membership of the stock exchange. For both commercial and investment banking institutions, it also means eventual removal of the last remaining cultural barriers to liberalization, namely, nurturing of an environment in which Japanese financial institutions can be acquired by foreign institutions.

In the latter part of 1987 and the first half of 1988, there were numerous indications from both the business community and the government that activities and policies which will promote the international use of the yen will continue, namely:

- The Japanese government inaugurated a domestic commercial paper market and opened it to foreign companies.
- In April 1988, the Ministry of Finance announced that it will permit medium- and long-term Euroyen loans for both domestic and foreign corporations.
- The Ministry of Finance has also accepted, in principle, the purchase of domestic securities companies by foreign securities companies.
- The Japanese Export-Import Bank is increasing loans to less-developed nations and the government is reported to be preparing a kind of Japanese Marshall Plan.

The putting into effect of these and other measures will obviously meet with domestic opposition; the pace of change may be slow, but the direction is clear.

Progress towards Yen Internationalization

One of the objectives of the Japan-US Yen-Dollar Committee recommendations was to make the yen more available as an international trade and investment currency. The rationale behind this move was to relieve the excess demand for dollars that had been cited as one of the reasons for the unusually high value of the dollar prevailing at that time. As a result of these recommendations, Japan has accelerated its program of deregulating interest rates, opening new financial markets, and revamping its financial system.

In retrospect, it appears that measures to internationalize the yen have created a very attractive alternative to dollar investments and funding, but may have contributed to the decline in the dollar's value. In the environment that has prevailed since September 1985, with large and lingering surpluses in Japan's current account and prospects for possible medium-term decline in the value of the dollar, yen internationalization may in fact have had the effect of stimulating the movement away from dollar assets.

Growing Role of the Yen in Bank Assets

All measures of the world's international banking assets and liabilities by currency indicate that the dollar is still by far the most commonly used international currency. Even though there has been an increase, for example, in the proportion of Japan's exports and imports denominated in yen in recent years, more than 60% of Japan's exports are denominated in non-yen currencies – mainly US dollars – and just under 90% of imports are denominated in dollars.

However, the strong position of the dollar by most indicators is a two-edged sword, since large international dollar positions may be unstable if the US continues to increase its external borrowings and has difficulty in lowering its current account deficit below $100 billion.

Various indicators show the yen making steady gains as an international currency. For example, data issued by the BIS show a substantial rise in the value of the cross-border yen asset positions of international banks in both Euroyen and domestic yen. A rough order of magnitude calculation shows total cross-border positions in yen at the equivalent of US$436 billion at the end of December 1987, compared to $223 billion in 1986. Part of this increase is due to a stronger yen, but much of it is accounted for by a continued rise in the lending and investment activities of Japanese banks.

The roughly comparable figures for cross-border positions in dollars (including both Eurodollars and domestic dollars invested outside the US) were $1,696 billion in December 1987 and $1,488 billion in December 1986. Therefore, over the course of 1987, cross-border yen positions rose to 25% of dollar positions, versus only 15% for 1986.

The yen is also gaining on or has exceeded other international currencies as a currency for international banking assets. Total cross-border positions in German marks, for example, were $325 billion in December 1986, considerably higher than the $223 billion in yen positions. By the end of 1987, however, this lead had narrowed considerably, with mark positions rising to $446 billion, versus $436 billion for the yen. The yen has long since overtaken the pound sterling and the Swiss franc in terms of cross-border bank positions.

Growth in Euroyen Bond Issues

Another measure of the internationalization of currencies is their usage in international bond issues. Since 1984, when Euroyen issues amounted to the equivalent of US$1.2 billion, these issues have expanded by leaps and bounds to $18.2 billion in 1986 and $23.1 billion in 1987. The greater flexibility of Euroyen issues has also had an adverse impact on the issuing of yen-denominated bonds in Japan, the so-called Samurai bond market. As the Euroyen market has expanded, the Samurai market has dropped from $4.7 billion in 1984 to $1.6 billion in 1987.

Use of the yen in international bond issues, including both Euroyen and domestic yen, exceeded that of the German mark in 1985, and was slightly above that of the Swiss franc in 1987. At the same time, use of the dollar for international bond issues has dropped from $121.7 billion in 1986 to $62.8 billion in 1987. Therefore, in 1987, international bond issues in yen were nearly 40% of the value of international bond issues in dollars.

Although use of the yen as the currency for bond issues will continue to vary widely from quarter to quarter, depending on market conditions, it appears that the yen is establishing a strong position in this area, just as it has in bank lending.

Growing Foreign Investment in Yen

Despite a net disinvestment in Japanese equities of US$41.5 billion in fiscal 1987, related to the October stock-market drop, foreigners have become net buyers again since early 1988. They have also been net buyers of public bonds in most recent years.

Figures for transactions by foreigners in stocks and bonds show a continued sharp rise in the level of buying and selling. For example, even though foreign investors pulled out on a net basis in fiscal 1987, their transactions were up to US$148 billion, versus $108 billion in 1986. Similarly, bond transactions moved up to $273 billion, compared with $221 billion in 1986.

As these and other data clearly show, the yen is now being used quite extensively by international investors, although the volume of international transactions in dollars remains far larger. As deregulation proceeds and more types of financial instruments are introduced in Tokyo and in the Euroyen market, the use of the yen as an international currency is very likely to increase.

This development will permit Japanese financial institutions especially to play an even greater role in financing the world's trade and investment. The principal problem – and this is difficult to quantify – is that the timing of yen internationalization may prove somewhat awkward for the dollar. With prospects for a medium-term decline in the dollar's value, rapid internationalization of the yen may hasten the movement from dollar assets. Nevertheless, the architects of the Yen-Dollar Committee recommendations have certainly achieved their goal of taking the demand pressure off the dollar.

4   CHALLENGE OF AND RESPONSE TO THE JAPANESE CENTURY

A Comparison of the US and Japanese Economies: Fundamental Strengths of the US Economy

Some Japanese commentators take a strong position on the relative roles of Japan and the US. A newspaper editorial by a well-known Japanese analyst contends that the US has mismanaged not only its economy, but the world's. The view is also expressed that Japan and several European nations ought to share leadership with the US. This analyst is not alone in thinking that the US must 'wise up' or 'wake up'; this attitude is also growing in the US. But before any drastic action is taken, we would be well advised to examine carefully the circumstances leading to the current problems in the Japan-US relationship. We should also look at the alternatives which are feasible within the context of the exceptionally high level of dependence between Japan and the US. Finally, we should examine what realistic options are open to Japan as it makes the long-awaited move towards sharing leadership with the US.

Japan's History of Protectionism

There is a tendency among Japanese economic commentators to place the blame for imbalances in trade, investment, and other areas on the US and on US corporations. It is true that the US and its business interests have made serious strategic errors in not realizing the potential of the Japanese market and making the needed investments in the 1960s and 1970s to establish a strong market position.

At least two problems worked to deter US investments in Japan. The first is that Japan, given its growing size and importance in the world economy, was one of the most highly protectionist nations in the world during the mid-1970s. This has resulted in the development of a highly competitive domestic industrial structure which is difficult and expensive to penetrate. Even though Japanese companies faced difficulties in entering the US market, and Japanese automobile and electronics companies have established strong positions despite what seemed to be impossible odds in the early 1960s, the fundamental attitude in Japan and the US towards the entry of foreign corporations is still very different even today. This is one of the key obstacles to penetration of the market and to the true internationalization of the Japanese economy.

Although leading Japanese companies faced difficulties in the 1960s in setting up and penetrating the US market, critics are right in pointing out that

Japanese companies overcame these difficulties. But the fundamental attitude in the US is that anyone with a good product at a good price is welcome. In Japan, newcomers – both Japanese and foreign – are immediately suspect. Japanese society is homogeneous and inward-looking, and establishing business relationships is a time-consuming task. But the reverse side of these traits, of course, is that such relationships are generally firmer and more stable once established.

The second problem restraining investments by US corporations in Japan has been the differing investment behavior patterns arising from differences in the financial systems of the two nations. US corporations are strongly influenced by quarterly earnings. A corporate planner in the US who presented a 20–30-year plan for penetrating the Japanese market would probably not have lasted long in his position. However, such long-terms plans may be necessary in some industries if the US is to enter the Japanese market. In Japan, the pressure to maintain and increase quarterly earnings is not as strong. Over the long haul, thus far, the Japanese financial system has proven itself superior in strengthening the competitiveness of Japanese industry.

Implications of Dependence

The suggestion of 'issuing some securities pegged to the yen to signal its seriousness about currency stabilization' and certain other comments would imply a major shift in the nature and tone of relationships between Japan and the US. Because of its current deficit problems, the US is already faced with the need to reduce government expenditures and to encourage a higher rate of savings, and these measures may lead to a decline in the quality of life in some sections of the country. This is probably not a suitable time for Japanese interests to come on too strongly in public about what the US should do.

Any slowdown in the US economy or decline in its standard of living is very likely to have a direct and immediate impact on Japan itself because of the extraordinarily high level of dependence between the two countries. Close to 40% of Japan's exports go to the US. In turn, Japan finances a substantial portion of the US government debt. To write off the capability of the US to recover and to maintain a strong world economic position would seem to be a serious mistake.

Even though Japan's industrial policy has been successful in developing corporations which are highly competitive internationally, the strategic error on the Japanese side appears to have been to allow the development of excessive dependence on the US market.

Japan's Options

Given that Japan wishes to take a stronger role and to share leadership with the US and certain European nations, what options are open? The most obvious ones appear to be what the US has already suggested. For example, Japan could shoulder a larger portion of its defense burden. The end of US hegemony will clearly bring a greater obligation for Japan to defend itself. Another area where Japan can play a greater role is in financing the economic development of the developing nations. A closely related step, which Japan is already taking, would be to accelerate the opening of the Tokyo financial markets and the internationalization of the yen. All of these steps would most likely be welcomed by the US at this time. The question, of course, is whether Japan will actually be able to achieve a consensus to move in this direction.

Some Suggested Responses

Yen Shock Not Enough to Slow Japan

In listening to US economists discuss the decline in the value of the dollar, there seems to be a fundamental lack of awareness of the magnitude of the shift in the value of the two currencies and its medium- and long-term implications. This is perhaps not surprising since most grew up and were educated during a period when Japan's long-term potential and the implications of its industrial and corporate strategies were not fully appreciated.

Consider carefully the magnitude of the change in the value of the yen versus the dollar. Prior to the freeing of the yen exchange rate in 1971, the dollar bought ¥360. When the yen moved temporarily very close to ¥120 to the dollar in December 1987, the US currency had in effect dropped to a mere one-third of its former value. In late 1988, it stood only slightly above this. Considering that the US is still a major industrialized nation with a GNP of over $4 trillion, and that it is still a leader in the development of new technologies, producing goods and services perceived to be of value both at home and abroad, the order of magnitude of this change is staggering.

Inflexibilities Abound

Another important development, no doubt surprising to those who have argued for flexible exchange rates, has been the lack of effectiveness of currency adjustments in bringing about a correction in Japan's surplus and the US deficit. On an annual basis, the US trade deficit has grown larger since the adjustment in the yen-dollar rate began in mid-1985. The US trade balance deficit has grown from $69.3 billion in 1983, to $123 billion in 1984, $148 billion in 1985, $169 billion in 1986, and $174 billion in 1987. The decline in the value of the dollar has therefore done little to reduce the US trade deficit; in fact, through 1987, it had only slowed the rate of increase.

Despite the rise in the value of the yen since mid-1985, the reverse set of trends was recorded in Japan. The trade surplus was US$31 billion in calendar

1983, but rose to $44 billion in 1984, $56 billion in 1985, $93 billion in 1986, and $96 billion in 1987. In Japan's case also, therefore, the appreciation of the yen against the dollar through 1987 had only slowed the rate of increase in the trade surplus, not reduced it.

The conclusion from this is that a simple adjustment of currency values is too blunt an instrument to deal effectively with the problem of achieving a better balance in trade between Japan and the US. Much more is at work than the 'J-curve' effect, which is the usual way of explaining the lag between changes in currency valuations and adjustments in trade flows. The currency adjustments since September 1985 have exposed a host of inflexibilities in buying patterns in both Japan and the US which changes in price have been only marginally capable of influencing.

Consumers in the US have proved willing to spend much more for what they perceive as the higher quality of Japanese automobiles and other merchandise. For some products, the Japanese are the dominant, or only significant, manufacturers in the world.

For their part, Japanese consumers, where they have had the opportunity, have not jumped at the chance to buy US products at reduced prices because their perception of quality is similar to that of the US consumer. Up-market European goods in fact have been the main beneficiaries to date.

A Long Time Needed for Adjustment

Advocates of flexible exchange rates will no doubt argue that rates of growth in Japan's imports are up and that US exports are now on a strong upward trend; a move back to a balance in trade is only a matter of time. While these observations may be true, it will take a long time to make these adjustments, even assuming some very high rates of growth in US exports and in Japanese imports.

Let us assume that Japan's imports in dollar terms continue to grow at an annual rate of 20% until the end of 1990. Let us also assume that exports expand at about 5% in dollar terms, much lower than in the past, but are still boosted by the development of new markets outside the US and increases in prices of 2–3% annually. Projecting recent trade figures forward at these rates, Japan will still have a surplus of about US$87 billion in 1988, $70 billion in 1989, and nearly $50 billion in 1990. Between 1988 and 1990, Japan will have amassed another $207 billion from the excess of exports over imports.

In the case of the US, assuming 20% annual growth in exports and 10% growth in imports, the trade deficit will still amount to $150 billion in 1988, $133 billion in 1989, and $100 billion in 1990. The US will therefore have spent $383 billion more than its export earnings between 1988 and 1990.

These results look even more alarming when we consider the current account, because Japan will continue to amass overseas assets and its inflow of income from overseas investment will continue to rise, probably more than cancelling out the increase in expenditure on overseas travel by Japanese. The US will continue to borrow abroad and will have to increase its interest and dividend payments to Japan and other foreign countries.

Although the blame for this state of affairs can be laid at the doorsteps of both the US and Japan, with a significantly higher stack of problems at the US doorstep, an urgent task for Mr Takeshita and the new US president will be to devise policy measures to hasten the adjustment in the underlying economies of the two nations. Interference in the currency markets is clearly only a stopgap measure and not likely to be any more effective than Japan, or America, bashing.

Japan – US Frictions

The pronouncements of US politicians relating to Japan appear likely to grow more strident. Responses from the Japanese side may also become considerably less tactful than in the past, and some sharp exchanges and conflicts of views may emerge. Some aspects of statements by US politicians about 'unfair' Japanese trade practices ring true, particularly as they refer to the highly protectionist policies adopted by Japan during the mid-1970s. But these instances are history, and US business and political interests are far from blameless for allowing US–Japan relations to take the course which they have.

The most alarming prospect is that the US electorate is probably not prepared psychologically and emotionally to deal with the notion of becoming financially dependent upon Japan, especially as this dependence increases into the 1990s. What will be needed most is a more sober awareness in the US that the economic accomplishments of Japan have been attained largely through the rules and practices laid down by the US itself. It is essential, therefore, that the US has a plan of action that includes a concerted program of re-establishing its industrial competitiveness, while at the same time insisting that Japan does not bend the rules to achieve an even greater advantage.

'Unfair' Trade Practices

A thoughtful analysis of Japan's economic development during the post-World War II period needs to address the many instances where Japan and Japanese interests recognized and took advantage of the potential for seizing competitive advantage. Some instances include: (a) the purchase of technology from the US and Europe on terms that now seem very favorable; and (b) the practice of using tariffs and other mechanisms (largely before the mid-1970s) to permit the emergence of strong domestic manufacturers in key sectors, thus making it very difficult and expensive for foreign manufacturers to enter with their products after the removal of various deterrents. Unlike West Germany, Japan thus far has not adopted a true policy of division of labor and production in international trade. The Japanese posture is expressed in the phrase *jimae-shugi*, the attitude that Japan must and will produce the vast majority of its needs, rather than rely on imports. Even though finished-product imports are now rising rapidly, this fundamental attitude will die hard.

In addition, Japan developed a highly effective structure of incentives to promote the development of strong domestic and export-oriented industries. One of the key aspects of this structure has been the financial system, which has tended to de-emphasize short-term profits and to place greater emphasis on the medium- to long-term building of strong, international market positions.

Now that Japan has become the principal external creditor of the US, the policies and industrial strategies adopted by Japan since the 1950s may seem sinister to the US electorate. Japan's unrelenting drive to become number 1 industrially and financially is very likely to come as a surprise to the average American who is proud of the low maintenance costs of his Japanese automobile. But now, important aspects of his destiny, including future growth in income, what interest rates he must pay, and even the international political and military position of his nation, can be made to seem much less certain, depending on how politicians present their arguments.

Avoiding Infantile Reactions

In a worst-case scenario, US politicians could seek to deflect towards Japan any criticism for the economic and fiscal policies that have led to the rising external debt of the US. Some, in fact, have already taken this approach. The response from Japan might be to point to the need to improve the quality of US goods, to make greater investments in entering the Japanese market, to consume less, and to work harder.

Perhaps the most important thing for the US will be to recognize and appreciate fully the magnitude of the problems involved. US competitiveness must be restored and the US must regain its ability to pay its way internationally. And, as the Japanese will probably say, in order to accomplish these objectives, US companies must concentrate on quality, make greater investments to enter the Japanese market, and consume less and work harder. But this is not likely to be a popular point of view. Advice of this sort from the Japanese business and financial community is also likely to meet with intense resentment.

Despite this resentment, it is essential that the US regains its international competitiveness and achieves a better balance in trade. The first steps should be to gain a realistic awareness of the problems facing the US, to increase capital investment, and to create a consensus on the need to postpone some consumption until the future. A realistic viewpoint will also involve the recognition that Japan, as the closest trading partner of the US, is an aggressive and competitive economic power. Japan has grown up and bettered its teacher in many areas. In some cases, this has been because the teacher has been slow to recognize the progress of the student. From now on, US business must compete seriously and with equal determination. The activities of Japanese competitors must be monitored carefully. Concerted efforts must be made to channel Japan's competitive energy, either to stimulate greater creativity and hard work in the US or into co-operative ventures.

The 'unfair' trade practices of Japan during the mid-1970s have also created a major economic power. It is an exercise in futility to focus on the unfairness of the past; focusing on how to stimulate and channel the energies of Japan and its trading partners into more productive directions will be the key to the future economic health of Japan and its major trading partners.

Clearing up Misconceptions: Japan versus the US

The policies which must be adopted in order to make structural adjustments and reduce the trade and other imbalances between Japan and the US have been summarized above. A greater problem, however, is clearing the way so that such policies can be implemented. Both Japan and the US appear to have certain misconceptions and attitudes which must be changed before the peoples and representatives of these two leading economies will be prepared to come to terms with the problems.

On the US side, there appear to be at least three misconceptions:
- *That the government cannot devise a viable industrial policy; its clumsy efforts only create problems.* The problem with this view is that the fabric of legal regulations, including tax laws, creates a de facto industrial policy, which may or may not be in the long-term economic interest of the US.
- *The invisible hand is infallible; the market mechanism will always come up with the right solution.* The problem with this belief is that the 'invisible hand' moves very clumsily when confronted by certain practical situations where production costs change over time, along with movements in market share and scale. Total reliance on the market mechanism may also be difficult where the US is obliged to compete with nations aware of the implications of global market share and changing costs and are prepared to use any and all means necessary to take and retain global market share.
- *The US will always remain the world's major industrial power.* This misconception is perhaps the most dangerous, since the rising external debt of the US may lead to an even higher cost of capital for US industry, creating an even greater competitive disadvantage. Some major US industries are already dependent for their existence on the continuation of 'voluntary' import restraints.

On the Japanese side, there are attitudes that are equally troublesome.
- *Because of quality and reliability problems associated in the Japanese mind with imported products, Japanese companies must seek to produce whatever they can on their own initiative.* Known as *jimae shugi* in Japanese, this underlying belief remains little changed despite the appreciation of the yen and numerous efforts at opening the market. For this

reason, the pattern of relying mainly on domestic production still prevails.

- *Japan has worked hard since the war, overcome many problems, and finally emerged with a highly competitive industrial establishment. The US should wise up and work harder.* This view shows little appreciation of the contribution of US and European technology, the access to overseas markets, and the defense umbrella, all of which have contributed immeasurably to Japan's success.

- *Japan is somehow 'different' from other countries.* This is Japan's exaggerated sense of cultural uniqueness. It reinforces the first two attitudes and plagues companies trying to establish a business foothold in Japan. As former ambassador Reischauer suggested in a New Year's TV message to Japan, perhaps 'Japan should join the human race.'

Setting the Right Economic Goals

If these attitudes can be changed, then both Japan and the US could move more deliberately towards a solution to their adjustment problems. For its part, the US must take steps to increase savings and investment. Japan's experience in increasing the savings rate in the 1950s should be instructive. Investment must be increased in basic and applied research and development, with the government taking the role of organizer and stimulator in high-cost, high-risk areas. Tax policies must encourage both R & D and investment in the reindustrializing of the US. Many US companies have moved operations offshore and are faced with a decision to move back now that the dollar is weaker. If Japanese companies can invest heavily in buying up US companies, then certainly US companies should consider the same.

The US should also stop trying to peg the value of the dollar. This will only make overseas investors reluctant to place funds in the US as reindustrialization takes place, thus placing further upward pressure on interest rates. This might mean the dollar would fall to ¥100 or less in the early 1990s, but as the US reindustrializes with greater domestic initiative, regains its international competitiveness, and begins to pay its way internationally, policy should aim for ¥150 or stronger by 1995.

The policies Japan must take are in many ways the reverse of those in the US. They include further measures to increase consumption and to raise investments to improve the quality of life, while continuing to take steps to facilitate imports.

Japan's imports are increasing in some areas and there are belated signs of a gradual adjustment. But the task of changing attitudes in Japan appears very formidable. After the US public is made more aware of the problems and the alternatives, action must be taken. After all, the US is now the world's largest debtor nation. In Japan, the underlying urgency for adjustment and cooperation with the US may be lacking. The reluctance of Japan to 'join the human race' is one of our biggest problems.

Why the US Needs a Sense of Crisis

A number of economists in Japan have pointed to the probability that the dollar might continue to drop in value against the yen through to the early 1990s. Japan can probably cope with a gradual increase in the value of the yen towards ¥100 to the dollar, but the possibility remains that the dollar could fall even faster in value if the US trade deficit begins to widen again. A further sharp drop in the dollar could very well lead to unsettled economic conditions. For this reason, one commentator has concluded, 'the US should have somewhat more of a sense of crisis.'

Slow Progress to Adjustment

It is amazing that the US does not have a greater sense of crisis. Even though there has been a substantial upward revaluation of the yen against the dollar since mid-1985, Japan's trade surplus is only beginning to decline and is still at a very high level by historical standards. The US trade deficit, on the other hand, is still very large and has shown no decisive downtrend. In addition, US reliance on external debt is rising rapidly, and net external assets may reach $1 trillion by the early 1990s, so the current account deficit, which reflects both the trade account and the outflow of funds to pay interest on debts to foreigners, is very likely to deteriorate even if the trade deficit diminishes.

Although comments about a 'sense of crisis' seem to point mainly to a need for more prudent monetary and fiscal policies, the crises facing the US, if current trends continue, appear likely to have implications far beyond government fiscal policy.

For example, from the point of view of corporate strategy, the US faces some daunting obstacles in the years ahead, particularly if the dollar continues to decline seriously. One scenario calls for a drop in the value of the dollar against the yen to the ¥120s or high ¥110s by the end of 1988, then into the ¥110s or high ¥100s in 1989 and 1990. If the trade deficit does not move towards correction because of the lack of price elasticity for imports, and external indebtedness continues to rise, the dollar may fall faster. Some analysts are even talking about values of less than ¥100 to the dollar for the early 1990s.

On the positive side, the cheaper dollar is beneficial to US export industries, and the growth in US exports is one of the factors supporting the uptrend in capital spending and the growth in incomes. The US export sector is regaining its competitiveness. Ironically, some of this is 'owned by Japan', as in the case of export of US-made Hondas to Japan.

But US companies in general are becoming more attractive – some might even say 'vulnerable' – for strategic acquisition by Japan and other nations. This may be desirable from the point of view of some US companies seeking strategic alliances with strong foreign partners. If more Japanese automobile companies, for example, begin to export from the US to Japan, more Japanese investment in the US will contribute to a solution to the trade deficit. President Reagan, in fact, reaffirmed in mid-1985 the importance of having a continued inflow of foreign investment into the US. A growing number of Americans work for foreign-owned corporations, and these companies pay local and federal taxes to support the public sector in the US.

However, a number of circumstances seem likely to lead to future problems. One is the potential volume and frequency of these investments. Because of high stock prices in Tokyo, the market capitalization of Japanese companies in a broad range of industries, for example, dwarfs that of competitors in the US and Europe. This has very serious competitive implications. For example, not only is the acquisition of Japanese companies difficult for reasons of different business practices, but in many cases they are also now extremely, or even prohibitively, expensive.

US companies are therefore faced with a situation in which they could become takeover candidates, but do not have the same strategic option in Japan. On the other hand, a growing number of Japanese companies are in a position easily to outbid US or other competitors for the control of US corporations. Concern about the possible dilution of earnings because of a high multiple paid for the company to be acquired is a much less serious issue in Japan. For most Japanese companies, international market position and its long-term implications take precedence over short-term profitability and movements in stock prices.

The other side of that coin is that if Japanese companies become more aggressive in takeover bids, it may become very difficult for US corporations to keep stock prices high enough to prevent a takeover.

Policies to Induce a Sense of Crisis

This is not an argument against foreign investment as such. But as Japan's own experience suggests, the government has a role to play as supervisor and referee. If it refuses to play that role, then competitive forces will take full charge. Where one side has an overwhelming advantage, that side is likely to win.

The role of government in Japan during the period when US companies were in a far stronger position, and the competitive positions of the US and Japan were reversed, was to supervise investments into Japan with the aim of stimulating competition, but assuring that domestic interests had a substantial share of the market. In retrospect, those policies were perhaps overly restrictive, but they certainly did not impair the long-term vitality of Japanese industries.

The US should indeed have a sense of crisis, not only about large government deficits, but also about the growing possibility of exceptionally high levels of foreign ownership of key corporations. The potential for this exists if current trends and rules of play continue. Even if Japanese companies become model corporate citizens in the US, differences in political, social, and economic goals are bound to arise, and extraordinarily high levels of foreign ownership, which are by no means impossible, may impair the integrity of the political process. This in turn may lead to unfortunate repercussions for the Japan–US relationship.

The adoption of two policies in the US might bring about a healthy sense of crisis. First, the US should develop a system to monitor foreign investments and to develop guidelines for the role of domestic industries, just as Japan did in the 1950s and '60s. Secondly, in order to reduce its dependence on foreign sources of funds and to stem the long-term decline in the value of the dollar, the US might introduce a requirement – similar to a progressive tax – that US citizens buy a new type of government bond. A portion of the proceeds from issuance of these bonds would go to fund the government deficit, with particular emphasis on infrastructure renewal and upgrading; the remainder would be used to finance industrial development in the private sector.

Can the US Implement Industrial Policy?

The idea of introducing an industrial policy to regain and maintain international competitiveness has been proposed many times in the US since the early 1970s. The prospect of a large and growing current account deficit in the years ahead seems likely to assure that such proposals will now be given more than passing attention. The example of Japan's success in achieving a co-operative relationship between government and business, rather than an adversarial one, and in continuing to set long-range goals and sustain industrial momentum has provoked renewed interest in the potential for implementing a similar set of policies in the US.

One of the principal problems standing in the way appears to be lingering doubts about whether such policies can be formulated and implemented in the US. Some economists, who have examined Japan's approach to industrial policy carefully, believe that the US has what appears to be a 'myth' that such policies cannot be implemented. Even allowing for the differences in economic background and structure of government, it seems appropriate, even essential, at this time to give industrial policy a new hearing. There have been some instances of US states actually implementing industrial policies successfully. At the same time, the framework of tax laws and other legislation in effect in the US in fact represents a de facto industrial policy.

Black Magic?

The negative views of industrial policy in the US are perhaps suggested by a few phrases from a leading US business magazine published in mid-1988: 'that old Democratic black magic, industrial policy', and 'Allocating scarce resources on an economic rather than a political basis is just what Washington does worst.'

If we examine Japan's experience in developing and implementing industrial policies over the past 40 years, there appears to be little that could be described as 'black magic'. There is also very little that would warrant the label of being either Democratic or Republican. Japan set out in the postwar period to take some very necessary and practical steps to raise savings and to direct resources into industries that would have the highest impact on increasing incomes. Emphasis was placed first on rebuilding basic industries, such as electric power and steel. This was accompanied by a restructuring of the financial system, with emphasis placed on generating a flow of funds through intermediaries that would work closely with government and industry in allocating resources. Initially, few resources were made available for housing construction, and consumer finance did not really become significant until the latter half of the 1970s.

In the late 1960s and 1970s, priorities began to change as more and more industries became internationally competitive, reached maturity in the domestic market, and began to generate cash rather than use it. Close supervision and direction of resource flows became less necessary, and more resources were available for housing and consumer finance. Japan's savings rate began a gradual decline, even though it remains the highest in the world.

The essence of Japan's industrial policy over the last 40 years has been its emphasis on savings and investment rather than on consumption. As national wealth and income have grown, this emphasis has changed, but Japan still places substantially greater priority on savings and investment than the US. For example, during the postwar period, numerous measures were adopted to make savings more attractive. One of these, the *maruyu* system, which exempted interest on small savings from taxation, was eliminated only in April 1988. Although many of the measures which stimulated investment have now been removed, in the late 1950s and '60s, for example, selective accelerated depreciation schedules were in effect what provided tax breaks for companies investing in equipment for modernization, along with numerous other measures.

More Savings and Investment Needed

When borrowing what seems appropriate from Japan's experience, consideration might be given to the following:

- Creation of a better domestic awareness that the US must begin to pay its own way internationally through reduction of its trade and current account deficits. This will involve devoting more resources to the development of a strong industrial base. There is no guarantee that US industry or individual companies will automatically remain on top internationally, without considerably more competitive effort than is now being made. The key motivating factor in Japan's postwar industrial policy was the realization that prosperity was impossible without the export earnings to buy the necessary raw material imports. For the US, the motivating factor will probably have to be the realization that manufacturing-based earnings must pay for finished-product imports.

- Generation of a new interest in and greater enthusiasm for the future potential of the US through the formulation of national goals, including an outline of what industries will contribute most to the long-term increase in income. Japan has sustained a sense of industrial direction through a series of well-informed reports, such as those prepared by the Industrial Structure Council, a bipartisan committee under MITI. Labelled 'visions' rather than 'plans', the latest report came out in January 1988 and outlines the likely direction of changes in Japanese industry in response to the stronger yen and other developments. For a report to have similar weight and influence in the US, it would have to be prepared by a Presidential Commission.

- Generation of a better awareness that the realization of future goals will involve increased saving and the shifting of resources away from present consumption. The US should implement stronger incentives to raise the savings rate and to encourage investments in capital, practical training, and improvement of the quality of the work environment.

US Exports Could Benefit from Industrial Policy

We seem to be witnessing a scenario that has occurred several times in the past: the dollar has declined in value, opening a 'window' of opportunity for US exporters. Exporting industries are thus presented with the opportunity to expand their shipments to overseas markets and to develop stronger, long-term overseas market positions. However, instead of this happening, a number of events occur that allow the 'window' of opportunity to close before US corporations can recover their competitiveness in the broad sense of the term – that is, becoming not only low-cost suppliers, but also reliable, long-term suppliers with sufficiently large export market positions to justify the development of products to meet the needs of overseas markets on a long-term basis.

If the US does not use this opportunity to recover its export competitiveness, then we may well be in for a further round of yen appreciation and dollar depreciation. Prospects for reduction of the overall US trade deficit and the US-Japan trade imbalance may begin to look poorer in the coming months.

Limited Progress to Date

Advocates of floating exchange rates have placed great faith in exchange rate adjustments to correct trade imbalances. However, exchange rate adjustments only open a window of opportunity for US industries to regain their competitiveness. If the underlying problems – such as lagging growth in productivity and a lack of determination and commitment to become reliable, responsive suppliers to overseas customers – are not addressed, exchange rate adjustments may be quite futile.

Examination of US-Japan trade figures to date does not offer much cause for optimism, and reports of the lack of adequate capacity additions in the US export sector offer cause for concern. US-Japan trade figures for calendar 1987 show an improvement in the imbalance of only about US$2 billion. In 1987, Japan exported about $85 billion to the US and imported only $35 billion, leaving a US deficit of $50 billion. This compared to $82 billion in exports from Japan to the US in 1986, as against imports from the US of $30 billion. More recent figures through mid-1985 show no significant improvement.

The most encouraging news to date has been the announcement of faster growth in finished product imports from the US since the beginning of 1988. Some of this is apparently accounted for by increased automobile exports from the US to Japan, including exports by Japan's Honda.   On a more global basis, progress toward reducing Japan's merchandise trade surplus and the US deficit seems much less the foregone conclusion than announcements by Japanese government agencies would suggest. Japan's exports, for example, have shown signs of recovery in recent months.

In volume terms, exports were up slightly more than 3% over the previous year between October 1987 and March 1988. This compared to a 1.2% decline for the previous six months, from April to September 1987. In dollar terms, the recovery has been almost mystifying. Exports were up an average of slightly more than 6% from October 1986 to September 1987. Growth accelerated to 15% in the October 1987–March 1988 period. Although this recovery may reflect some 'J-curve' phenomena, the bulk of the increase appears to be the renewed success of Japanese companies in introducing new, high-value-added products and in holding product prices down.

There is also ample evidence that Japanese imports are rising rapidly. In volume terms, Japan's imports were up almost 8% from April to October 1987, and by almost 18% for the October–March 1988 period. Over the same period, growth in dollar terms rose from nearly 22% to 37%. If these rates continue, Japan's trade surplus will drop gradually from recent levels by the early 1990s.

But what about the US? Progress to date in reducing the trade deficit has been limited and erratic, and the latest information is not very encouraging. Exports have risen, but because of the combination of a strong growth in domestic demand and limitations on capacity, manufacturers seem more likely to raise prices and forego significant increases in capacity than to expand their export positions aggressively.

US imports have continued to expand, reflecting both the willingness of consumers to pay higher prices for imports and the necessity of importing some types of capital equipment that are no longer manufactured in the US because of 'hollowing out' in the past.

A Good Time for Attention to Industrial Policy

Some of the factors deterring US exporters from increasing capacity include: (a) concern about the possibility of an economic downturn in late 1988 and early 1989, following the presidential election; (b) a reluctance to make a full commitment to establishing, holding, and expanding positions in export markets; (c) the higher cost of capital; and (d) an orientation towards increasing short-term profits, arising in part from the demands of the US financial system.

When in a similar situation during the 1950s and '60s, Japan maintained momentum in capacity expansion through a number of measures, depending on the industry in question. In the case of the steel industry, ongoing five-year plans for capacity expansion were implemented; low, fixed-interest loans were provided from long-term credit banks and other institutions, including government banks; depreciation provisions were liberal; MITI supervised production levels and additions to capacity (most problems centered around restraining companies from over-investing, rather than encouraging them to do so); and when recession threatened, MITI was authorized, under special exemptions to the anti-monopoly legislation, to set up cartels and to provide guidance for production and exports, thus avoiding a sharp decline in prices.

The introducion of such measures in the US would no doubt raise some eyebrows. But the Japanese experience is there for reference. At the very least, national and local officials should take up the issue and make the public aware of the importance of exports. Another nearly costless measure would be to introduce a system of Presidential awards for companies that have significantly increased their exports. Special tax relief might also be considered, based on export earnings or on investment to expand the capacity for exports. Special low-interest rate financing would also be helpful.

Japan's Exports Recover

The principal objective of the September 1985 meeting of the Group of Five (G5) in New York was to seek a means to correct the overvaluation of the dollar and thus reduce the large and growing US trade deficit. The G5 proved very successful in accomplishing the objective of reducing the value of the dollar, especially against the yen and in varying degrees against other currencies. By the end of calendar 1987, for example, the dollar had dropped to nearly half its mid-1985 valuation against the yen.

Common sense would tell us that such a sharp decline in the value of the dollar should make it much more difficult to sell Japanese products in the US and much easier to sell US goods in Japan, thus contributing to a correction in the trade imbalances between the two countries. In fact, the appreciation of the yen against the dollar has only gone part way towards making a really substantial reduction in Japan's trade surplus and the US trade deficit. Latest trade data suggest that Japan is still running a surplus of about US$90 billion, down only marginally from $96 billion in fiscal 1987. In addition, all recent indicators of exports suggest that many Japanese exporters have made the needed adjustments to restore their competitiveness by such means as lowering costs through increased automation, targeting a higher-valued-added selection of products, and shifting a portion of manufacturing production to areas with lower costs. As a result of all these measures, combined with a strong uptrend in demand in Japan and other major markets, Japan's exports give all the indications of moving into a period of recovery.

A number of reasons have been advanced for the failure of currency adjustments to have a significant impact on trade imbalances. Some of the most recent data on Japan's exports by product point fairly clearly to the effectiveness of Japan's export and industrial strategies in preventing it from slipping from its position as the world's leading export surplus nation.

Product Targeting Effective

Indicators of the volume of Japan's exports began to show reasonably clear signs of a moderate upward trend in late 1987. One of the most important, 'acid test' indicators for recovery in exports is the value of exports in yen terms. Latest information shows Japan's exports in yen rose above last year's levels in June 1988 by 2.7% and in July by 3.2%. In US dollar terms, rates of growth in exports have been far higher, averaging 15.8% from January through July 1988.

A close look at the trends in exports by product suggest that the recovery can be accounted for in part by the success of careful product targeting. The items showing the most rapid rates of growth are those for which Japan is either the sole or the dominant international supplier.

The highest rates of growth in exports in recent months have been for machine tools, principally exports to the newly industrializing nations, semiconductors, television sets, and office automation equipment, especially facsimile machines and personal computers. For many of the successful export items, Japan is the principal or dominant supplier.

Facsimile machines are a particularly interesting example of product targeting. Japanese companies have strongly, and very successfully, promoted the use of these machines in Japan when they came into their own less than a decade ago. Anyone working in Japan and familiar with the convenience and low cost of being able to send documents by facsimile rather than telex or courier would have been a bit surprised to find how few US and European companies were using these machines 18 to 24 months ago. Japanese companies followed the pattern often repeated in the past of developing the home market, realizing economies of scale, and then beginning a drive to export to other markets.

The facsimile example is also interesting because the Japanese presence in the international market is virtually uncontested and represents another important oversight by non-Japanese manufacturers. Careful monitoring of developments in Japan by leading foreign electronics companies would seem to have suggested the prospects for a large international market, but Japanese companies gained the lead. Facsimiles thus follow a long line of import products including VTRs, watches, CD players, DRAMS, and bullet trains.

Implications for the Rest of the World

The decline in the value of the dollar appears to be having one of the desired effects, that is, of stimulating US exports. It does not seem to have had much effect in restoring the relative industrial sophistication of the US compared to Japan. Instead, the stronger yen has stimulated Japan into higher-value-added industries and probably narrowed the gap in industrial sophistication. If this is the case, appreciation of the yen to date may have brought only a brief respite. Adding insult to injury, the largest-selling US automobile in Japan now is not a Ford or a General Motors car, but a US-manufactured Japanese brand.

The appreciation of the yen, in the absence of any US policy to target certain industries that are regarded as being of strategic importance, may in the longer term only complicate the problem. The strengthening of the yen has essentially had no impact on Japan's ability to export its managerial capabilities. Instead, the competitive problem for non-Japanese companies may have only exploded in scale. Japanese companies are moving into Thailand, for example, at the rate of one a week, and this will form a base for supplying lower-cost intermediate products to Japan and finished products to the rest of the world. Japanese companies are also very likely to continue to expand their presence in the US and in Europe.

The only real long-term solution will be for the US to develop a 'vision' of what its strategic industries are. Will these include steel? Semiconductors? Superconductive materials? In the absence of any clear US industrial policy and plan, the US may be moving on an accelerating decline to become a second-rate economic power. Indeed, which US industries should be regarded as strategic?

US Economic Successes and Failures

Some leading Japanese bankers, economists, and other commentators have responded with disbelief to rhetoric in the US that praises US economic performance over the past eight years. They are willing to acknowledge certain very important accomplishments, such as the reduction in inflation and interest rates, the creation of new jobs, the reduction in unemployment, and the rise in incomes. But as Japan has become the leading banker to the US, supplying substantial amounts of capital to finance the government deficit, concern has grown over the ballooning external debt of the US and the less-successful aspects of US economic policy and performance since 1980. Some of the most obvious problems have been large fiscal deficits, a decline in the savings ratio, and a drop in the percentage of GNP devoted to capital investment, which is needed to build new factories to help close the large trade deficit.

These views from Japan bear careful attention and thought among Americans. As both candidates for president must realize, important tasks confronting the winner will be bringing the budget deficit under control and seeking to restore lasting competitiveness to US industry.

The Accomplishments

The accomplishments of the 1980s in the US are numerous. These include bringing inflation in consumer prices down from an average of 13.5% in 1980 to 3.6% in 1987. Along with this drop in inflation, interest rates have also fallen dramatically since the early 1980s. For example, the prime lending rate came down from an average of 21.5% in 1980 to 8.75% in 1987, and mortgage rates came down from an average of 12.7% to 9.3% over the same period.

In addition, the employed labor force swelled from just over 100 million in 1980 to slightly more than 114 million in 1987. Along with this, unemployment dropped from more than 7.5% to just over 6% average for 1987.

Important increases were also recorded in incomes. GNP expanded in real terms from just under US$3.2 trillion in 1980 to more than $3.8 trillion in 1987, or about $660 billion. Hourly wages in manufacturing were up nearly 20% over this period, and consumer spending rose from $2 trillion to more than $2.5 trillion. Despite the drop in stock prices in October 1987, new wealth was created as the Dow Jones average, for example, moved from an average of 891 to an average of 2,275 for 1987 and still stands at around 2,000.

Even though expenditures on private capital investment have lagged behind overall growth, they rose from an annual rate of $379 billion in real terms in 1980 to $445 billion in 1987.

These are all substantial accomplishments. But commentators in Japan, based on their own experience in bringing an economy from virtually nowhere to second place during the postwar period, have quite a different perspective, especially since such a high percentage of Japan's trade is with the US, and since the US is the prime recipient of Japanese investment.

The Problems

From Japan's perspective as the leading international creditor nation, the US has become far too consumption-oriented. The rate of savings from disposable income has dropped from 7.1% in 1980 to 3.3% in 1987. Even though interest rates have come down since the peaks of the early 1980s, 9.5% is still a very high level for the prime lending rate when compared to the costs of money in Japan.

Furthermore, the US seems to have ceased to think seriously about the future of its industrial sector, as evidenced by the continued low percentage of GNP devoted to private capital investment in comparison with Japan and many European nations. In real terms, the percentage of private investment to GNP has remained at just over 11% for most of the 1980s versus about 15% in Japan. In contrast, the percentage of GNP accounted for by consumer spending has gone from 62.8% to 65.5%, compared to about 55% in Japan. The percentage of real GNP accounted for by government spending has increased from 16.8% to 18.4%.

Although these are seemingly small percentage changes in the composition of GNP, they translate into mind-boggling amounts of money. The annual GNP of the US in real terms increased by about US$660 billion from 1980 to 1987. A very high $500 billion of this was accounted for by the increase in consumption. Only $66 billion was due to increased investment spending. Also, at recent exchange rates, the dollar value of investments in the US has fallen behind the dollar value of investments in Japan. In 1987, private capital investment in the US was $445 billion at an annual rate, compared to $461 billion in Japan.

In part as a reflection of this, even though the dollar has dropped sharply in value since 1985 and US exports are booming, the principal problem for some export industries is the lack of sufficient capacity to keep up with the growth in export demand. The excessive emphasis on consumption therefore is preventing the US from correcting its trade deficit, despite the sharp fall in the value of the dollar over the past three years.

Judgment

When the history of the 1980s is finally written, the persistent trade and fiscal deficits appear likely to be weighed more heavily than the accomplishments of the 1980s. A shift in economic policies to place slightly less emphasis on consumption and more emphasis on investment could have made an enormous difference in the rate of productivity increase in the US and gone a long way towards reducing the trade deficit.

Over the period from 1980 to 1987, real GNP rose by about 20%, but consumer spending was up 26% and private capital investment by only 17%. Instead of permitting consumption to increase by 26% over the 1980 period, and holding its rise to about 20% while providing incentives for more investment, the US would have been better prepared to cope with the rising demand for exports that followed the drop in the value of the dollar.

Japanese bankers will no doubt have more to say about this in the years ahead as the US external debt heads almost irreversibly towards US$1 trillion and more.

THE JAPANESE CENTURY – A PERSPECTIVE

US Trade Legislation: Too Little Too Late?

The trade bill passed by the US Senate in August 1988 is probably the most significant piece of legislation regarding trade passed over the last 40 years. Although the bill has widely been described as protectionist, the underlying message is that the US is striving to set clearer rules in the interests of maintaining and expanding international commerce, with the US continuing to be a major economic power and participant in trade. In short, the trade bill puts some teeth into US trade policy, but most of the details of implementation are left to the discretion of the president. The trade bill could therefore be either a powerful weapon in helping the US to reduce its trade deficit or just a limp wash rag, depending on how it is used. One shortcoming of the trade bill is the lack of any link with a co-ordinated industrial policy. Without this, trade measures run the risk of being only stopgap measures.

What the Trade Bill Tells Us

The passage of the trade bill gives several clear messages to Japan and the rest of the world. One of these is that a consensus is emerging in the US that trade itself and the large US trade deficit are significant issues that need serious attention. Continuation of a large trade deficit is bound to put further downward pressure on the dollar, especially as the large, and possibly more intractable, fiscal deficit is expected to lead to a deficit in US international financial accounts in the near future. The US may therefore soon have deficits in trade, government fiscal, and its invisibles account of the balance of payments. A steadily weakening dollar will undermine the ability of the US to maintain its defense commitments and to provide assistance for development programs in the industrializing nations.

Another message seems to be that there are limits to the willingness of the US to continue to give up its industries. Despite the arguments of the 1970s and early 1980s that a post-industrial US economy might emerge where manufacturing plays only a minor role, Japan's example provides clear evidence that wealth and, ultimately, the quality of life are closely associated with the industrial structure. A strong, competitive manufacturing sector must be part of the industrial structure to maintain the value of the currency and the international position of the US. A question of utmost importance for the future of the US is the health of its steel, automobile, semiconductor, aerospace, and many other industries. In view of the not-so-healthy state of some of these industries, the trade bill, together with a co-ordinated industrial policy, is perhaps long overdue.

Another message seems to be that the US has recognized the need for working closely with its principal trading partners in developing a trading system that assures long-term development of world trade. Since US negotiators in the past have had little scope for taking quick action to make their negotiation points clearly, even when inappropriate trade practices were recognized to exist, the approach of Japanese negotiators has been to wear the US negotiators down. Shifting of authority to the US Trade Representative in cases where the President has given no instructions reflects an appreciation of this point in the US Congress.

The section of the trade bill dealing with intellectual property rights reflects the growing concern about, for example, the differences in patent practices between Japan and other nations. As the experience with a proposal regarding computer software protection in Japan several years ago suggested, Japan tends toward an 'opportunistic' view of intellectual property. To obtain a patent in Japan, the contents of the application must be disclosed for a significant period, thus opening up the possibility of inventing around a patent before protection can be obtained. This is in contrast to the practice in most other nations that are signatory to international patent conventions of not disclosing details of applications until protection has been obtained.

What the Bill Misses

The trade bill needs to be followed up in at least two areas. The first is the development of a co-ordinated national industrial and economic policy. The second, yet largely unaddressed, is the development of a stance and appropriate legislation on foreign investment in the US.

In many ways the trade bill is defensively oriented. Greater latitude is given to the president and the US Trade Representative to take action when problems arise. Anticipation of problems and the adoption of appropriate measures under the trade bill will no doubt assist in the development of competitive industries in the US. However, more specific legislation and focused efforts are needed to provide direction for industrial development.

In addition, the US has yet to come to grips with the issue of how it will take the best advantage of foreign investment, while not permitting foreign ownership of productive assets to interfere with the integrity of the political process. Japan's experience in this area is most useful since policy makers were very successful in using foreign competitors to stimulate domestic manufacturers into becoming internationally competitive, while keeping most of these companies on a rather short leash.

Japan's Reaction

Needless to say, the passage of the trade bill has met with a strong response in Japan. Most comments reflect the view that the new legislation is protectionist. The head of the Federation of Economic Organizations was quoted as saying, 'It is most unfortunate indeed that protectionist legislation has been passed.... We can only hope that when the bill is put into practice appropriate measures are taken.' Another leading business figure was quoted as saying, 'To prevent a deterioration in Japan-US relations, the members of the Japan and US business communities should open up opportunities for discussion as quickly as possible.... Maintaining the free trading system is absolutely essential.'

If anything, the new trade bill reflects a growing recognition of the importance of free trade practiced on an equal footing by countries with strong industrial bases. One of the implications of the bill, however, may well be that the US needs to rebuild and revitalize its industrial base before it can return to the degree of freedom prevailing in previous years. This may become a new fact of business life in the US in the coming years.

Japan's Rising Influence in the US

Leading US and European business magazines ran a series of feature stories in 1988 on Japan's growing influence in the US. Some of the questions the articles raise include: Is Japan's influence becoming too great in Washington and in the politics of other major cities of the US, such as Los Angeles? Is the acceptance of financial support from Japanese companies and other interests by a growing number of US opinion leaders likely to have a significant effect in shaping policies adopted by the US in the years ahead, and, if so, what difference will this make? Is the growing financial support from Japanese interests to US universities and think tanks likely to provide Japanese companies with priority access to new technologies and thus give them an additional edge over US companies?

The articles do not really present a conclusion, but introduce opinions that range from strongly positive in the case of companies and individuals working closely with Japanese interests, to mildly negative. The one conclusion that seems inescapable is that opinion leaders in the US have not taken, or perhaps cannot take, a decisive stance regarding the role of foreign versus domestic interests in spearheading economic growth and development in the US. In fact, with the exception of the activities of the USSR, it is doubtful that most citizens of the US have the same concept of 'foreign' and 'foreigner' that is so common in Japanese speech.

In the US, investment by foreigners, be they British, Arabs, or Japanese, has become a fact of life. Despite the growing role of foreign investment, the magazine articles suggest an underlying current of concern in the US about where growing investments and the buying of influence through the use of lobbyists and other means are likely to lead.

Benefits of Japanese Investment

This nagging concern is mitigated by the growing benefits that investments by Japanese companies are beginning to have in the US, including the creation of jobs, the introduction of sophisticated manufacturing and quality control technology, and the potential expansion in US exports which seems likely to come from having internationally competitive Japanese plants in the US.

Even though the growing interrelationship of the Japanese and US economies may have distinct, and very likely increasing, benefits for the US, the continuing imbalances may very well lead to an escalation in friction between the two nations. This arises from at least two sources.

Imbalances Remain

The first source of friction is the one-sidedness of the relationship. For example, the areas where Japanese influence is growing in the US are those where US and other foreign interests have exceptional difficulty in gaining any influence in Japan. Except at the government-to-government level, the influence of the US in the Japanese political process is virtually non-existent. The flow of information and technology coming from the support of research in the US is not matched by a reverse flow from Japan. Nor is it likely to be, since most of the significant research in Japan takes place in companies, not in universities or think tanks.

The second source of friction is an absence of a sense of crisis and national industrial/economic direction in the US. The US is a consumer-oriented society. Low prices and high quality are to be desired, regardless of the maker of the product or the effect on the US industrial structure. In Japan, the tacit rule is still *jimae shugi*, ie Japanese companies should retain a strong manufacturing presence in key industries. Purely domestic *jimae shugi* seems to be giving way to a selective, global *jimae shugi* as the yen has grown stronger.

A more balanced, but still competitive, Japan-US relationship is important for both nations and their trading partners. But unless more efforts are made to reduce the one-sidedness of the relationship and the US becomes serious about mapping out its future as a nation, the years ahead may be filled with growing frictions that will detract from what Japan and the US might accomplish through a more balanced, but still competitive, relationship.

Need to Reduce Frictions

As Japanese influence in the US continues to grow, some of the benefits may become more apparent. In the interim, a priority task for Japanese management will be to work to de-escalate growing frictions in the Japan-US relationship. One of the most important tasks for Japanese business interests will be to establish close, two-way communication with a range of interest groups in the

US. Even though estimates show that Japanese interests spent almost US$50 million on corporate communications in the US last year, these expenditures seem to be less effective than they could be.

This lack of effectiveness comes from a number of sources. For example, Japanese companies often fail to anticipate problems, then choose inappropriate tactics after issues have become serious. For example, large sums of money are spent on product advertisements, but relatively little is spent on acquainting various key publics with the corporation's objectives and contributions. This product advertising approach needs to be supported by broader, ongoing corporate communications programs to gain the confidence of the US. Viewed in the worst light, Japanese companies seem to be saying that US public opinion can be bought when necessary. If there are no problems, then silence is golden.

In addition, communication programs of Japanese companies are often one-way. There is often no provision for feedback from the target audience. Companies tend to spend much of their money and energy in translating statements written from the point of view of the head office in Japan, then fail to follow up to determine what information was missing, what further questions people may have, and what the next step in the public relations program should be.

Greater Role for Top Management

Perhaps the greatest difficulty is the perception that good relationships and corporate communications can be divorced from corporate strategies. As the operations of Japanese companies become more global in scope, corporate communications should be of central concern to Japanese management. The concepts of 'corporate communications' and 'corporate responsibility' are really quite new to Japan, and are often very difficult for the current generation of top management to understand. Strong support from national and regional governments and reasonably strong support from labor has been taken for granted in postwar Japan.

But as Japanese corporations become more involved in the US and other overseas economies and societies, top management needs to be closely involved at the headquarters level to provide better coherence and direction in corporation communications.

The feedback that is essential for planning any good corporate communications program can also provide important inputs into corporate strategy. Just as top management have learned to listen to customers about products, they should also listen to key publics and make full use of qualified professionals to establish effective investor relations and corporate communications programs.

Conclusions from the US Experience

Between the 1870s and the early 1900s, the US experienced a period of rapid growth. Its rise to a high economic standing was in many respects similar to

Japan's experience since World War II. As the following quotations from *Dynamics of Ascent – A History of the American Economy*, by W. Elliot Brownlee suggest, there are some striking similarities between the experience of the US as it moved to prominence as an economic power and that of Japan:

- *Rapid growth by the standards of the 1800s.* 'Economic growth had, of course, been impressive before the Civil War, but per-capita output increased only slightly more than 1 percent per year during the years 1800–1860, reaching an average of 1.45 percent per year during the dynamic 1840s and 1850s. By way of contrast, the annual rate of per-capita output growth reached 2.1 percent for the period 1870–1900.' (page 269)
- *Very high rates of saving and investment.* 'While savers and investors devoted only 14 to 16 percent of national product to capital formation prior to the Civil War, by the 1870s they devoted almost one-quarter to capital formation, and by the 1880s they had increased the rate to 28 percent.' (page 277)
- *A key and growing role for finance.* 'The success of investment bankers stemmed also from the fact that they proved to be the leading force in promoting industrial innovation. The investment bankers not only engineered the organisation of the largest manufacturing combinations of the day but also led the internal reorganisations that were designed to maximise the returns from the use of the new, large accumulations of capital.' (pages 295–296)

    One important distinguishing feature between the US experience and that of Japan is that a limited group of investment bankers was extremely influential in the industrialization of the US, whereas in Japan commercial banks played the principal role during most of the postwar period, collecting deposits and making loans to finance industrial development. Another distinguishing feature was that the banking system was subject to only minimal regulation in the US, and the lack of a central bank and other circumstances led to a very unstable system that was subject to periodic panics and bank failures which impaired economic development. In restructuring its financial system after World War II, Japan drew on these experiences and put together a bank-centered financial system that would act as a very stable and reliable conduit for channeling savings into industrial development.
- *Until the early 1900s, antitrust regulation was limited.* 'Not until Theodore Roosevelt's presidency did the federal government initiate vigorous antitrust prosecutions. That series of attacks culminated in the dissolution of J.P. Morgan's Northern Securities in 1904 and both Standard Oil and American Tobacco in 1911.' (page 306)
- *The late 1800s were a time of rising exports and falling prices.* 'American exports soared, roughly tripling (in current dollar value) between the late 1860s and the late 1890s and then more than doubling during the rest of the period up until World War I. This expansion reflected the growing effi-

ciency of American producers and, in the period prior to the late 1890s, falling prices, which declined more dramatically than those of any other country in the world, making American products available at bargain prices.' (page 350)

- *The US was an export powerhouse.* 'Yet even though world prices proceeded to fall relative to domestic prices, increasing American productivity resulted in the persistence of a favorable balance of trade. [In fact, until 1971 the annual merchandise trade balance since 1896 had always been favorable.] . . . Despite fluctuations in the trade balance, the dominant element in America's international commercial relations, from the Civil War through World War I, was the strength of her highly efficient export sector.' (page 351)
- *Even though conventional economic theory would argue against it, like Japan during much of the postwar period, the US was highly protectionist.* 'One of the paradoxical political facts of rapid growth in trade and increasing American productivity, particularly within the manufacturing sector, was the enactment of high tariffs on imports of manufactures and agricultural products. . . . Although the [Civil] wartime excises were lowered rapidly during the 1860s, the high tariffs were retained. Revisions . . . failed to change the fundamental structure of the tariff system, and until the Underwood-Simmons Tariff of 1913 significantly reduced Civil War rates, the ratio between duties and the value of dutiable goods rarely dropped below 40 percent and was frequently close to 50 percent. The highest rates were imposed on manufactured goods, particularly on metals and metal products, especially those of the iron and steel and related industries, cotton textiles, and certain woollen goods; on many such items the rate of protection was as high as 100 percent.' (page 355)

Japan's Economic Strategy

Following Japan's defeat in World War II, the country essentially retired from the political and military arena and devoted its attention almost exclusively to economics. Over the postwar period and with Japan's growing economic successes, economics has therefore come to replace ideology as the key theme for interaction between Japan, the US, and the rest of the world. Economics, not ideology, is the key theme of the Japanese Century. Here we include both political and economic ideologies that at present blanket arguments against protectionism and the formulation of industrial strategies.

Japan has clearly had an industrial strategy characterized by hard-headed pragmatism and minimal attention to economic ideologies. Some of the principal aspects of this strategy have included:

- Selective use of protectionism and the threat of market-opening to stimulate its infant industries to grow into world giants.
- Clear industrial targets and a sense of mission and direction based on a

consensus established between industry, finance, and the government.

- A rolling, long-term game plan that has moved the country through at least three identifiable phases since the 1950s. Phase I: A movement into heavy industry, and a de-emphasizing of prewar and early postwar industries such as textiles. Phase II: A drive into high technology which, among other things, has resulted in world dominance in many key sectors, including semiconductors. Phase III: The emerging period of dominance in world finance and expansion of Japanese industry to truly global standing.
- The adoption of policy measures needed to assure the maintenance of high savings and investment rates, and not basically altering the essentially frugal mind-set of the Japanese populace.
- The avoidance of involvement in geopolitical issues and restraint of expenditures on the military, in line with the postwar constitution.

Many aspects of Japanese society have come together to support Japan's ascent to a high economic standing. For all intents and purposes, Japan's elite is monolithic. Business, the bureaucracy, and the Liberal Democratic Party are cut of the same cloth. In many respects, the elite in Japan is the most exclusive in the world and brooks little dissent. Its successes and the general downplaying of conspicuous consumption among the real elite have reinforced its authority and status.

Peace between labor and management has been another major contributor to Japan's rise to prominence. Much has already been written on this, so we will not repeat the facts here, except to say that in many respects there are stark contrasts with the US experience.

For all intents and purposes, unlike the US, Japan is still closed to corporate takeovers from the outside. Any US or European company thinking of taking over a leading Japanese company is dealing with 'Fortress Japan.'

Unlike the US, in Japan the financial sector is still the handmaiden of industry. In the US, much merger and acquisition activity suggests that industry there may be the handmaiden of finance. At the same time that the financial sector in Japan has been obedient, it has also been highly protected until recently, when it has become enormous and very competitive.

Japanese attitudes have also played an important role in its success, and, put baldly, these have included keeping the foreigners out and keeping the stock-market and shareholders out of the picture as much as possible. The general docility of the Japanese populace and their conviction that they are nearly all part of the middle class have made it possible to de-emphasize consumer spending, so that the quality of life has taken a back seat to the country's industrial development.

In retrospect, the yen shock has ironically been an enormous boon for Japan, enabling it to move easily into Phase III of the game plan where it will be a dominant force in world finance and its industries will become truly global, not just in terms of having a large share of major markets but also in terms of the ownership of the means of production and the employment of foreign labor forces.

Even though some in the US might have thought that a stronger yen would deal a telling blow to Japanese manufacturing, in fact it seems to have shown, among other things, that profitability in the manufacturing sector prior to the yen shock was probably greatly understated.

With a currency doubled in value since mid-1985, the resources of Japanese banks are now worth twice as much and have risen to the top of ranking tables. In addition, the financial resources of many leading Japanese corporations, backed by astronomical price-earnings ratios and, in many cases, leverageable land holdings, are astonishingly large.

In taking steps to devalue the dollar against the yen in order to increase exports, the US appears to have forgotten that an increase in exports also requires an industrial base that does not run out of capacity within a year or two after the currency adjustment.

Perhaps the most important implication of the yen shock is that Japan can now buy in the US at bargain basement prices. Perhaps the currency adjustment should more appropriately have been termed the 'dollar shock'.

Implications for the US and the Rest of the World

In Phase III of Japan's game plan, Japanese financial institutions will play an increasing role in financing growth and development around the world. These institutions will also work closely with Japanese industries as they establish global positions. For example, Japanese companies are already going offshore in growing numbers into Asian nations to establish lower-cost manufacturing facilities. US companies, of course, moved into Europe and elsewhere in the 1950s and 1960s. Unlike the US companies, Japanese corporations may provide not only the technology but also the management skills that US companies have yet to master and implement effectively at home, such as total quality control systems. We should perhaps not be surprised to find Deming prizes for statistical quality control given to many Japanese companies in Japan and in many other countries before one is instituted in the US, despite the fact that Dr Deming is an American.

Investment in Europe is also on the increase and, with the integration of the EC market in 1992, Japanese companies are likely to step up their investments as a result of the strong yen and a fear of being shut out of 'Fortress Europe'.

The Japanese Century will also have far-reaching implications for the US. Japanese companies will most likely prove to be a powerful force in revitalizing the US economy. Japanese corporations will move from the domination of many US markets to the ownership of key US industries. Some Americans might be disturbed by the following statement: 'In the future, your children will be trained and work under Japanese management.' Americans are used to an open-door policy for new additions to the labor force through immigration, but the introduction of a new management class might cause concern. This is particularly the case since senior management posts could be closed to all but the Japanese.

Automobiles and automobile parts, of course, are prime examples of the wave of the future. To maintain quality, Japanese companies are already selectively producing many key components in Japan and have established distribution chains embodying computerized tracking systems and intelligent warehouses that provide 'just in time delivery' of parts at assembly plants in the US.

Some Clues as to How the Economic War Was Lost

In the context of the liberal view of economics current in the US – though not in Japan – a state of economic warfare between Japan and the US never existed. The consumer can only benefit from the survival of the fittest and most competitive corporations. Nationalities are irrelevant.

Those of a less ideological and more pragmatic turn of mind might be interested in two closing insights.:

- Much of Japan's success in business seems to have been based on the fundamental mind-set expressed in Japanese as *jimae shugi*, ie the desire and drive to be self-sufficient, a kind of restlessness that will never let things be and motivates the Japanese to tinker constantly with things to make them better, especially if they were invented or manufactured outside Japan. *Jimae shugi* is closely linked to the sense of nationalism of the Japanese. It is closely akin to being very clannish and having a strong sense of being culturally unique and different. It is also a very good mind-set for winning in economic contests. With this frame of reference, in simplest terms, you do it yourself whenever you can and you do not sell the family farm.

  In the US, the consumer buys the product he wants, regardless of where it was made. Selling the family farm is not a major issue; indeed, one idea of success in the US seems to involve selling out and retiring in Maui, or buying and selling businesses according to the latest strategic whim or fashion. In contrast to the way in which Japanese businesses grow through internal diversification and now globalization, the haphazard restructuring of US industry through mergers and acquisitions looks quite primitive, even aimless or unreasoned. Unlike Japan, restructuring is not taking place within a well-integrated and supportive system.

- Japan's success also seems to be closely related to the fact that it has kept almost exclusive control over the three most important aspects of business activity – and, by extension, the economy itself – namely industry, markets, and finance.

  Foreign business accounts for only about 3% of sales in Japan, hardly a threatening presence. Japan has been skilful in keeping its industry

Japanese. With the yen worth about three times what it was in 1970 and twice what it was in mid-1985, and with price-earnings multiples in Japan averaging 70 times, we can be reasonably confident that a wave of takeovers will probably not start tomorrow, even if all other deterrents were removed, such as close holdings of shares.

Japan's Control over its Industries

Until very recently, Japan has not welcomed imports. It has retained its markets for its own industries, making it possible for them to expand and to become competitive internationally before becoming export industries. With the appreciation of the yen, these companies have responded by upgrading the value-added of products manufactured in Japan and globalizing their operations through overseas investments.

Japan's Control over its Markets

Japanese regulatory authorities have also carefully circumscribed the role of foreign financial institutions and have provided Japanese institutions with the necessary sources of revenue to build their operations in Japan and to establish strong positions overseas. In the international financial industry, for example, the market for Eurobond underwriting has dropped to minimal profitability because Japanese institutions – with large revenues from fixed-equity commissions in Japan – are buying their way into the market.

Japan's Control over its Money

Attitudes in the US are, of course, very different. The US will essentially let anyone supply its markets. The underlying philosophy is that competition is good, and the best way to give the consumer the best deal.

In Japan, the consumer takes a back seat to two other priorities, expressed in Japanese as *kuni no tame* (for the country) and *kaisha no tame* (for the company). The Japanese have a very strong sense of economic nationalism. This ethos is shared by both management and employees, not to mention the bureaucracy.

Many in the US already seem to sense the problems which may arise during the Japanese Century. The trade bill is but one example. In retrospect, perhaps the US has been wrong in negotiating to open the Japanese market. The Japanese simply have no intention of throwing the market open, except on a piecemeal basis, since a closed market and careful management of the growth of Japan's economy has been a key to its success. The problem with the US policy approach is that it is free trade-oriented in a world that is not free trade-oriented. Instead of spending energy in trying to open Japan, the US should have been developing its own industrial policy and game plan.

In Conclusion, a Puzzle

Many of the trends discussed in this book will continue for another 10 years or more. In the interim, Japan's influence in US financial markets and elsewhere will continue to rise. Tokyo will have an increasing influence on interest rates in the US. The strong emphasis on consumption in the US will come under increasing comment and scrutiny by the Japanese. Many key industries in the US will be dominated by Japanese companies. US investors, including pension funds that have the monies of employees of US companies, will be faced with a dilemma: Should funds be taken out of US companies, even out of the companies where the pension beneficiaries are employed, and be invested in Japanese companies that are winning the battle?

We leave you with a puzzle. We do not know the correct answer. Economics has replaced ideology as a key theme of the Japanese Century. Many aspects of US foreign and economic policy are based on deep-seated beliefs in ideologies. Japan will be formulating its domestic and international policies based on what we might call *real economique* . Japan's political power will rise as it provides more aid and invests more and more around the world. Will Japan be able to formulate policies that are not in conflict with those of the US? Can Japan be relied on as an ally? Can Japan be relied on to move in line with US foreign policy, based on ideologies? If not, then what?